# The Leap

Presenting an Enlightened Path toward Marriage
to Create Greater Social Stability and
Personal Happiness

## by
## Nasser Rida

authorHOUSE™

*1663 Liberty Drive, Suite 200*
*Bloomington, Indiana 47403*
*(800) 839-8640*
*www.AuthorHouse.com*

*Copyright © 2003. Dar Al-Ousra. Beirut, Lebanon. Arabic Language. All Rights Reserved*
*Copyright © 2006. Dar Al-Ousra. Beirut, Lebanon. English Translation. All Rights Reserved*

*First published in English by AuthorHouse 01/18/06*

*Website: www. alousra.com*

*ISBN: 1-4259-0819-5 (sc)*

*Library of Congress Control Number: 2005911360*

*Printed in the United States of America*
*Bloomington, Indiana*

*This book is printed on acid-free paper.*

# Dedication

To the children of all the men and women
who have suffered disappointment in marriage

* * * * *

# Acknowledgments

The author expresses his deepest gratitude to the many who assisted him throughout his work – the thinkers, researchers, librarians, writers, editors, translators, designers, and the men and women who responded to his surveys. He also thanks those whom he interviewed for their time and generous sharing of ideas. Without all the contributors, The Leap would not have been born.

# Table of Contents

# Preface

Is anything on Earth more wondrous than human beings and their capacity for thought, creation, kindness, love, empathy, and offers of assistance to those in need? It is these positive human traits that are best nurtured and expressed within the framework of a stable and moral family structure. If the framework is shaken or removed, it becomes likely that many people will stumble down the wrongful paths of life and the dark side of human nature will triumph over the decent side. Such danger exists in our society today. The cause of the danger is the alarmingly high rate of divorce that tears apart families and, most of all, victimizes children.

It is the recognition of this danger threatening society as a whole, and on a personal level clouding the future of the author's young children, that propelled him to spend many years investigating the problem and searching for a solution compatible with the letter and spirit of Islamic law. The publication of The Leap is the result of that effort.

As its subtitle suggests, The Leap presents an alternative path toward marriage tailored for our modern world, but never in contradiction to the *Qur'an* or *Shari'ah*. The author found this path by traveling back in time to the original source and intention of his religion and by bypassing customs and traditions that arose in response to ancient societal needs but that have lost their relevance today. The author's aim is to offer a system that will greatly reduce the number of divorces and thereby stem the family's disintegration and its negative impact on individuals and on society as a whole.

The Leap is divided into seven sections. The Introduction reviews the background and early thinking of the initiator of the search for a cure to society's current ills.

Chapter One goes deeper into his analysis and details his efforts at lone research, his formation of a research team, and the first interactive presentation of the team's findings at a seminar attended by university students. This first seminar focuses on divorce – the size of the problem, its causes, and its negative effects. Throughout the entire book, issues related to marriage and divorce continue to be presented and discussed during a series of seminars in the university setting.

Chapter Two examines acquaintance and the lack of acquaintance between a man and woman before their marriage, with an emphasis on the importance of compatibility in ensuring a successful marriage. Three different types of marriage practiced in some Islamic countries are defined and explained.

Chapter Three discusses the elements of marriage – the proposal, dowry, witnessing, guardianship, competency based on rationality, and age of maturity. Scholarly arguments are detailed for whether the latter four elements are obligatory.

Chapter Four introduces The Leap and its relationship to morality and timing in the marriage contract. Proof is presented for the religious lawfulness of making The Leap.

Chapter Five clarifies the many issues raised by introducing the new social system and delves deeply into the features of temporary marriage. Discussions include conditions needed in the marriage contract, the role emotions play in a relationship, freedom of choice, misconceptions about sex, and the responsibilities of parenthood.

Chapter Six contains an overview by The Leap's initiator, final questions and answers about the new system, and each team member's summation of The Leap's meaning.

At the back of the book, a list is presented of conditions to be considered in the permanent marriage contract. This list is intended to stimulate thought and debate by a couple before they enter into a marriage agreement.

The Glossary is a guide for the pronunciation and definition of Arabic terms found in this book. The many variations in spelling of Arabic words when translated into English make this section useful for Arabic and non-Arabic readers of English.

The Documents section quotes in English and Arabic from 19 of the main bibliographic sources consulted in producing this book. The *Qur'anic* verses and *hadiths* cited herein are compiled in two sections. The Bibliography contains only Arabic language sources and is selective. The Index includes words and phrases used in the book plus value-added concepts that assist the reader in finding all the discussions on a particular topic.

The Leap was written in Arabic and completed and published in 2003 in Beirut. The translation into English was published in 2006 in the USA and is intended mainly for Muslim readers living outside the Arabic countries. The book will soon be available in Farsi and is also now being translated into French. The translations, while not absolutely literal, do thoroughly present all the ideas in the original work and do totally reflect the spirit of the original work. The text of the book and its translations are also available online at the website **www.alousra.com**.

The Leap is not signed with the author's real name because of the sensitivity of its subject in the Arab world and because not everyone may understand the author's good intentions and deep religious devotion. The author is conscious of his responsibility to God and proposes nothing that challenges God's laws. God knows who wrote The Leap and sees his intentions.

The author seeks neither gain nor recognition, but he does welcome ideas, suggestions, questions, and opinions. Please take the time to contact him at the e-mail address **dar_al_ousra@hotmail.com**.

The new system presented in these pages will not entirely rid society of divorce, but full application of the system will substantially reduce the current divorce rate. The ideas are not for now because people need time to change and adjust. They are presented now because we must start somewhere. It is hoped these ideas will find a following, one that grows each year as adoption of the system makes evident its soundness. If we work together under the umbrella of Islamic law, we will find ways to implement this system for creating greater social stability and personal happiness and thereby solve most of the problems facing the family in today's society. May we be with God.

Respectfully,

*Nasser Rida*

# List of Characters

Nasser Rida - sociologist, lecturer, and relationship counselor; initiator of the marriage project and the seminars
Latifah Rida - Nasser's wife
Ayad, Salma, Iman, Alia - Nasser's and Latifah's children
Amal - Latifah's cousin
Ahmed - Amal's husband
Nura - Amal's and Ahmed's eldest child
Mustafa Naqib - university librarian; Nasser's best friend; secretary of the seminars
Seyyid Hussein - highly respected scholar of Islamic religion
Seyyid Mohammed - scholar of Islamic religion; pupil of Seyyid Hussein
Dr. Afaf Badran - university professor of sociology
Hadeel - Dr. Afaf's daughter
Su'ad - Dr. Afaf's neighbor
Dr. Omar Abu Zakaria - university professor of sociology; visiting from Morocco
Dr. Elias Munir - Dean at the university
Dr. George Hana - Trustee at the university
Seminar attendees and participants - numerous male and female university students, plus professors and employees from the university and several citizens from outside the university

# Members of the Team

Nasser Rida   (Shi'ite, male)
Mustafa Naqib   (Shi'ite, male)
Seyyid Mohammed   (Shi'ite, male)
Dr. Afaf Badran   (Shi'ite, female)
Dr. Omar Abu Zakaria   (Sunni, male)

# INTRODUCTION
## Past and Present

***** 

### Nasser's Journey

It was Nasser Rida's favorite time of day. The sun had set hours ago, and the moon and stars lit up the sky. A sweet-scented breeze cooled the evening air. All around him houselights were clicking off, one by one. The silence of the dark was replacing the buzz of the day. It was the perfect time to take a long walk, the perfect time to be alone with his thoughts.

Lately, Nasser had a lot on his mind. Next month his son Ayad would return home to Beirut, a proud graduate of a fine American college. Already, Ayad's mother and grandmothers were talking about whom he should marry, about which girls to introduce him to. Nasser smiled as he imagined a comic scene. Ayad steps off the airplane and, after passing through customs inspection, he notices 20 girls lined up in a row and then he sees his family. His mother and grandmothers rush at him, and kiss and hug him so hard that he nearly faints. As soon as the kissing and hugging are over, they point to the line of girls and say, "Ayad, which one do you choose to be your wife?"

In real life, it would not happen this way. And yet, to Nasser, it felt emotionally closer to the truth than not. The process of choosing a partner for the rest of your life could be, in his world, almost that abrupt, that pushy, that arbitrary.

1

If Nasser was worried about Ayad and his future happiness, he was even more worried about his younger children – his three daughters Salma the scholar, Iman the promising artist, and little Alia the jolly one. The years were passing swiftly. It would soon be time to think about husbands for Salma and Iman.

He loved them all so much and wished it were possible to guarantee their happiness. With his heart full of this feeling, he strolled farther into the night. The sounds of an intense quarrel coming from one of the houses suddenly drove his thoughts 40 years back into the past. When he was a child, his parents argued like that often. They were almost complete opposites in personality, beliefs, likes, and dislikes. Their quarrels were loud and full of cruel words. Afterwards, they did not speak to each other for days.

Nasser remembered, even as a child, he did not find one parent right and the other wrong. The problem was that they were so different, so mismatched in every way, that constant disagreement was inevitable. Even more strongly, he recalled the deep pain he and his brother and sister felt from the arguments and the long silences that followed.

The marriages of his uncles, aunts, grandparents, and older cousins were not much better. The young Nasser sensed the tension, dissatisfaction, and disappointment in all these marriages. He grew up believing this was normal, this was what to expect, this was what marriage was – until, that is, he found himself in college in America.

During his first year away from home, Nasser shared a room in the college dormitory with another student. The small space and lack of privacy were hard on him. On many nights, his roommate's noisy friends kept him from sleeping.

By the end of this year, Nasser learned that rooms were available in private homes near the campus for the same money as the dormitory rent. After convincing his father to let him try living in a private room, he began searching through the ads in the school newspaper. And that is how he met the Moores, an elderly American couple with grown children and an empty room for rent.

Nasser grinned at the memory of the Moores being "elderly." He guessed now that they may have each been around 60 years of age or less, but, to his 19 year old eyes, they seemed almost ancient. It was at the Moore home that a small revolution occurred in Nasser's mind. For the first time he had met real people who were truly compatible and happy together. The Moores enjoyed the same activities and liked to do things together. They laughed at the same jokes. They spoke respectfully to each other, but also knew how to tease with good nature.

To Nasser, this was so strange at first that he wondered if the Moores had come from another planet. Or maybe they were senile. Or on drugs.

After he and the Moores became better acquainted, they chatted with him about their single years. He learned they had dated a lot and had romances with other people. Mr. Moore had nearly married someone else. They finally met each other on a long line for buying movie tickets. They talked, exchanged phone numbers, had a lunch date, and then another and another. They dated happily for six months, after which they decided to move in together. Two years later Mr. Moore proposed marriage, according to Mrs. Moore. Mr. Moore claimed this was untrue, that Mrs. Moore had proposed. It was one of their many "fun" arguments. Nasser was amazed to learn that arguing could be fun.

As time passed, Nasser made many friends at college. They went together to cafes and ballgames and theaters. Because of the Moores, Nasser found himself listening and talking to his friends with only half his brain while observing the couples around him with the other half. He saw couples, young and old, in love and not in love, attentive and inattentive, compatible and incompatible. He was invited to spend holidays in friends' homes, where he met divorced parents, miserable parents like his own who, in his opinion, should get a divorce, wonderful couples like the Moores, and just about everything in between.

Nasser now realized the Moores and those resembling them were not from outer space, senile, or addicted to drugs. They were merely happy. They had chosen a lifelong partner carefully and wisely and had also known how to treat each other after marriage.

Nasser's fascination with watching couples led him away from studying engineering, as his father wanted, and toward studying psychology and sociology. He took his bachelor's degree and spent two more years in obtaining a master's degree. He wrote his thesis on the psychology of argument in marriage. His intention was to teach at a university back home and also offer relationship counseling to couples before and after marriage. In his society, this was a very unusual plan.

* * * * *

## Nasser at Home

The longing for something to chew on drew Nasser back into the present. He checked his pockets, found a few hard candies, and popped them into his mouth. He looked around and realized that he had reached a park at the edge of the city. Walking always tired him, so he sat down on a park bench. He needed the solitude. He had much to think about.

Nasser was now remembering his return from America 25 years ago. Coming home to Lebanon made him feel like he was traveling from the future back into the past. This was in some ways good and in some ways not. The good was the closeness of families, the food and the communal meals, and the feeling of his religion being all around him. Before his years in America, he had taken religion for granted. Despite finding much to admire in America, he also often felt like a fish out of water in a non-Muslim country.

What he preferred in America was the work ethic, the acceptance of the social sciences, the freedom and rights that women enjoyed, and especially the way men and women got acquainted and chose whom to marry. There was no way in his society that he and a young woman could copy the Moores and remain respectable.

After returning home, his first aim was to find a job teaching at a good university. He succeeded easily in this, and, as the years passed, gained many academic honors, including being appointed assistant director at his university's Center for Sociological Research. A year after he began teaching, he opened a private office for relationship counseling. Years passed before this counseling service attracted enough couples to pay for itself.

As soon as Nasser had secured a good job, his mother and sister went to work on finding him a wife. Nasser was very nervous at this time, but he had a pleasant surprise. He liked and agreed to marry the first young girl who he was introduced to and she also agreed to marry him. In his view, the marriage had been successful. It was not perfect, but nothing human is. He was not perfect, his wife was not perfect, but they were understanding and kind to each other and they were raising four bright children together.

Nasser believed he had been lucky. He did not really know the shy girl he was marrying. In some ways, even after 24 years of marriage, he was still learning more about her. The main thing was that it had turned out well and he would choose her again if he had to. He hoped she felt the same.

Nasser credited his successful marriage to three reasons. The first reason scared him for he knew his mother and sister had chosen well by accident. They could just as easily have picked the wrong person for him and how would he have known she was the wrong one when pre-marital acquaintance was so limited by custom?

The second reason was all the years he had spent under the Moores' roof. He had learned there that marriage could be fun and fulfilling. Marriage could build people up instead of tearing them down. He had witnessed the value of a happy marriage and had promised himself that he would aim for this in his own life.

The third reason was the self-awareness that his psychology and sociology studies had given him. He had learned to recognize his father's behavior inside himself and to suppress his first impulse to raise his voice and start an argument, a destructive argument, when he had had a bad day at work or something displeased him at home or he was feeling ill. Nasser had become an adult mentally as well as physically. Nasser had learned how to treat a wife.

In practicing his profession as counselor, Nasser tried hard to help couples achieve the kind of healthy marriage that he and his wife enjoyed. Though he felt that he had assisted some couples in solving minor problems, mostly he knew he had failed. The couples were too incompatible to be helped. They never should have married.

Nasser became so expert at his job that he could with much accuracy predict, when he met young couples, whether they would still be married 15 years later. He needed to observe them together for only five minutes to judge their level of compatibility.

He followed the statistics and saw the divorce rate climb and climb to be one out of every three marriages. Knowing all the misery that came with divorce saddened him, especially when he considered the effect on a couple's children. He also knew that staying together despite an unhappy marriage could harm the couple and their children.

His thoughts now shifted to his own children as he sat on the park bench on that cool spring night. Because he loved his children so much, he wanted them all to be as happy as the Moores. He did not want his son Ayad and his three daughters to marry by chance, find themselves in bad marriages, raise sad and troubled children, or get divorces. He knew success in marriage cannot be guaranteed, but he also wondered if there was a better way to help young people find the right partner.

"This is the most important decision of your life," he said to himself. "How can you leave it to chance or to the opinions of others?"

And, so, as he stared up at the stars in the sky, the exact question to ask formed itself in his mind: How, on the one hand, can you be a good Muslim and follow the *Qur'an* and, on the other hand, also have the freedom to choose your marriage partner yourself and to choose one who is not a stranger?

He now had the question, but not the answer. He sighed and admitted to himself that finding the answer would not be simple. He resolved to think about it intensely and to do research in the library by studying the religious literature. After he learned more, he might contact an old acquaintance, a revered Seyyid, to see if he had similar concerns or feelings. Yes, this was the direction to travel in. And, yes, this research might take much time – months or perhaps years. He was confident, if the effort were made, the answer was almost certain to be found.

This thought considerably lightened the weight on Nasser's mind. Hidden by the darkness, he did a few stretching exercises. This helped him to feel less tired and less restless. It was now very late at night and time to leave the park and go home to bed.

The way home seemed shorter than the way to the park. Nasser smiled as he walked.

\* \* \* \* \*

# End of a Marriage

Nasser found his wife Latifah in bed, not asleep but reading a book. Latifah was educated, though with not as much formal schooling as her husband. She had attended a local university and, despite never having been to America or Britain, she spoke English even better than Nasser. She loved reading, in Arabic and in English.

Latifah was accustomed to Nasser's long evening walks. She trusted him and never asked with suspicion where he went or whom he saw. But, being an educated person, she was always interested in his ideas and willing to share her own.

Tonight she greeted him with the same question she had asked many times before. "So, did you solve the world's problems?" Nasser had to admit he had not.

Instead, he described how Ayad's impending return had made him confront his anxieties about their children's future. How could they best insure their children's happiness in adulthood? How could they help prevent their children from marrying the wrong person?

Latifah replied that they must examine the marriage candidates very closely and look into their backgrounds thoroughly. With Nasser's training, it should not be hard to recognize a person who has serious problems or who is insincere or inconsiderate.

Nasser was less sure of his or any "expert's" ability to uncover insincerity and other character flaws that a marriage candidate would try hard to hide. He explained that her solution was still the same old custom of not choosing for yourself. And it is the person getting married who should best know whether the right partner has been found. Young people should be taught how to judge who has decent character and who has enough similar interests to make a good companion for life. He added that, given the lowly position of women in their society, his anxiety was the greatest for their three daughters. He had been remembering his student days in America and wondering if some of the answers would come from studying and applying the better parts of Western culture, where there was much to admire when strong family ties and values were present.

Latifah pointed out that the divorce rate in the West was very high. Nasser agreed that this was a human problem everywhere and that much improvement was needed in Western society too. However, he was not ready to tackle the problems of the West. His immediate concern was his family and the society they lived in. But there were a few things he had esteemed when living in America. When the two right people finally found each other, the happy life they led together was enviable. And, he believed, this happiness was due in part to the equality or near equality that women had with men.

By this time, they had both grown sleepy. Latifah was eager to hear more, but it could wait for tomorrow.

The next day Latifah had a story waiting when Nasser returned home from work. Her cousin Amal, who lived in Kuwait, was getting a divorce. Nasser, who had lunched that afternoon with his divorced friend Mustafa Naqib, felt sorry to see himself being proved right yet again about the sorry state of marriages in today's world.

Nasser knew Amal's history. That she would want to divorce was not surprising. The surprise was more in why it took so long to happen. And yet, at the first news of a divorce among people he knew, Nasser always experienced a little shock.

Amal was from the side of Latifah's family who had settled in rural Lebanon. They were well off and owned a large farm. When Amal was 16 years old, her family married her to Ahmed, a very religious man of 24. Amal saw Ahmed for the first time a few days before their wedding day. By the time Amal reached 22 years of age, she had a daughter and two sons.

Amal now insisted on returning to school and there was no stopping her. She was an amazing student and won a top scholarship to the best university in Kuwait. She earned a Master's degree in economics and was one of the first women to be offered a managerial job in banking in Kuwait City. She accepted and Ahmed and the children then joined her there, where Amal became the main wage earner in the family. Amal was ambitious. Her husband was not.

Amal liked living in Kuwait and adapted easily to modern Kuwaiti urban society, while Ahmed clung to the old ways. Only the densest person could overlook their incompatibility. Amal was not happily married, but she found fulfillment in her children and in her employment.

Amal and Ahmed rarely argued and had a proper Muslim marriage till a crisis occurred. When their daughter Nura was 16, she wanted to have dinner with her girl friends at a restaurant. Boys might be there too. Ahmed forbad it. There was a big fight between Ahmed and Nura, but she could not convince her father to let her go. Nura spent a miserable evening at home. The next day she disappeared.

Amal was out of her mind. She called the police. She called all Nura's friends. She walked through the streets of Kuwait City for miles, not because she knew where to search but because she could not sit still. Ahmed refused to search.

On the fifth day, the police found Nura hiding at the home of a friend. She had been there the entire time and the friend had lied when Amal had phoned.

Those four days had been the most terrible of Amal's life. She never forgave Ahmed for not helping to search for Nura and their marriage became a marriage in name only. This was what Nasser knew.

"Why a divorce now?" he asked Latifah. "The mess with Nura occurred eight years ago. If that did not cause a breakup, what would?"

"The cause was," said Latifah, "on the surface a small matter, though not so small to Amal. It was apparently the last straw. A few weeks ago, Amal had a bad case of the flu. She was lying in bed and burning up with a high fever. She felt dizzy and her throat was so dry that she could hardly swallow. She asked Ahmed to make her a cup of tea. He replied that he was tired and that it was the woman's duty to serve a man and not the other way around.

"Amal told me that she made her way from the bed to the kitchen by holding on to the walls. She was so dizzy that she nearly fell. As she was doing this, she made herself a promise. When she recovered from the flu, she would get a divorce. And that is what she is doing."

Nasser whistled in astonishment. It took a minute for it all to sink into his mind, and then he erupted in anger, "A man does not serve a woman, even if she is ill? This is not what our religion is about! From where did he take that idea? Ahmed is a fool. He will be lost without Amal."

"They are like oil and water," concluded Latifah. "These two never should have married."

"That is exactly my point," said Nasser. "If it were left up to them, these two would not have chosen each other. And, to arrange a marriage for a 16 year old defies common sense."

"So," asked Latifah, "what is the next step? What is to be done?"

* * * * *

# CHAPTER ONE
## A Hope Becomes Real

\* \* \* \* \*

### Thought and Research

"What is to be done?" For the next few days, Latifah's question echoed in Nasser's mind. More and more his thoughts confirmed the need to go beyond university lecturing and relationship counseling and toward very specific research. He must examine whether Eastern marriage customs might be improved within their religious context to ensure a better life for married couples.

Contemplating the state of women in his world, where women had customs of family, marriage, and divorce pushed on them – and the social fragmentation resulting from divorce – scared him. His concern was not confined to his daughters. It spread to become a social one and left him asking, "Are there practical solutions for bettering the state of the Eastern woman?"

He admired those Western individuals and social institutions that shunned advertising agencies and other industries that used women as merchandise and abused their dignity. At the same time, he began participating in lectures calling for preserving morals among youth and for avoiding irresponsible conduct that is dangerous to society.

In his intellectual and social discussions with colleagues and friends, he became uneasy when "the woman" was the center of those discussions. This is because an Eastern woman is marginalized. She is a second class citizen at best, while the Western woman has the freedom to express her energy, capabilities, and ambitions. The Western man has no authority over her except within duties and rights in which she joins with him completely in all aspects of life: marriage, work, expenses, children, divorce, and custody. Often, the woman in the East may be controlled by the authority of her father, brothers, and society and may have little say in her affairs. If the Western woman is sometimes sneered at as merchandise, in the East also, through oppressive social practices, the man indirectly treats the woman as merchandise, by treating her as he pleases.

Nasser, with anguish, compared the actual status of Muslim women with the true Islamic view of a woman as an individual having freedom and dignity. He saw that customs and traditions contradict Islamic morality in their view of woman, because these traditions are based on the assumption that women lack intelligence. Under such traditions, she is unqualified for political and administrative responsibilities, often does not enjoy the right to vote, and may be killed legally in some countries by her father or brother as revenge for "dishonoring" the family. All this must damage her state of mind and undermine her hopes and ambitions.

Nasser understood the deep chasm between Islam and what some Muslims practiced regarding women's rights. He saw that Islam had established a complete system that preserved women's rights and gave them a role that complemented their feminine nature. However, some Muslims, both men and women, did not believe in women's natural and humanistic role. Using divorce as an example, the woman is the greater loser as she struggles to care for the children and to obtain the financial support that the man should reasonably give her. This is not how the Western woman lives. The law protects her by determining adequate financial support before separation or divorce and it searches for and prosecutes the man who tries to avoid paying this support.

As Nasser painfully learned from studying the statistics, divorce may occur in one out of three or four Eastern marriages. Nasser also knew how women marry and divorce, and what is pushed on them. He saw that this way is affected by fog and ignorance, and how women suffer from the system that controls them.

He thanked God that, when he married, the choice had been successful, even though he had had little say in the matter. Reality shocked him, and he viewed the situation with a sense of great obligation. When he looked at Islamic law in the *Qur'anic* verses and in the *hadiths* that honor women and protect them from injustice, he saw how this honor had been obscured in day to day living. It was as though some people had not learned a thing from Islam, or they had learned one thing and practiced another.

More recently, when comparing Eastern society and Western society, he found many negative points concerning women in both, but he also saw many positive points because both societies have laws that protect all people, and that includes women.

Nasser wondered, if the Western woman had complete freedom to build a relationship with a man whether it was legalized by marriage or not, and if the law was as much on her side as on a man's side, and if she could start a relationship with a man and end it the next day when she found it was not in her best interests, so why cannot Muslim women have this right? He came to believe that, within Islam, women were able to have these same rights without tarnishing their honor. The question was: Within which system is this possible?

Since each sex is attracted to and cares for the opposite one, how could they meet and date in an acceptable way, Islamically speaking? When the *hadith* states **No man and a woman get together without Satan becoming the third**, it makes aware and reminds Muslims of the importance of having the meeting between a man and a woman be Islamically lawful. But, how may it be made so that God rather than Satan is "the third"?

Nasser also asked himself: How should we marry, and what are the steps to take that would meet our expectations and achieve this future plan? The questions came to be always in his mind, because he could not find a system in society through which reasonable people may approach marriage.

The questions then became apprehensions. He saw that society was interested in everything to do with politics, economics, and sociology, but it did not pay enough attention to the issues surrounding marriage.

It followed that, if enough attention were not paid to issues involved with starting a family, then forming a stable and safe society would be impossible, because the family is the image of society. Men and women are the elements in developing a family. If they do not get a chance to choose each other as life partners, they will not achieve the best kind of family.

Nasser was searching for a clear system that embraced both Islamic law and his society. Now, his society swung between Western and Islamic concepts, customs, and traditions, and the result was not a clear system.

He wanted to enter into the minds of the youth. He saw that religion did not attract them completely due to all its prohibitions and due to the lack of well-studied scientific methods by those who preach.

People needed solutions, thought Nasser, particularly those young Muslims who did not want to sin, but were filled with uncertainty. Music is forbidden. Mixing with the opposite sex is forbidden. How was the satisfaction of desire to be Islamically allowed?

He was looking for modern, humane answers for those young men and women, and for how society could untangle reality from confusion and from social, mental, and family problems. Finally, he went toward Islam, not the West, for the answers.

Nasser began his researching and learning, eagerly reading everything that was pertinent to his quest. His childhood friend Mustafa Naqib, who was in charge of the library at the country's largest university, helped him greatly. They met regularly, especially as Mustafa was emerging from a failed marriage. He needed Nasser's advice, mainly because of his children. Their mother had left the children with him when she married another man.

For three years, Nasser collected information on the relationship between men and women, from *Qur'anic* verses and *hadiths*, Islamic law texts, and books on education, sociology, and psychology, until he reached the essence of the subject. In Islam, he found realistic solutions for every time and place, especially in terms of the relationship between men and women. But, as he expected, the Islamic beliefs associated with marriage, family, divorce, and men and women contradicted what is practiced in reality. The hoped-for aim of marriage – to build a stable family – was not being achieved. As a result, the relationship between men and women was undermined and divorce rates were rising. He found a missing link in the chain. Where was the missing link? This became the focus of his thoughts, but he did not expect to find the link by himself.

Now that Nasser had collected a large amount of information, how he could turn what he had faith in into reality? He saw the urgent need to find other researchers and scholars to share his concern and to form a close team. He would share his quest with others, both men and women, both married and unmarried. Putting their heads together would surely lead to interesting ideas and solutions.

* * * * *

## Formation of the Team

The first to join the team was Mustafa. He had gradually become part of a team informally by all the assistance he gave Nasser, but now he formally agreed to join.

Next, Nasser remembered that the research he had just completed had its seeds in discussions with the religious scholar Seyyid Hussein, whom Nasser saw regularly in his youth before studying in America. The cleric had listened to him and understood his youthful anxiety and criticism of the state of society. The Seyyid had advised him and given him all the information he needed regarding the Islamic viewpoint on raising a family and society. Though Nasser was keen on keeping up their relationship after returning to his country, his absorption in family and career had kept him from visiting the Seyyid for many years.

Nasser felt there was no one better than Seyyid Hussein to be on the team as he held the scientific and religious qualifications compatible with the needs of the era. He talked this over with Mustafa, who wholeheartedly agreed. Nasser then went to the cultural center that the Seyyid ran and was greeted with, "Your absence has been long Nasser. I hope what prevented you from coming were not bad thoughts."

Nasser said, "They were good thoughts, Sir, especially regarding the same subject from the old days, the one I had many questions about. You never held back in answering them. I come here today after having done much research. The relationship between men and women still preoccupies me, along with marriage and divorce."

The Seyyid replied, "Is the thrust of your research still knocking on this same door after all these years?"

"Yes," said Nasser, "and I will keep knocking on this door until I have peace of mind!"

"When will you be satisfied?" wondered the Seyyid.

"When you have accepted my invitation," answered Nasser.

The Seyyid said, "What is your invitation, Nasser? I am ready to hear it."

Sensing the Seyyid's care for him, Nasser replied, "I have come to ask you to be a part of a dedicated team working on my marriage project."

At this point, Seyyid Mohammed entered the room. He was one of the most alert and charitable of Seyyid Hussein's students. After greeting them both, he sat down and listened as Nasser described the project. When Nasser finished, Seyyid Hussein said, "Nasser, you do realize how busy I am with my engagements. Such work needs a team that has enough time for it. My time is very tight. I suggest that Seyyid Mohammed join your team. I am sure he will not object and I will help with anything you need."

Seyyid Mohammed could only comply with his tutor's wishes. He accepted readily, also because he had experienced many marital problems. He was happy that Seyyid Hussein trusted him, and this trust reflected well on Nasser too.

Nasser was full of happiness when he left the Seyyids. His hopes of completing his project rose. He called Mustafa with the news that Seyyid Mohammed had joined the team. They then made an appointment to meet that evening.

Mustafa came a little late because of the needs of his children, who were in the care of his mother. Nasser and Mustafa began to discuss how enlarge their team of three. Mustafa suggested inviting a female with experience in sociology. Nasser liked the idea. Mustafa and he thought of names, but they did not make a choice.

One morning Nasser went to see Mustafa at the university's library, but he was in a meeting. To fill his spare time, Nasser began to look for a book that Seyyid Hussein had advised him to read. He noticed a woman trying to return a book to a top shelf and, thinking she worked in the library, he asked, "Excuse me, do you have *The World of Women*?" [1]

She looked at him strangely, not because she did not work in the library, but because the book meant a lot to her. Her mind drifted – to the extent that he felt he had offended her. He realized his error and quickly added, "Sorry, I thought you worked in the library."

Quickly she erased the picture of the event that had been in her mind and smiled, to assure him and alleviate the uncertainty that he may have made a mistake. She began to talk to him calmly, "Do not worry; no offence. What caught my attention was the book's name. It is a good scientific product. A great thinking mind is behind it, and I respect the mind of that God-blessed author."

Nasser realized he was talking to a highly educated person. He said, "The mind that does not work paralyzes society, so blessed is the working mind."

She showed her appreciation for that by responding, "I did not think the man who stood before me was so educated!"

"I am flattered," replied Nasser with true spontaneity.

"What you said about the mind shows wisdom," she stated. "You place a high value on the working mind. Well said!"

She now stopped talking, embarrassed. Nasser realized there had been no introduction. He said, "My name is Nasser Rida."

"I am honored," she replied. "I am Afaf Badran, professor of psychology at the College of Social Sciences."

Nasser thought he may have found the person he was looking for. He asked her, "Why did this book catch your eye?"

Dr. Afaf sighed. She felt it wrong to talk about a personal problem with a person she had met for the first time. Instead, she gave a general answer: "It is good for my research. I have put all my efforts

---

[1] Seyyid Mohammed Hussein Fadlullah, *Dunyal Mar'ah* [*The World of Women*] (Beirut: Dar Al-Malak, 1997).

17

into it for years. This book supports my ideas and opens up even more thoughts."

Nasser interposed to say that, if this book had accompanied her efforts for years, it would continue to do so. He had discovered another like-minded person researching the subject of women and family. He was daydreaming when he heard Dr. Afaf taking her leave. She informed him that he would find the book in the library, but, if he wanted a copy to keep, she could mail one to him, as she had several, or she could give him one the next morning in her office at the university. He said farewell full of hope. He could not sleep that night, kept awake by wondering whether Dr. Afaf might agree to help in his research.

The next morning, Nasser knocked on Dr. Afaf's office door. She understood, from how he looked, that he was apprehensive. She tried with all the modesty and intelligence God had given her to take his mind off his anxieties. She presented him with *The World of Women*. He began to speak, but she interrupted him politely and said, "Do not thank me till you have read the dedication, as I am not one who gives gifts to get repeatedly thanked!"

This comment made Nasser feel more comfortable. He opened the book and read: "To Mr. Nasser, on whose face glows the determination of the researcher who will not rest till he finds the elusive truth. Afaf Badran." Nasser read the inscription and felt he would be unworthy of her praise unless he worked on the project much more than he already had. He said simply, "Thank you, my teacher."

She stopped him, saying, "We are not in the position of teacher and student. Take this in the name of knowledge" – he could not believe what he was hearing – "and we will work together." Nasser felt this was the right moment to describe his project and propose that she join the team.

She thought his idea good. They made an appointment to meet three days later, as she was busy with her work. During this time, Nasser sat every night with his wife, who shared the burden of his project, and they discussed ideas

Nasser's face showed concern as he went to meet Dr. Afaf. He felt it was his job to find out how determined she was to tackle the subject. He feared his request might be seen as interfering in her private life. She put him at ease as soon as he had raised this issue. Without embarrassment, she asked, "Why do you think I have been researching this subject for years?" He did not answer out of surprise, so she added, "I am waiting for your reply, Nasser."

"I was going to ask that question," he said, "but I was too shy. So, what made you research issues concerning men and women, marriage and divorce?"

"The reason goes back eight years," she replied. "Hadeel, my daughter and only child, was 15 years old when my neighbor Su'ad suggested marriage between my daughter and her brother-in-law, newly returned from abroad. It was the first trial for me as a mother and a widow. I felt awkward, so I said, 'My daughter is still young and she is studying.' Su'ad suggested an engagement, for two years. Hadeel would then be 17 years old and they could marry and agree on finishing her education. All I could say was, 'Give me a few days to ask the girl and think about it.' Su'ad encouraged me to accept her brother-in-law, whom she described as pious and hardworking. He was 25, owned an apartment in Beirut, had a good income, and seemed in all ways respectable.

"My neighbor and I agreed to meet in a week. Meanwhile, I arranged a meeting among my daughter, me, and the young man to get to know him. Our neighbor came with the young suitor, who – in a meeting that took a little more than half an hour – showed us documents to demonstrate his financial independence, and gave us other detailed information. After the visit, I asked my daughter's opinion and she agreed to marry him. Everything happened quickly. They got engaged through preliminary marriage. The marriage contract was drawn up, under which they would move into the marital home after two years. But, it did not take long to discover that this young man did not possess any stability whatsoever. His aim in this engagement was to tap into the wealth of the mother. He started to create problems, so we asked for a divorce. He said he would divorce only if we gave him $5,000 in addition to returning the full dowry. We had to accept. Imagine a 15-year-old girl being unable to go to school. Every time we went out it was a struggle for her. She was called the divorcée of that man, even though full marriage did not become a reality."

As Dr. Afaf concluded her story, Nasser sensed she would have broken into tears were it not for her shyness in front of a stranger. He felt much sympathy for her and it showed on his face. Dr. Afaf noticed this and finished by saying, "This story is now a memory, though still raw. We must be aware of it in the research and not ignore it. This is why it was not awkward for me to tell you. My daughter has continued living her life with strength and determination. She is now 23 years old and is specializing in chemistry."

Nasser was happy to hear of the girl's determination. He thanked God the girl had gotten divorced before full marriage. If she had given birth and then separated, she probably would never have finished her education.

Nasser felt a sense of care toward Dr. Afaf, who was searching for the truth in addition to peace of mind, for he was on a journey toward these goals too. Here, he realized, was a person who shared his hopes of propagating a social system that protected the family from disintegration.

Dr. Afaf now addressed the subject of the team. She proposed that, in addition to the Shi'ite Muslims, a researcher of the Sunni doctrine should join. This would give the work its strength, the understanding that the subject does not concern one sect, but rather all people. She suggested Dr. Omar Abu Zakaria, a delegate from the University of Morocco who was teaching at the university and who had written many research papers on the family in Islam.

After he had assented to her proposal, Dr. Afaf, without revealing the idea of the project, phoned Dr. Omar and asked him to meet with Nasser. He agreed to a meeting the next day. When Nasser saw this white-haired man, he was reassured. They began to talk about the subject of family. Nasser soon realized this man had great understanding. Nasser saw the reason Dr. Afaf chose Dr. Omar, for she had spoken of his general understanding of women topics and the family, and his scientific knowledge of people's problems and anxieties.

Nasser summed up the aims of the project in terms of the relationship between men and women, marriage, family, and divorce; what elements these issues are built on; how society deals with them positively and negatively; the impact of the rulings based on religion and traditions; the danger of the control that men exercised over women; and also men's oppression of them. Dr. Omar listened and asked Nasser to specify how he could help. Nasser replied, "We aim to produce an educational project, enlightened by modern ideas, that is totally consistent with Islam. The research should go beyond sensitivities with doctrines, and should illustrate a path for young men and women to use to reach a future place where they can achieve their hopes and ambitions. This will not happen without the cooperation of thinkers and scientists. They have a responsibility to serve the younger generation and to open their minds to what Islam offers in terms of forgiveness and a welcome that embraces all."

As Dr. Omar listened, in his mind was the image of his two daughters in Morocco, for whom he had worked hard to bring them happiness and comfort in life, to guide them toward a safe future, and to offer them the benefits of his experience and education to help them avoid the thorny paths of life. He now asked Nasser, "How may I assist with this project?"

"It would be a great honor if you would join our team," said Nasser. We are four Shi'ite Muslims – Dr. Afaf, Seyyid Mohammed, Mustafa Naqib, and me. Your perspective will contribute in developing an idea that will benefit our society."

Dr. Omar answered gravely, "Thank you for the great confidence in me. If I accept, I will try not to disappoint you. However, I need time to think, so I may reach the correct decision."

After Nasser left Dr. Omar's office, he felt, from the type of questions Dr. Omar had asked, that Dr. Omar needed more time and more details about the project – what was its basis and what were the aims, means, and tools to guide the research. Nasser thought Dr. Omar suspected him of wanting to draw Dr. Omar to ideas he did not believe in. Nasser went straight to Dr. Afaf and told her this. She knew Dr. Omar's research interests well and advised Nasser not to give up. Nasser met with Dr. Omar several more times, each time getting deeper into the project. Dr. Omar finally agreed to join because the project contained features of modern Islamic social research, though he still had personal reservations.

Now the team was complete and they could start meeting. Mustafa was chosen to be the team's secretary. He would organize the meetings, create the agendas, and record the opinions and ideas. The team members met once or twice a week, depending on need. They might sometimes agree on a subject, and disagree on another, but would collect all points of view that were not fueled by fanaticism or prejudice. After two years of meetings, discussions, and document collection, they came out satisfied with similar opinions and practical solutions to put forward for more deliberation. "Where should these ideas and opinions now be discussed?" was the question Nasser raised.

"At the university," suggested Dr. Afaf. "Who are more suitable to deliberate with and listen to than students? Such a subject cannot be discussed intelligently unless it is with university students in the form of seminars. High-school students are too young to analyze such issues. As for older people, these are fathers and mothers. Some of them may to be an obstacle in a project such as this because of their ties to traditions."

The team felt she was right. Nasser offered to contact his university, but the other three preferred their university because it was the country's largest and most prestigious. So it was agreed. Dr. Omar would talk to Dr. Elias Munir, the Dean at his university, and briefly outline the project and request that he meet with Nasser. Dr. Omar then immediately contacted the Dean. On behalf of the team, he asked the Dean to reserve a large room for discussion and promised that Nasser would fully inform him about the project when they met. Because of the Dean's respect for Dr. Omar, he made an appointment to meet Nasser early the next morning.

When Nasser arrived, the Dean welcomed him and asked for his news, for he knew of Nasser as the reputable deputy director of the Center for Sociological Research at Beirut's second largest university. The Dean's personal office was full of the Center's publications. Nasser thanked him for his interest and told him about the background research – research on issues central to the social, psychological, and emotional aims of all human beings, in society and in life. Nasser gave the Dean the proposed titles of the seminars, and expressed the hopes of the team regarding the Dean's contribution to the project's success by allowing use of the university facilities and ensuring that the essentials would be provided.

The Dean's trust in Dr. Omar and Dr. Afaf, two eminent professors at the university, and the subject's importance, impelled him to contact Dr. George Hana, the university Trustee. He informed him of Nasser's visit to confirm the reservation for a lecture hall and the start of the seminars. A few minutes later, Nasser was meeting with Dr. Hana, who offered him the hall that seated 170 people. Nasser was elated.

* * * * *

# The First Seminar

Nasser phoned the rest of the team with the details of his agreement with the Dean and the Trustee. They all shared his joy. After consulting with Mustafa about how to announce the seminars, Nasser had banners printed that would create suspense and make students eager to attend without preconceived ideas.

Next, the university was decorated with banners throughout the various departments. Students began noticing the time and place of the seminars. They were, however, confused by the vague invitation. The banners read: "All university students are invited to attend a seminar on Thursday at four o'clock in the afternoon – an event concerning research on *an important social issue.*"

Finally, the day came. The hall doors opened and the five members of the team took their seats at a table on the stage. On top of the table were stacks of books and piles of papers. Each lecturer had a glass and pitcher filled with water.The students, who had turned out in small numbers, also took seats. Nasser had arranged for audio tapes and cameras to be turned on as soon as the seminars began with Mustafa's welcome to the audience and his colleagues. "Thank you all," said Mustafa, "for responding to our announcement and coming here today. Most of you may already know me and my fellow lecturers. For those who do not, I am Mustafa Naqib, the head librarian at this university. I will act as the secretary for these seminars. Seyyid Mohammed is an eminent scholar of Islamic law. Dr. Omar Abu Zakaria is a professor of sociology at our university's College of Social Sciences. Dr. Afaf Badran is a professor of psychology at the same College. Mr. Nasser Rida, the initiator of our project, is the assistant director of the Center for Sociological Research at our sister university at the other end of the city. He also lectures there in sociology and has a private practice for relationship counseling.

"We will hold seminars here. They will be about men and women, and the relationship between them. This subject, with all its complexities, has been the central focus of my colleagues' research for many years, as each one had an interest in the issue long before our team was formed two years ago. Now this team is determined to conclude its work by bringing its findings into a university, since an educational environment offers the best chance for producing recommendations to serve all society."

Then Mustafa added, "We appear before you as lecturers and discussion leaders on a subject on which we have become expert. To put you in the framework of the discussion, we will start by studying marriage and divorce. The 'important social issue' that we advertised for today's seminar is 'divorce' and its causes and its effects on the family and society. The problem of divorce is found in Islam, Christianity, and other religions, but our focus will be only on Islam. I leave the discussion to the lecturers and I call on Seyyid Mohammed to talk about: Why is divorce a problem?"

After welcoming the students, the Seyyid began, "The family unit is a microcosm of society. If the family unit crumbles, so does our larger family – society. The greatest threat to the integrity of the family today is divorce. Each divorce dissolves a particular family, but divorce as a whole, if it occurs in large enough numbers, burdens and destabilizes the entire society. Among the impacts and costs of divorce to society are the strain on the legal court system, the rise in criminal behavior among children from a broken home, the financial inefficiency of maintaining separate households, the need for treatment programs for physical and emotional illnesses suffered by many divorced parties and their children, and the toll taken, not just on the couple, but also on their children, families, friends, employers, and co-workers. During the last few decades in our country and in the surrounding region, the divorce rate has been very high and it continues to rise. The future implications of this are ominous."

Mustafa took notes as the Seyyid spoke to keep track of the main points. He now asked Dr. Afaf to talk about the effects of divorce on the family and she said, "Generally speaking, divorce marks the ending of that enduring basis on which the family should be established. 'Family' is a social organization, with divorce signaling a failed marriage for those people who were unable to steer their family life on to the right path. This results in the family's fragmentation. Divorce assumes significance, and becomes imperative as the only way out of a nightmarish situation, when marital life becomes a hell that swallows all members of the family. But, far from being an ending of life, divorce may serve as the needed remedy for ending prolonged marital suffering. It does, however, cause deep psychological stress on the concerned parties. The main victims are the children, who are exposed to the anguish of losing one of the parents and being deprived of that parent's love and compassion. They also suffer added tension and stress as they see most other children having a stable life filled with love and compassion and being close with both parents. The worst damage from divorce occurs when one parent paints a distorted image of the other to the children and fills their hearts with anger and hate. Added to the enmity between the divorced couple, and often also between the two families of in-laws, are the financial problems that arise over adequate support for the wife and care of the children. These problems occur when the divorced husband and wife fail to carry out their legal, moral, and social responsibilities as parents toward their children following divorce.

"Another negative impact of divorce is how it restricts a woman's freedom in our society. Divorce compels her to return to her father's and brother's authority and power, and so subjects her to their continuous control and supervision, whereas a man walks away with all the compassion and sympathy of his relatives and friends."

Here, Nasser requested to amplify on what the Seyyid had said about the increase in divorce in the Islamic community. Nasser said, "I will quote from an article in the magazine *Kullun Naas* by the Egyptian lawyer Mohammed Hijazi, who wrote, 'The Arabic Lawyers' Union and the United Nations report 100 million separations and divorces occur worldwide yearly among all peoples. The victim is the family, and most of the time it is the children who pay the price of divorce.'" [2]

The audience began to take an interest, as the importance of the subject became more evident. From then on, it seemed that every student felt the need to combat this problem. Their interest was seen growing even stronger when Nasser quoted more specific figures: "The book in my hands is *Women and Divorce in Kuwaiti Society,* by Dr. Fahad Al-Thaqib. It highlights the statistics from the Kuwait Ministry of Justice, which recorded 2,594 divorce cases in 1993.[3] Statistics from the Kuwaiti newspaper *Al-Anba'a*, July 28, 1999, reveal 3,096 divorce cases in 1997 in Kuwait.[4] According to

---

[2]  *Kullun Naas* [Egypt], ﹍﹍ Jan. 1997: 27 (no specific date).
[3]  Fahad Al-Thaqib, *Al-Mar'aa wat-Talak fil Moujtam' Al-Kuwaiti* [*Women and Divorce in Kuwaiti Society*] (Khaldiya: Kuwait University, 1999), 47.
[4]  *Al-Anba'a* [Kuwait], 28 July 1999: (no page no.).

the Kuwaiti newspaper *Al-Qabas* of December 6, 2003, the divorce percentage in this country reached 44%.[5] This number is very high for a nation whose population does not exceed 950,000. As for here in Beirut, in 1996 one of its *Shari'ah* [Islamic law] offices reported 899 divorces resulted from 2,906 marriage contracts that were made between September 9, 1985 and the end of 1995.[6] This means a third of those marriages in Beirut ended in divorce after a certain time."

Nasser added to the students' surprise at the figures by saying, "According to Bahrain's central Department of Statistics, 2,233 marriage contracts were recorded in 1985, with 535 divorces, so the divorce rate was 24%.[7] In the 1990s, four researchers in the U.A.E. found half of all their marriages ending in divorce.[8] More recent data cited a divorce rate of 46% in the U.A.E., 38% in Qatar, 35% in Kuwait, and 34% in Bahrain. Also, separate studies in 2003 by the Prince Salman Social Center in Riyadh and by the Saudi Ministry of Planning revealed alarming annual increases in divorce in Saudi Arabia and other Gulf countries, whose divorce rates ranged from 30% to 35%. In Saudi Arabia, an average of 33 women divorce daily and Riyadh has about 3,000 divorcées.[9] However, some government agencies in Arab countries often report official statistics for divorce that are lower than the numbers I have quoted here. This is because their calculations are based on limited time periods that do not portray the complete picture."

Mustafa then offered a comment. "Putting aside the tragic reality that children of divorce face, most marital disputes stay in the home and do not reach the courts. In many such homes, a crime worse than divorce is committed daily: violence against women!" As he finished, Dr. Afaf nodded in strong agreement and added her own comment.

She said, "While the West has the courage to publish studies and figures on the violence practiced against women there, the studies

---

[5] *Al-Qabas* [Kuwait], 6 Dec. 2003: (no page no.).
[6] Beirut *Shari'ah* Office, *'Ahada 'Ashara 'Aman fil Khidmat Al-Moujtama'* [*Eleven Years Serving the Society*] (Beirut: Beirut *Shari'ah* Office, 1996), 6.
[7] *Al-Yawm* [Bahrain], 9 July 1986, 14.
[8] Ali Abu Abdullah Abdul Mohsin, *Ta'addod Al-Zawjat Bainal-'ilm wal-Din* [*Polygamy between Science and Religion*] (Beirut: Dar As-Safwa, 1997) 11.
[9] *Khaleej Times Online* [U.A.E.], 5 Sept. 2005: www.khaleejtimes.com.

in Islamic society remain prisoners of fear. Yet even with the media limitations, we know it is rising to the roof."

At this moment a student raised his hand. Mustafa gave him permission to speak, and the boy asked, **"What prevents a wife from rebeling and taking her case to court?"**

Seyyid Mohammed answered, "Many women do that. They take refuge in the courts or tell their families, but other women have become used to surrendering to the customs within which they were raised. Women who surrender to this bad state of affairs and accept it fear the weapon of divorce, as it would make them homeless, especially when their families cannot take them in and or will not stand by them. Under such circumstances, they stay with their husbands, even though suffering."

Mustafa then asked the students, "What are the causes of divorce?" He gave time to allow each student to form an opinion. A few moments passed in silence, as if each was recalling cases he or she had heard of or experienced. Then, one by one, they raised their hands for permission to speak.

Mustafa chose a male student, who looked to be about 18 years old, to speak first. He said, "The age difference between a couple is a major cause of divorce."

"A logical and acceptable reason," said Mustafa and then called on a female student.

From her appearance, she seemed composed and well educated. She said, "The woman could be barren or the man could be impotent. The couple might accept the suffering this brings, but the insistence of the families on having children and implied blame against the sterile person could lead to a separation."

The seminar participants carried on discussing this opinion, till a male student said, "One main reason for divorce is when a husband is not wealthy and must live with his parents and brothers and sisters. This makes the wife feel awkward and causes problems between her and the husband. As he cannot provide a stable home, divorce results."

The audience's interest in what their fellow students were saying began to increase. Mustafa made sure he was writing down all the causes he thought valid and then he called on a male student in the back row. The student said, "One of the reasons for divorce is the belittling of the man's position in the family. I speak of the woman who tries to be masculine or takes the man's role. She wants her husband to be the feminine one – she is like an aggressive cat! Some men cannot put up with it and they divorce her."

Mustafa allowed another male student to speak. He said, "The breadwinner was financially secure, and his family had a comfortable lifestyle. Then he lost his job and could not provide the essentials for his family. His wife hates living in poverty. They begin to differ and she asks for a divorce."

A third male student jumped in and said, "One reason for divorce is the difference in sects and religions."

Mustafa was about to write down this point when a female student jumped up with obvious enthusiasm and offered, "Religions do not cause differences among people, but bring them together. Those who interpret religion incorrectly cause the differences."

The same male student who spoke before now rose without permission and called out, "Religions are one of the causes of divorce, though not a main reason." The same female student answered that the ills are found in souls, not in laws of religion. Mustafa intervened to calm them down, for such disputes could ruin the seminar. He stopped the chaos that was about to unfold and he requested that the discussions be objective to keep the seminar running smoothly, without agitation.

Mustafa then called on a male student, who was patiently waiting his turn. "A couple can disagree about choosing a marital home," he said. "They argue over location, size, style, furnishings, renting vs. buying, what they can afford, and so on."

Mustafa gave every student time to voice an opinion. Most of the students spoke, and most spoke several times. The lecturers were happy that the students mentioned so many problems leading to divorce and destroying the family. After quickly removing the most of repetition and grouping similar concepts together, Mustafa read aloud the list he had made of the many reasons mentioned for divorce:

- ❖ The couple disagrees over where to live, especially whether to set up an independent home or move in with relatives.
- ❖ One party's inability to adapt to the in-laws results in constant conflict and ends in divorce.
- ❖ The families of the couple constantly interfere in their private life. The main interferers are the women. In most cases, the husband submits to the will of his family. He obeys them blindly, to the extent that he loses his individuality.
- ❖ A man has a hidden motive for marrying: to make his wife a caretaker for his disabled mother. Tending to her mother-in-law overwhelms the wife.
- ❖ An event causes the husband or wife to become disabled, and one is unable to live with the other's disabilities and the constant need of a caretaker.
- ❖ The couple disagrees over the location or type of marital home.
- ❖ False information: one partner learns the other was deceitful before marriage. For example, the wife discovers her previously divorced husband pretended to be marrying for the first time.
- ❖ The wife experiences tension because the husband has another wife, wishes to marry another woman, or resume a relationship with his ex-wife.
- ❖ There is a long separation. For instance, the husband must work outside the country and cannot afford to bring along his wife.
- ❖ The husband lacks the knowledge to raise a family and run a household.
- ❖ Ignorance about sex puts a strain on the couple, and their sexual needs go unfulfilled. Conflict follows and leads to anger, then separation.
- ❖ One partner falls in love with another person.
- ❖ One partner discovers the other has a sinful relationship outside the home.
- ❖ The husband feels neglected after the couple has children.
- ❖ One of the partners is incapable of producing children.
- ❖ The birth of a disabled child puts great stress on the relationship.
- ❖ The wife wants to finish her education or have a career, even after childbirth.

- ❖ The couple is unequal in education. If the husband has a diploma and the wife is nearly illiterate, it creates conflict in marital life as they are not well-suited.
- ❖ The husband was attracted only to his wife's wealth, or the marriage was undertaken to achieve higher social status.
- ❖ One sees the other as inferior because of a difference in social status.
- ❖ The lifestyle the husband offers his wife is inferior to that of her family.
- ❖ The husband cannot support his wife and family financially.
- ❖ One partner is accused or convicted of fraud and goes to prison.
- ❖ The husband chooses a sinful path, such as drug or alcohol addiction.
- ❖ Physical abuse occurs. The husband hits the wife. Sometimes the wife may be the abuser.
- ❖ Psychological abuse occurs. One party is demeaned in private and/or in public.
- ❖ The couple did not know important things about each other before their marriage.
- ❖ The husband and wife have incompatible interests due to a big age difference.
- ❖ The couple's immaturity prevents discovery of each other's faults before marriage and acceptance of these faults after marriage. Later, such faults become unbearable.
- ❖ Great responsibility and pressure undermine the marriage. Life before marriage was simple, but now one or both partners fail to meet the challenges of marriage.
- ❖ One partner changes and becomes almost a different person, due to maturity, higher education, career advancement, or wartime experiences.
- ❖ The wife changes after marriage from obedient to rebellious.
- ❖ The wife is aggressive and tries to take over the husband's role in the home.
- ❖ Negative traits, such as selfishness, emerge or worsen after marriage.
- ❖ One makes rash decisions. The other is shocked to find the partner is not whom he or she seemed to be, and realizes having been blinded by physical attraction.
- ❖ One partner has so many outside interests that he or she ignores the other. The ignored partner experiences loneliness.

- One partner suffers from boredom and desires a change.
- The husband or wife lacks concern about problems and struggles they face outside the home. The couple does not behave as a team.
- One of the partners has a suspicious nature.
- Unjustified jealousy arises in one of the partners and this drives them apart.
- The wife practices black magic or she assumes the husband or his family is using black magic against her.
- A difference in sect or religion makes the relationship tense and unstable, especially where there is interference from both families. This stems from the lack of religious tolerance in families and society.
- The couple has a conflict over values, customs, politics, or personal wishes.

While he was presenting the lists, Mustafa recognized some of the reasons for divorce given by the students were similar to others. He paused to consolidate them and said, "I have sorted your specific answers into these main general categories:

- Conflict with the partner's family, including the wish for an independent home.
- Physical or mental illness, including jealousy and suspicion.
- The existence of a second wife.
- Sexual problems, including adultery, sterility, and long separation.
- Financial issues.
- Sinful behavior, such as drug or alcohol addiction.
- Ill treatment.
- Lack of understanding between the couple, including not behaving like a team.
- Lack of satisfaction and growth of hostility.
- Conflict due to different religions or sects or values."

After the input from the students had been narrowed down in this way, Seyyid Mohammed felt the session could not be concluded without making this point: "As the causes are added up and listed, let us be aware that, were it not for divorce being easy – for men, of course, but not for women – such a big rise in divorce cases would not have occurred. For the Shi'ites, two legal witnesses are enough and divorce can be granted in court in minutes. For the

Sunnis, though most use the court system for divorce, a husband may divorce his wife by simply saying the words 'you are divorced' at home. A judge, both Shi'ite and Sunni, may postpone the divorce for a week, for example, in hope of reconciliation. After that, it is easy for the man to get the divorce paper. It is evident that in the past, the wife was able to get used to her husband, to accept a domineering husband. She accepted his wishes and sacrificed her personal freedom. The woman was oppressed. Because of her limited knowledge, her husband did not hear her voice."

He continued, "She did not know her lawful rights – the opposite of what it is like now. Today, after educating herself and competing with men at work, her choices are greater. She does not accept what she did in the past. This is an essential cause in the increase in divorce: her unwillingness to tolerate the oppression she accepted in the past. It is for men to be aware of this reality, to understand a woman's rights, and to respect her as a human being and regarding her role in the family. Men should follow their religious obligations, which include treating women well.

He concluded with, "Here, we are interested in the opinions of others, and hope to come up with solutions that may limit the increase in divorce cases, generation after generation. We have heard of true causes that lead to the breakup of a family, and other well-reasoned points. Having identified some of these causes, we should now search for ways to prevent the husband and wife from ruining this sacred relationship."

The voice of Seyyid Mohammed was like a bell announcing the time for serious thought. During the silence that followed, the lecturers and students looked around as if their eyes were searching for the solution.

Nasser broke this silence. "Having noted all the general and specific causes of divorce that the students brought up – and I believe the lecturers will agree with my opinion – I noticed a point many students made directly or indirectly, that husband and wife did not truly know each other before marriage. I believe what drives most divorces is the discovery after time that our partner has many negative traits we were unaware of before the marriage. This is because we decided to marry without serious and realistic research on the partner we chose. Divorce also stems from incompatibility, that is, the degree of mismatch between the two people if they do not experience the spiritual element of marriage and if one feels the other does not complement his or her needs and hopes."

"In my opinion, most causes of divorce – conflict with the partner's family, mental problems, sexual problems, sinful behavior, ill treatment, lack of understanding, lack of satisfaction, and differences in religion or values – may result from not truly knowing each other well before marriage. If we do get to know each other well, it is fair to say about 70% of the problems may be solved before they begin, that is, before marriage. An example of this from our list of the causes of divorce is family interference in the couple's marital life. If the boy and girl got to know the nature of each other's families before marriage, they would see the potential family problems and make an informed decision to marry and live with this reality or break up before marriage."

Nasser found the audience appreciated his opinion. It was as though he had expressed what was inside of everyone. He realized this after seeing a smile of approval on Seyyid Mohammed's face, a nod from Dr. Omar, and signs of agreement on the students' faces.

After witnessing this positive atmosphere, Mustafa ended the session by saying, "This opinion was welcomed by the audience because it is the kind of solution we seek, so I ask this question: How can we make a young man and young woman get to know each other before marriage? Who has an idea for this? I am not waiting for an answer to this question now – we have already spent two hours at this seminar. We – God willing – will be waiting for you here in this hall at 3 pm next Thursday, so what do you say?"

The students found this appointment suited them, and it did not conflict with studying for their exams. Mustafa now said, "Open the subject among yourselves and your friends, your fathers, your mothers. We will not conceal anything. Our efforts and your efforts are revealing the truth about how to achieve family stability in our society. Examine, search, and ask, 'How can boys and girls get to know each other?' We will be waiting."

* * * * *

# CHAPTER TWO
## On the Journey of Life

* * * * *

### Acquaintance Before Marriage

Nasser sat at the desk in his office. He was organizing his papers for the upcoming seminar on the new subject, acquaintance before marriage. The team had spent months documenting, organizing, and drawing conclusions to reach a logical result after weighing the negative effects of entering a marriage without knowing each other against the positive effects of being acquainted with one another before marriage. It was important to him that the lecturers and the students reach the result he hoped for.

At three o'clock on the appointed day Nasser stood amazed at the entrance door of the lecture hall. Students in large numbers arrived to reserve their seats, ready for the commencement of the seminar that everyone had heard of around the university. The students had understood that issues concerning men and women, marriage and divorce, and the family and society were the top priorities for educated persons. Five minutes before the seminar was to start, the 170-seat hall was almost full. Now whole groups came, whereas the first time random individuals had come for a total of not more than 30 students. This full attendance was the result of the students having been discussing the subject for days. Nasser could see excitement on their faces because the subject was no longer a mystery. Nasser realized the lecturers would now need the microphone so he made sure it was turned on and working properly.

The seminar began when the lecturers entered. Mustafa, as seminar secretary, summarized the first session by listing the causes for divorce that the audience had pointed out, and by stating that the session had concluded that the main reason for divorce was the lack of acquaintance before marriage. Then he said, "As it is clear that acquaintance is necessary between a boy and girl before marriage, I open this session by asking: How can this acquaintance be lawful, Islamically speaking?"

Before listening to the students' opinions, Nasser asked to speak. Mustafa gave permission by passing the microphone to him, and Nasser said, "Before we delineate the lawfulness of the acquaintance between the two people, we must think about the importance of the marriage succeeding. It is a journey of a lifetime – an entrance into an institution controlled by a system of relationships, rights, and obligations. The family is one of the distinctive elements in this system. To live successfully within this institution depends on the compatibility and understanding of men and women before marriage. It is natural to study a person's personality, ideas, and aims before entering into a partnership with that person. Partners should know their compatibility so that the relationship's outcome is not unexpected. This acquaintance needs enough time to develop. It is a natural right for everyone, and this applies also to marriage, which is considered more than a partnership. As marriage is a lawful social institution, it is the man's right to know the nature of whom he wishes to marry – to get to know her mentality and the way she thinks – to judge their compatibility. It is also the woman's right to know the kind of man he is before marriage: his education, lifestyle, and what he strives to achieve in life. For both sides to understand these issues, a period of acquaintance is needed for mature and realistic study, isolated from superficial attraction. An opportunity should be made available for the two to pinpoint the negative and positive traits in each other."

Dr. Omar then spoke. "I want to add to Brother Nasser's remarks. The period of acquaintance is a true and realistic test if the two sides refrain from role playing and show their true selves free of artificiality. Honesty should rule the relationship. Our beliefs at this time stem from the possibility of there being compatibility or not."

Dr. Omar opened one of the books in front of him and continued, "I will quote from Dr. Adnan Al-Shati's book *Marriage and Family*. 'Compatibility, as William Law defined it, is present between two people who accept mutual feelings and achieve the expectations of marriage for each other.' Dr. Adnan adds, 'According to Spanier and Thompson, marital harmony includes mutual gratification and solidarity, and agreement on important issues. The authors identified these requirements for marital harmony:

- ❖ Coherence of opinions,
- ❖ Solidarity and the guarantee of the marriage, and
- ❖ Emotional expression and the satisfaction of essential emotional and sexual desires.' [10]

"I will now read a selection from Dr. Sana'a Al-Khouly's book The Family and Familial Life. On page 177, she says, 'Every boy and girl should realize that to achieve [marital harmony], they should have enough time [to get acquainted]. This [type of negative discovery] is avoidable, provided they have the chance of knowing and understanding each other prior to marriage, rather than uncovering traits under new and changed circumstances that limit their freedom of choice. Such a situation leads to a lack of consensus, often breeding stress and conflict, which is avoidable through tolerance, an attitude of flexibility, and a redefinition of their expectations of each other. One of the major factors affecting marital harmony and leading to failed marriages is the inability to accept each other the way they are. Marriage between a boy and girl, without fully knowing each other, may result in both rejecting the other as marriage partners.'" [11]

Now one of the male students stood and spoke. **"Getting married without knowing each other – especially when the family chooses a husband for their daughter or a wife for their son where there is no desire or attraction – is venturing into the unknown. Many constraints face young men and women who want to get to know each other before marriage. Customs and**

---

[10] Adnan Al-Shati, *Az-Zawaj wal-'Ailah [Marriage and Family]* (Khaldiya: Kuwait University, 1997) 166. William Law, 1686-1761, was an independent Protestant Christian clergyman and writer who lived in England. Spanier and Thompson are American sociologists. Al-Shati is quoting from Graham Spanier and Linda Thompson, *The Rewards and Costs of Ending a Marriage* (unpublished manuscript, 1981), later incorporated into *Parting: the Aftermath of Separation and Divorce* (Newbury Park, CA: Sage, 1984; revised 1987).

[11] Sana'a Al-Khouly, *Al-'Ailah wal-Hayat Al-'Ailah [The Family and Familial Life]* (Beirut: Dar Al-Nahda Al-Arabia, 1984) 177.

**traditions prohibit this, so how is it possible for a young man to get to know a young woman in Islam?**"

This question had attracted the audience's attention, so Mustafa took control of the dialog by asking, "What are the lawful limits? To what extent does Islam allow a boy and girl to get acquainted? We put this question before you all. We wish to hear your opinions and thoughts."

The students were eager to give their opinions. The first to respond said, **"Why do we burden ourselves? The solution is available. The engagement is enough."**

She said this while looking at Nasser, who took over the discussion by saying, "This suggestion opens up important horizons. I remind our Christian brothers and sisters present in this hall that our study falls within the framework of *Shari'ah* [Islamic law], as applied by all Islamic sects. Therefore, we do not speak of the system for engagements between Christians, but we will come to this later. It is more suitable to ask Seyyid Mohammed for the *Shari'ah's* view of the student's suggestion."

The Seyyid then addressed her question. "The kind of engagement widely practiced in most Islamic countries does not include the term 'lawful contract' that would allow the boy and girl to feel free – as regards the law – to sit alone together and go out together. How can they get to know one another when the restraints of *Shari'ah* prevent them from reaching beyond this in terms of being intimate, and discover what the other person is really like, and decide whether to go ahead with the engagement? We say this without stating that Islam, nevertheless, allows the boy to look at the girl's face and hands, if they are serious in their engagement. In the past, a boy often sent a woman whom he trusted – some women did this professionally – to see more of the girl's behavior and appearance and also to look at the body almost naked. This is not needed today. A boy may see for himself if the girl is decent by getting to know her through her manners and her body language.

"At times, some religious clerics permit the face and hands to be seen. Other groups say he may see her with tight-fitting clothing that outlines her body. A third group, which includes Sheikh Mohammed Abu Zahra, forbids even the face and hands to be seen. Some clerics let the couple talk to each other in the presence of a relative.

In light of what has been said, engagement is not a solution for truly getting to know one another lawfully."

After receiving Mustafa's permission, a female student got up quietly and with composure to say, **"There is no doubt that marital problems and difficulties stem from the lack of knowing each other well, and I mean in acquaintance in knowing all the details, from manners to physique and other matters. Therefore, if we discuss our families allowing the fiancé to sit with his fiancée only in the presence of a relative, how will they be able to choose? All eyes will be on them, and ears pick every word they utter. Second, if the law allows the boy to see only the hands and face, does the appearance of these show the girl's beauty? As we know, beauty is a requirement for many boys. Third, can women be trusted with discovering the manners and behavior of the girl? What they like is not necessarily what the boy likes. It is the person alone, whether boy or girl, through companionship, who can discover the other's character."**

Nasser praised her well-reasoned words. Just as he was about to review her contribution, another female student interrupted him. **"Why do we concern ourselves with what is lawful and unlawful? Companionship alone should be the solution. With companionship, we are free from the constraints forced on us, and acquaintance between the boy and girl may take place."**

Seyyid Mohammed smiled and offered an answer. "We are distinctly talking about the relationship between females and males or, on a larger scale, human's relationship to human through a system that God made for his worshippers. Our nations have tried other ideas and systems, but they led to many problems and we still are feeling the negative effects. As we search for a solution to the problem of lack of acquaintance, we will ask for it through Islam because Islam presents us with solutions that fulfill the needs of humankind."

During the Seyyid's reply, Dr. Omar had been organizing his papers while waiting his turn to speak. The Seyyid had just finished when Dr. Omar was permitted to comment. He said, "Companionship means that a certain relationship ties a boy and girl together. This relationship is not controlled by any kind of frame. Companionship cannot even be put under the heading of friendship because friendship will not go beyond brotherhood between the two people. Companionship is a meeting between two people that starts with emotions. This is why the girl believes that this boy is the man of her dreams as the relationship progresses into a kind of intimacy. Isolation can lead to sexual acts, possibly even to the loss of virginity."

Agreeing, Seyyid Mohammed inserted, "How many girls have confided in me on this issue! Within the Islamic concept, it is a forbidden relationship."

After that, Dr. Omar concluded, "The danger in befriending someone is that some of our societies do not allow this. If the girl's family find out about her relationship with the boy, there may be an outcry. The girl may even be killed to defend the family honor. This companionship is not a solution to getting acquainted because, as one of its disadvantages, it lacks a proper sanction, and sanction is not forthcoming."

One of the female students wanted to prove these opinions on companionship were illogical. She stood and said loudly, **"But why? Many of these relationships ended in marriage."**

Nasser quickly replied, "It is correct that some companionships lead to marriage, but, as Seyyid Mohammed clarified, any such relationship before marriage is forbidden. From my field studies, I concluded most of these companionships were unfocused, non-productive, and in vain.

"It affects a girl badly if she foolishly thought her relationship with a boy would lead to marriage and it did not. Nothing becomes of this girl in such a situation except for the pathetic light in which the boy sees her. To add to what Dr. Omar has said about crimes of honor, these punishments fall solely on the girl. The boy walks away without loss."

It seemed that some of the audience, Muslims and Christians alike, agreed about the dangers of dating, while being convinced of its lawfulness. After this, a silence fell over the room, till one of the male students spoke. **"The problem of acquaintance may be solved by some kind of engagement, especially the lawful engagement done in some places – mainly the Gulf countries – and called** *milcheh* **[preliminary marriage with delayed sex]. It is a lawful marriage that forbids sexual contact between the couple till a wedding celebration occurs. Is not** *milcheh* **the solution to acquaintance before marriage?"**

Seyyid Mohammed responded, "The solution is not that simple. A so-called engagement may be done in two ways. First, as we have said earlier, a couple may agree to marry later, without a lawful agreement in the beginning. They only put their hands on top of each other and read *Al-Fatiha* [the opening verses of the *Qur'an*]. So how can we let acquaintance happen in the shadow of an unlawful engagement? We cannot accept this. True acquaintance of one another means knowing everything about the other person. The girl wants to feel safe and assured: Is this boy the one she has hoped for? The boy wants the burdens of married life to be shared: Can this girl handle the responsibilities?

"There are also temperamental, psychological, and moral issues. Understanding these can lead to detailed answers on compatibility, which must include the right of both parties to know about each other sexually. Dr. Adnan Al-Shati says on page 176 of his book *Marriage and Family*, 'It may be that problems with sex are the most important ones, yet many authors believe achieving compatible sex in marriage is not a priority. They do not see it as a reason for marital problems or unhappiness in families. Even so, it is one of the reasons that causes trouble in family life. No doubt, when sexual needs are not satisfied in marriage, they may lead to differences and then hostility and repulsion.'" [12]

Seyyid Mohammed read from the book because he saw the importance of quoting a professional on this subject. He paused for a sip of water and continued, "As we have heard, sex is essential for a stable married life. However, how can a fiancé and fiancée understand their sexual compatibility through an engagement that has started just with reading *Al-Fatiha*?

"The second way of getting engaged is the lawful contract. However, if the couple breaks up due to incompatibility, many financial and emotional problems may result. I have witnessed some of these problems and can give examples of what may happen when a girl wishes to break the engagement. She can struggle with the boy's injustice, such as his demand for a large payment that her parents can hardly afford in addition to receiving back half the dowry if the marriage was not consummated, that is, if she is still a virgin. Or he may demand a payment even though the full dowry is rightfully hers if the marriage was consummated. Or he may travel away without

---

[12] Al-Shati 176.

41

divorcing her, making her future depend on his whim. This is not to mention the quarrels and disputes between the two families."

Here, Dr. Afaf interrupted to mention one of the significant effects of an engaged girl's divorce, based on her experience with her daughter's divorce before full marriage. "I will add to what the Seyyid has said. One of the negative effects is to brand her a divorcée. We are aware how this affects a girl when referred to by this word."

The Seyyid acknowledged Dr. Afaf's words and then continued, "*Milcheh*, as the student has mentioned, is a lawful engagement. However, the few days or few months before the wedding celebration do not allow enough time for becoming acquainted. Even if some of the traditions imposed on the boy and girl are suspended – and we know how strict these are, especially in the Gulf countries – there will still be harsh restraints. When that is the case, how can they get to know each other?"

The Seyyid finished by saying, "Finally, it must be understood that calling *milcheh* an engagement is technically incorrect. It is an actual lawful marriage, requiring a divorce for termination. For a girl, getting out of it is complicated. *Milcheh* is contrary to our entire search for a means of lawful acquaintance because we want this to occur before marriage, before the damage is done."

This left the students sifting through their thoughts to find lawful solutions for getting to know one another. Silence had begun to dominate. At last, a female student stood and asked, **"What is an 'urfi marriage?"**

\* \* \* \* \*

## The Different Types of Marriage

Mustafa looked at the Seyyid, as if to say that it was still his turn. The Seyyid answered, "The 'urfi marriage is 100% lawful. The married couple sometimes celebrates it with a group of friends. However, this marriage is not registered in court for certain reasons concerning one or both parties. Not registering it does not annul its lawfulness."

This subject aroused the students' curiosity. Most of the audience knew nothing about it except for its name. A male student now asked, **"What is the reason for concealing the marriage?"**

"Some businessmen travel often and are married," the Seyyid answered. "Their journeys sometimes take as long as few months. They may be living in their country or working or studying abroad. They feel in need of a wife and long to satisfy their desires, but they do not want to go to forbidden places for sex. They marry in this way because the marriage need not be announced. However, this marriage may be registered in court later if the couple finds it beneficial, particularly when the woman gets pregnant."

Here, Dr. Omar commented, "This type of marriage stems from poverty in Islamic countries. It is popular among the poor and middle class, especially with students in their country or abroad and especially in Egypt. Young men and women dream, but economic restraints make their future bleak. Responding to their desires, they go to a ma'thoon [licensed cleric] and write a marriage paper without their parents' knowledge. Shari'ah recognizes this marriage, but the courts reject it."

**"Why should the courts reject *'urfi* marriage?"** a male student wanted to know.

Dr. Afaf handled the question. "Government offices are responsible for the courts' rejection of *'urfi* marriage. This rejection makes people think it is forbidden and against Shari'ah. The excuse these offices use for not registering *'urfi* marriage is that a child born through *'urfi* marriage needs a proper ancestry. But they harm the child this way: when the marriage is not registered, the child cannot benefit from the right to have a nationality and passport, education, and health insurance. We must, however, differentiate between the lawfulness of this marriage and denial of registration when there are children. That is why we say, 'when this *'urfi* marriage produces a child, it is a legitimate one,' and the father must acknowledge the child is from his descent and must be responsible for raising, educating, and providing the child with all that is obligatory.

"The parents have no excuse to undermine the child's full right to education, a good upbringing, health care, and the proper home atmosphere so that the child may develop as other children do. The government offices do hold the father responsible if he fails to register the child right after birth. In this case, they consider him an unfit father for not carrying out his duties, and will punish and pursue him if necessary. This is because he has committed a big sin by not fulfilling his duties toward his child, and has also done wrong because a child is vulnerable and should not suffer neglect. With this, we support the work of government offices that rigorously combat the problem of negligent fathers. However, we must differentiate between the nature of the marriage when not registered in court – an issue of lawfulness – and not registering the child, which is an injustice.

"This responsibility falls on the parents. That is why the courts' request for the marriage to be registered is void in itself, because the marriage does not have to be registered to be lawful. Yes, if the couple want to register it to gain certain social benefits, like a raise in salary, or to benefit from certain privileges from the government, like receipt of a home in some countries, they are free to do so. And, if they do not wish to register, we cannot say anything. Parents should, however, be required to register a child to give him or her security, protection from life's dangers, education, health care, and citizen rights, because the state does not recognize the child's citizenship unless the name is found in the registry of personal status.

One of the female students stood as Dr. Afaf finished speaking and raised an important point. **"About 100 or 200 years ago, the marriage contract was not written. To be precise, the marriage was not registered at all. So, any *'urfi* marriage is a lawful one, if there are witnesses, a dowry, and the consent of both parties, regardless of whether it is or is not registered in court."**

Nasser, happy with the student's contribution, volunteered to explain this. "The student's observation is correct. Regarding proof by legal marriage certificate, it began in Egypt on August 31, 1931 and was stated in such a way that the law of registration spread to all other Islamic nations. Before this, marriage took place by uttering the vows – as cited by the counselor Mohammed 'Alamuddin, head of the civil court in Egypt, during an interview with the Sharjah magazine *Kull Al-Ousra* in the January 4, 1995 issue: 'A man gave his word and stuck to it. If he left his wife, he would tell her and everyone who knew he was her husband. Then everyone made sure this man was no longer her husband, and she became free. A man's word was like a sword until his trustworthiness was destroyed. But, because some men denied their relationship with wife and children, the rights of wife and children came to need proof by contract. This developed till we arrived at the most recent recognized contract.'" [13]

---

[13]  *Kull Al-Ousra* [U.A.E.], 4 Jan. 1995: 166.

Seyyid Mohammed had something to add. "It is true that trustworthiness has been destroyed, but the world is not empty of people who fear God and are of good conscience and manners that prohibit them from suffocating the hopes and dignity of others. Many who pledge their word and make promises, stick to them. There are also many who cannot keep their word or promises. Still, I emphasize this marriage, even unregistered, is lawful in Islam. Were all lawful marriages throughout history registered in courts? Of course not, because the law of registration was not established until 1931.

"I must finish the discussion on *'urfi* marriage by quoting the late Al-Azhar Sheikh Jadul Haqq Ali Jadul Haqq (may God rest his soul) from the Lebanese magazine *Al-Watan Al-Arabi*: 'The spoken contract of the *'urfi* marriage has its counterpart in the legal marriage, that is, the one documented in the registry office. If the *'urfi* marriage satisfies all the requirements specified in Shari'ah, it becomes accepted and binding with all its legal obligations and rights, including allowing sexual activity and ensuring the children's ancestry and inheritance, without obligation to register the marriage. I emphasize this so no one may think this marriage is not Islamically lawful.'" [14]

The time was now suitable for the Seyyid to mention other types of marriage. "We have digressed from searching for a lawful way for two people to get acquainted before marriage. To further this search, I must first discuss the other lawful marriage choices. I will now talk about *misyar*. Abdullah Kamal quotes the Saudi writer Abdullah Abu As-Samah as defining *misyar* to be a practical solution in which a woman marries a man whom she wants and accepts, a man compatible to her intellectually, while giving up some of her rights."[15]

Noise from the students discussing the issue among themselves rose in the hall. Most had never heard of *misyar* marriage. The noise was not made to deny or reject this kind of marriage, but rather it was a kind of questioning. To prevent the seminar from getting out of control, Mustafa politely asked everyone not to talk among themselves.

A male student rose to ask the honorable Al-Azhar's view of *misyar* marriage. Nasser wanted to answer. He had done his research,

[14] *Al-Watan Al-Arabi* [Lebanon], 8 May 1986: (no page no.).
[15] Abdullah Kamal, *'Adda'ara Al-Halal* [*Lawful Prostitution*] (Beirut: Cultural Library, 1997) (no page no.).

and his study, which was based on legal documents and legal and social information, was in his hands. He stated, "In the Lebanese newspaper *As-Safir* of February 12, 1999, the Al-Azhar Sheikh Mohammed Seyyid Tantaoui, announced *misyar* marriage was legal. It contains all the elements of marriage. This is found in the 31st seminar advertising the Sheik's book, in which he says, 'This marriage is not found in Egypt, but I have heard of it in some countries, and, recently, that the woman asks the man for nothing except the dowry.'" [16]

Another male student asked, **"What does the word *misyar* mean?"**

The Seyyid answered, "Dr. Abdul Wadood Hanif's book *Spinsterhood* defines *misyar* as derived from the word 'visiting,' meaning uncompleted things at the time they are agreed on.[17] The husband makes a deal with his wife that he will see her once or twice a month, or once a week. It is essential to the marriage that the man is honest with his wife in staying over and assuming expenses. However, there is no harm if the woman backs down or reduces the number of nights with her husband. The man must abide by that, as the *misyar* marriage is considered legal in Islam. I do not want to open a door widely without controls and conditions, but it is constructively restrictive for older women, widows, or divorcées. For a widow with children, perhaps in her 30's or older and afraid of gossip, *misyar* marriage may make sense. It gives her partial independence and allows pursuit of goals she may have without a man's interference."

A third male student asked, **"The honorable Seyyid mentioned earlier that in *misyar* the wife can give up her rights to sex or reduce the number of nights her husband sleeps with her. What is the minimum that the man should sleep with his wife?"**

The Seyyid said, "This varies among scholars. Sunni opinion is detailed in the book *Fiqh As-Sunnah*, volume 2, by Sheikh Seyyid Sabiq, in the chapter on the rights of the wife. There, he quotes Ibn Hazim Al-Andalusi: 'It is obligatory for the man to have sexual intercourse with his wife at least once every month.' [18] He must be able to do so, otherwise he will have disobeyed God. Proof of this is in Allah saying, **but when they have purified themselves, you**

---

[16] *As-Safir* [Lebanon], 12 Feb. 1999: 7. See Document 5 at the back of this book.

[17] Abdul Wadood Hanif, *Al-'Unoosah* [*Spinsterhood*] (Mecca Al-Mukarramah: Dar 'Arraya, 1998) 38.

[18] Sheikh Seyyid Sabiq, *Fiqh As-Sunnah* [*Doctrine of the Sunnis*], vol. 2 (Beirut: Dar Al-Kitab Al-Arabi, 1971) 188.

**may approach them [in any manner, time, or place] ordained for you by Allah, 2:222.**

"Many scholars disagree with Ibn Hazim on the man's obligation, assuming he has no good excuse to avoid sex with his wife. Al-Shafi'i said, 'He does not have to, because it is his right, and he does not have to back down from his rights.' Also, a text by Ahmad Ibn Hanbal states that it should be about once every four months.

"As for the Shi'ites, they also hold this opinion, but we as a team, especially concerning permanent marriage, lean toward a month. We considered the monthly cycle of the woman's purification from menstruation and the fact that no book specifies four months. This is in addition to the sexual desire that has increased in modern times from various temptations, attractions, and seductions. You all know about these, and there is no need to discuss them here."

At this point, a female student directed a question to Dr. Afaf, as though she was asking for her assistance by citing an example of society's injustice toward women. She asked, **"Does this represent injustice toward a woman? A husband leaves a wife for this long time, yet what of her need for his companionship?"**

With her scientific and natural logic, Dr. Afaf answered, "The injustice lies in the conditions that go unnoticed in this kind of marriage. When the man proposes *misyar* marriage to the woman and (1) he is aware that he cannot satisfy her needs for companionship in the usual way for a married couple and (2) she is aware of his situation and still accepts him as a husband, then she has agreed to this and abandoned the condition of companionship as one of her wishes. He has not forced her into accepting his proposal. The offer was hers to accept or reject.

"But, what if the husband is brought before the law over issues concerning his absence in bed? What if he knows he will be absent for two months, or six, or more? Should he ask for her permission? If she gives permission, it is not his responsibility any more. If she does not give permission, he commits a legal infringement during his absence when traveling without her permission. He must also take responsibility for her actions if she sins as he drove her to this. But, if she does not insist on her rights, the responsibility for sinning falls on her when she is without her husband."

Seyyid Mohammed now spoke. "It is important to clarify the meaning of this marriage. From the past to the present, among those choosing this type of marriage, there are merchants, businessmen, or workers whose jobs require constant travel abroad. These men may be married with families living with them in a certain city. Because of the traveling, sometimes lasting for weeks or months, they propose *misyar* marriage – just as some propose *'urfi* marriage. They are far from their wives and cannot suppress their sexual needs. So as not to sin by practicing forbidden sex, they propose in the *misyar* way by informing the woman that her husband cannot always be in the city where she lives.

"Therefore, the man visits his *misyar* wife perhaps five times a year. He may, however, come only twice. This is why he should say he does not know when he will return, as it is unknown in his kind of work. If she agrees on legally canceling the terms of living together in the usual way and the money to be given for expenses, the husband will be free of commitments and of his obligation. Here we must correct the definition *misyar,* which some think means 'he comes to her when he wants.' This definition is imprecise because the man visits depending on his circumstances and situation – that is, when he can. The wife must understand that."

**"What about the living expenses?"** The question came from one of the students just as the Seyyid had finished. Seyyid Mohammed looked up to find the source of the voice. A male student raised his hand to show he was the one.

"I thank you for this question," said the Seyyid. "The costs are related to the conditions. In the past, if not wealthy, the husband was not required to give his wife money when he was away. Then, there were no checking accounts, wire transfers, or ATMs. Some men could not afford to maintain a *misyar* wife during the months of absence. They would ask her to cede her rights till their return.

"Today, money may be received in various ways during the husband's absence. Nevertheless, some men's poor earnings do not allow for financial support. If so, the wife must await his return, or she might receive some money when it becomes available to him during his absence. I should add that a man in a *misyar* marriage may also announce his willingness to have a wedding party, with witnesses and a formal announcement of the marriage. Even if a ceremony took place, he may still ask his wife to excuse him from the conditions of living together and covering expenses, because of his poor circumstances. If she accepts this, it is a choice that she has agreed to willingly. If she refuses, then she is free from any commitment."

The students were becoming acquainted with this type of marriage, especially with what drove a man to *misyar*. The conditions that drove a woman to accept *misyar* were still a mystery to them.

That is why a female student raised that point. **"If male travelers and those leading a life with special circumstances are choosing *misyar* marriage, whom are they proposing to? Why and under what conditions are their proposals accepted?"**

Nasser was waiting for the opportunity to say more about *misyar* marriage. He had collected what he believed to be a reference for all who have studied it and asked about it. He took a document from his papers and read, "The magazine *Al-Majallah* reported that a survey by the Central Agency for General Mobilization and Statistics in Egypt showed 4 million men and women have passed the natural age for marriage [30 years of age]. Among them are 2.5 million single women who are more than 30 years old. This includes divorcées and widows.[19] Also, a survey from 1960, found in the book *Polygamy Between Science and Religion* by Ali Abu Abdullah Abdul Mohsin, states there were 1,066,000 widows [before the wars in 1967 and 1973, and before the fight between the Egyptian authorities and the armed Islamic groups] and 147,000 divorcées.[20]

"These numbers are from the past. Imagine what they would be now. How many widows are there today in Iran and Iraq? The war devastated these countries. The number of widows must have increased even more after the first and second Gulf wars. Also, in a country like Lebanon, people are refraining from marriage because of the poor economy. How many Lebanese girls will miss out on marriage? The head of the Office of the Sunni Law Court in Beirut, the Seyyid Salah Yemoot, observed in his interview with the Lebanese newspaper *As-Safir* on June 17, 1999, that marriages increase only in the summer with the arrival of migrants. It is as though the residents of Lebanon do not think about marriage. In winter, there are no more than 170 marriages! That young people are refraining from marriage can be proved by the statistics. In 1993, 2,147 marriages were registered, but in 1991, 2,585 marriages were registered.[21]

---

[19]  *Al-Majallah* [London, U.K.], 20 July 1996: 70.
[20]  Abdul Mohsin 72.
[21]  *As-Safir*, 17 June 1999: (no page no.).

"In a study directed by the Society of Women's Awakening in Dubai, published in the magazine *Zahratul Khaleej,* December 18, 1993, the researcher Nura Ali 'Ubaid Al-Zu'bi cites evidence from Planning Ministry surveys in the U.A.E. It states there are about 11,432 female citizens and 23,794 male citizens of marrying age [15 to 60 years of age] still single. This was in 1980. No doubt, the opportunity was unavailable for most of those women. In 1993, the postponement of marriage in the U.A.E. reached many times this figure. The researcher says about this postponement: 'It has many negative effects, including harm to morals and health. The moral harm derives from young people refraining from or delaying marriage for a long time. It is difficult for many of them to preserve their chastity at a time of increasing temptation. Denial or sinful satisfaction of desires may also be accompanied by a rise in reproductive and emotional illnesses among both sexes.'" [22]

Nasser concluded by posing these questions: "Tens of thousands of divorcées and widows may be still young, so what should they do to satisfy their sexual needs? Should they hide their faces in the sand? Should they submit to these desires and risk coming into contact with adultery or prostitution? Should they realistically be asked to display a moral and sexual passivity that would cancel out patience in their life? What should they do in these circumstances?"

Nasser looked to Dr. Afaf for her opinion as a female and as a researcher on women's studies, for this subject focused on women. Dr. Afaf said, "In addition to dealing with desire, the divorcée, widow, or spinster searches for safety and stability and for ways to avoid solitude and anxiety. I know many women, many who are still young, who have sacrificed their future to raise brothers and sisters after the parents died. They vowed to serve in this way, but they are the ones in need of marriage. Also, how many chaste girls still in their prime, with a mature sexual energy, have sacrificed their lives to serve elderly fathers and mothers by offering humane service to those needing care? Why do we not answer their good will with the good will of another as a reward, to offer the love, security, and care they need? Future husbands should run after these girls, because they have humane feelings that will help them raise their children. Instead, we see society has lost much of its unique humane characteristics. Men look at these divorcées, widows, and spinsters as though they

---

[22] *Zahratul Khaleej* [U.A.E.], 18 Dec. 1993: 88.

were unworthy of receiving dignity and respect and being treated as equal to men. For all these women, *misyar* would be suitable."

The whole audience rose to clap excitedly, reflecting their sympathetic reaction to her frank and faithful expression of women's feelings.

When the applause ended, a male student stood and posed a question. He had the accent of a Gulf country resident. Maybe, as a man living far from his country, he wanted a solution for his personal situation. He said, **"I have heard of *zawaj bi-niat al-talaq* [marriage with hidden intention to divorce]. Does this act in the same way as *'urfi* or *misyar* marriage?"**

Mustafa passed the question to Dr. Omar, who answered, "In his book *Fiqh As-Sunnah,* volume 2, page 30, Sheikh Seyyid Sabiq says scholars agree, if a man marries without setting a time limit yet [secretly] intends to divorce after a certain time or after he finishes work in the country he is staying in, the marriage is legal." [23]

"Sheikh Ibrahim Ibn Mohammed Al-Dubai'i, a scholar from Saudi Arabia, has published a book called Clarifying the Order of Marriage with Hidden Intention to Divorce. He states on page 14, 'This is one way to preserve fidelity and avoid sin. Those compelled to resort it, do so to protect their dignity and complete the other half of their religion [that is, marriage]. It originated from the need to prevent a man from falling into forbidden acts at home or abroad. It is needed by expatriate students who mix with girls at the university and at the home of the family they live with, by embassy and consulate employees, and by those sent on da'wah [missionary work] and guidance missions or for those sent to conferences and training courses. It is also needed at home by those with limited income, by students until they graduate and God blesses them with more subsistence, by employees appointed to remote areas, by husbands whose wives are ill for a long time, and by bachelors who fear succumbing to adultery if they are surrounded by degrading environments, seductions, and wide-open doors of corruption. The Muslim has an Islamic duty to protect himself. This kind of marriage is needed when no other way exists to preserve his dignity.'" [24]

---

[23] Sabiq 30. See Document 1 at the back of this book.
[24] Sheikh Ibrahim Ibn Mohammed Al-Dubai'i, *Idah Hukmu Az-Zawaj Bi-niat Al-Talak* [Clarifying the Order of Marriage with Hidden Intention to Divorce] (no city or publisher, 1995) 14.

51

The same student replied, **"This marriage is based on deception. The man conceals he will divorce, when he should be standing by his wife and providing her with security and peace of mind. Are there scholars who have ruled to legalize this type of marriage?"**

After this students comment, there was a buzz of discussion among students. This confirmed that they did not like this kind of marriage, which made Dr. Omar try to calm the audience and retake control of the discussion. When it was quiet, he said, "These are not my words. I am only repeating what some scholars say."

While seated, another male student said, **"Islam has no deception in its Shari'ah, which God provided for the good of humanity. So, I ask if any present-day scholars think this type of marriage is lawful?"**

Dr. Omar said, "Yes, Ibn Baz (may God rest his soul) and others issued a fatwa [Islamic ruling] to allow this kind of marriage. Ibn Baz says in the book A Total of Various Rulings and Articles: 'Yes, a fatwa from the permanent committee, and I am its president, allows marriage with hidden intention to divorce, if it is between a man and God, if he marries in expatriate lands and intends to divorce when he his study or work is finished. The jomhoor [majority] of scholars have no problem with it. The intention is between him and Allah and is not a condition.'" [25]

The student spoke again. **"Did such marriage exist at the time of the Prophet (pbuh) and his companions?"**

"Sunni scholars who gave a legal opinion to allow this marriage found nothing in the Islamic scripts to forbid it," commented Dr. Omar. "They considered it a new order, and new orders are interpretative. So, no, this kind of marriage was unheard of at the time of the Prophet (pbuh) and his companions."

Dr. Omar took a sip of water and continued, "Shi'ites do not accept this kind of marriage, but Sunnis differ among themselves. The Imam of Al-Awza'ai, for instance, objected to it. Sheikh Salih Ibn Abdul Al-Aziz Al-Mansour, one of the Saudi scholars, was also against it. Sheikh Al-Dubai'i stated in his book Clarifying the Order

---

[25] Sheikh Abdul Aziz Ibn Baz. Majmoo Fatawa wa Maqalat Mutanawwi'ah [A Total of Various Rulings and Articles], vol. 4 (Mecca Al-Mukarramah: no publisher or year) 30. Also quoted by Al-Dubai'i 40. See Document 2 at the back of this book.

*of Marriage with Hidden Intention to Divorce* that, according to Al-Mansour, marriage with hidden intention to divorce is unlawful and cannot be allowed in Islam. Even if it were allowed in the past, it is invalid. Also, if the married man's intention to deceive becomes known, the Shari'ah court will invalidate the marriage." [26]

Dr. Omar added that he leans toward this view. "Whoever thinks this marriage is allowed must see it is only in a man's interest. It selfishly neglects a woman's needs and circumstances, which are no less great than a man's needs."

The student was trying hard to be sure of the ruling on lawfulness. He faced Dr. Omar with a fourth question. **"If some Sunni scholars permit marriage with hidden intention to divorce, why do they prohibit temporary marriage, popularly known as *mut'ah*? The conditions of *mut'ah* are clear to both parties from the start. The time of their separation is written in the contract. In marriage with hidden intention to divorce, the woman's position is weak while the man has options. She is deceived when in need of continuing the marriage. She is subjected to terrible injustice."**

Before Dr. Omar could respond, Mustafa intervened. He informed the audience that discussing *mut'ah* was postponed to a future seminar to be devoted especially to that subject. The time remaining in this seminar did not permit starting a new discussion.

At this, Seyyid Mohammed found it was time to call it a day. He said, "What Brother Mustafa says is correct. While we are closing the subject of marriage for today, we are still on it, and still seeking a lawful solution as to how a boy and girl may get to know each other while retaining the freedom to accept or reject a future relationship. We must present a solution that causes no problems for us or our parents, relatives, or neighbors. We will leave this for the future seminars, God willing."

Nasser then requested the agreement of the audience and lecturers that – as the discussion on marriage had turned to what is lawful and what is not – the next seminar should specifically be on this subject. The silence was a clear signal of acceptance.

He set the seminar for the next week on the same day, at the same time.

* * * * *

---

[26] Al-Dubai'i 14.

# CHAPTER THREE
## The Elements of Marriage

* * * * *

## The Proposal and the Dowry

During the week between the second and third seminars, they became the talk of the university. The outcome of the discussions was a daily topic among the students. This delighted the Dean of the university, and he sent for Nasser to congratulate him on the success so far.

On the appointed day, the lecturers arrived on the auditorium stage for the third seminar. They saw this audience was not only students and teachers. There were new faces – scholars and elderly people probably from outside the university – that gave variety to the audience. The hall was filled beyond capacity and people were standing. The lecturers asked the university staff for more chairs. When they arrived and everyone was seated, Nasser checked with the technicians to make sure the audiovisual equipment was working and then Mustafa began to speak.

He welcomed the audience and presented the results from the first two seminars. He finished by saying, "Everyone agreed that 'not knowing each other' before marriage is true for married couples in our society. This lack of acquaintance is one of the main reasons for rising divorce in Muslim countries. We studied this in the hope of finding an ideal way to allow acquaintance before marriage and so reduce divorce."

Many hands were raised, especially at the back of the hall. Mustafa chose a girl who stood and exclaimed with youthful vigor, **"We thank you for summarizing the discussions. However, something is missing. You should turn your attention to it and so be able to deal with the subject from all angles. You talk about the increasing divorce rates and about the need of acquaintance before marriage, but, before all that, we want to know what marriage is and what its requirements are. How can we speak about the ideal marriage before we talk about its substance – its *arkan* [pillars] – and not just the types of marriage?"**

The person who most appreciated what the student was saying was Seyyid Mohammed, but he looked at Dr. Omar and then at Nasser as though inviting them to speak first. When Dr. Omar made no move to speak, Nasser came forward. "There are requirements to be met for marriage to occur between a man and a woman. Lawfulness must be created in the relationship between the couple. One of the meanings of 'lawful' is that this relationship is based on a system of values, rules, and requirements. One of these requirements is the marriage contract, for marriage is a type of contract between a man and a woman. On this basis, the marital bond is controlled by a system of rights and Islamic and legal obligations. *Shari'ah* considers the nature of males and females, and what is given to them to take up their roles and responsibilities in life."

The student stood again, her eyes on Nasser, and asked, **"We understand that marriage is a contract, but what makes this contract legal in Islam?"**

"The elements of marriage," Nasser replied, "are in *Shari'ah* books – (1) the proposal, its acceptance, and the contract that embodies this acceptance, (2) specification of the dowry, (3) witnessing, (4) competence, (5) guardianship, and (6) age of maturity. Each must be examined. I will start with the proposal and its acceptance.

"In the sacred bond of marriage, there must be a contract that ties the two sides together. Of this, Sheikh Abdullah Ni'mah said, 'All Islamic schools agree there is no marriage without a contract. It cannot be lawful by only mutual agreement, or by an unclear proposal. This is the difference between marriage and the adulterous relationships that often take place by mutual agreement.' [27]

"The contract's lawfulness depends on the proposal and acceptance. Seyyid Izzuddin Bahrul Uloom comments in his book *Marriage in the Qur'an and Sunnah*: 'As marriage is a contract between the two parties, one party must propose and one must accept to gain (1) the contract and (2) the process of contracting between the two parties. Imam Mohammed Al-Baqir explained that 'covenant' from: **...and they have taken from you a solemn covenant? 4:21** is the word by which the marriage should be executed.' The complete verse is: **But if you decide to take one wife in place of another, even if you have given the latter a whole treasure for a dowry, take not the least bit of it back; do you take it by slander and a manifest wrong? And how could you take it when you have gone in unto each other, and they have taken from you a solemn covenant? 4:20-21.**

"This covenant binds together two people, before which there was no relationship between them and no commitment by one to the other. The *Qur'an*'s description of the covenant strongly portrays an enlarged image of the word 'marriage' that is made up of the proposal and the acceptance. It enriches the bonds of married life for the couple. The Prophet (pbuh) said, **You have taken them by the trust of Allah, and had them become sexually allowable to you by the word of Allah.**'" [28]

A male student stood and addressed Nasser. **"Do the proposal and its acceptance on their own convey the complete readiness of the proposer and the accepter, since it is part of the agreement?"**

"Yes," said Nasser. "For the contract terms to be complete, the terminology used should be uttered with precision. It is not enough to accept without a formal proposal. Also, the acceptance must be in the past tense. As Sheikh Mohammed Jawad Moghniyeh says: 'The engaged woman or her proxy begins accepting by saying: 'I have married....' The engaged man or his proxy then accepts by saying: 'I accept.' He should say that immediately. This is the common ruling.' [29] We must not forget the importance of saying the

[27] Sheikh Abdullah Ni'mah, *Daleel Al-Qadaa' Al-Ja'fari* [*References for Shi'ah Judges*] (Beirut: Dar Al-Balagha, 1996) 9. Ni'mah was Head of the *Shari'ah* Courts in Lebanon
[28] Seyyid Izzuddin Bahrul Uloom, *Az-Zawaj fil Qur'an was-Sunnah* [*Marriage in the Qur'an and Sunnah*], 3rd ed. (Beirut: Dar Az-Zahra', 1974) 158.
[29] Sheikh Mohammed Jawad Moghniyah, *Al-Fusool Ash-Shari'ah* [*Sections of Law*], 3rd ed. (Beirut: Dar Ath-Thaqafah, 1974) 9.

words of acceptance of marriage. That acceptance is not just one of making sex allowed, but rather all the responsibilities that come with marriage. Each party is declaring a commitment to carry out these responsibilities."

After his talk on the first element of marriage, Nasser expected questions about it. Many hands were raised, but, when Mustafa chose a male student, he asked Nasser to talk now about the dowry, the second element of the marriage contract. No one objected, so Nasser made sure the first element was clear to all and began describing the dowry.

"It is" he said, "the payment in money or goods that the man offers the woman who he wants as his life partner. Both must agree on the dowry, whether it is small or large. The *Qur'an* says, **And give the women [on marriage] their dowry as a free gift, 4:4**. This may be interpreted as 'give women their dowry as a gift from Allah' because Allah created the enjoyment that is shared between the couple. *Shari'ah* does not specify an exact value for the dowry, because marriage is a form of contract. Since the dowry is a symbolic expression of love, specifying the amount or value is left to the couple. It is for the woman to specify what she believes is suitable. She may agree to a small symbolic dowry. She may also raise the dowry's value, subject to her husband's approval. This becomes her right and property, which she can request whenever she likes. It is a promise that must be honored exactly as agreed on within the contract. [30]

"The dowry is called *sadaq* since it is the result of agreement between the two from *tasadaqa* [the two agreed on]. Also, it may be called *'iwathun 'anil bith*." [31]

A girl who had spoken at the first seminar now stood to object to what Nasser was saying. **"The dowry – considering what you have said about the contract or agreement – is buying and selling! The woman sells herself and the man buys her at a price! What is your opinion, honorable Seyyid?"**

"Some do say," answered the Seyyid, "the woman sells herself. This idea is false and comes from misunderstanding a *hadith* [narration by a prophet]. It is not what Mohammed (pbuh) meant when he said, **The woman is a seller and the man a buyer and the selling**

---

[30] The dowry is divided, by tradition, into two parts: the first is supposed to be paid before or at the beginning of the marriage contract, and the second is to be paid in the event of divorce, whichever happens earlier.

[31] That is, in exchange for allowing the man to have sexual intercourse with the woman.

**cannot be done without a price.** [32] The woman is not selling her body and soul, only the right to her body in exchange for living expenses and she can take back that right and get a divorce if the man does not meet his obligation to support her. The reply to this *hadith* is the *Qur'anic* verse **And give the women [on marriage] their dowry as a free gift, 4:4**, which means it is a God-given right because enjoyment – as Seyyid Mohammed Hussein Fadlullah sees it – is not only for men. The woman benefits from this enjoyment, which cannot be achieved without participation from both parties. The majority who request the dowry, due to their nature, are men not women. A man makes approaches to his future wife and tries to interest her. When she accepts, it is as though she is giving the man this right of enjoyment, even though she will benefit from it too. If she is selling, though not in the trade sense, the man is buying as he is the one paying. That is how it may seem though the real purpose of the dowry paid to the woman is to make her feel worthy and honorable. After marriage, it is considered a kind of security because women are weaker in the social structure and lack the job opportunities that men have."[33]

Mustafa thanked Seyyid Mohammed for his speech and asked him to continue clarifying the meaning of the dowry from the legal angle.

The Seyyid said, "From the legal angle, specifying the dowry is left to the couple. They name it, and it becomes be known and agreed on. The dowry, small or large, will be what satisfies her. Al-Shawkani said, 'It includes small or large amounts, in addition to what was stated in so many stories and the holy verses about giving complete freedom to the couple to agree on it. As an example of small dowries, the Prophet (pbuh) said the husband must give a dowry to the wife when he said: **Seek even if it is an iron ring.**' [34]

"That concerned offering specific things. As for the immaterial, anything may be accepted – even teaching a chapter of the *Qur'an*. Things offered may also be valuable, for Allah says: **...even if you have given the latter a whole treasure for a dowry, take not the least bit of it back; do you take it by slander and a manifest**

---

[32] *Wasa'il Ash-Shi'ah* [*The Ways of the Shi'ah*], section 21 (Beirut: Dar Ihya'a Al-Torath Al-Arabi, 1991) 267.

[33] Fadlullah, *Dunyal Mar'ah*, 269.

[34] Mohammed Ibn Ali Ibn Mohammed Al-Shawkani, *Naylul Awtar* [*Achieving Aims*], vol. 6 (Beirut: Dar Al-Fikr, 1994) 192.

**wrong? 4:20**. The *qintar* [treasure or massive amount] in this verse is a huge amount. Scholars define it differently. It could be 40 *oukeya* of gold or silver, 1,200 *oukeya* of gold or silver, 100 pounds of gold or silver, or 70,000 or 80,000 dinars. [35]

"*Shari'ah* has not specified an exact dowry for marriage, but has left it to those who have agreed and are satisfied with it. It has encouraged a modest sum for the dowry, which resulted in a saying by people: 'It is a bad omen for the woman if her dowry is high.'"

One of the male students stood and asked, **"In some countries, such as India, Pakistan, and Egypt, women pay dowries. What is the Islamic position on this?"**

Seyyid Mohammed answered, "This is false information. In these countries it is the girl's mother or brother, if her father is not present, who should pay for the wedding, from the invitations to the wedding dress to the party. This is influenced by the customs and traditions of each country. Here in Lebanon, the woman takes the first part of the dowry and spends it on furnishing the house and on her personal belongings. In other countries, the father takes the dowry. However, according to *Shari'ah*, the man is the one who pays the dowry to the woman, since the philosophy of the dowry is that, if the woman refuses to give the man sex, she is violating her obligation and thereby breaking the marriage agreement. She is also committing a sin, punishable by God. In that case, the man may divorce her and go to court to recover the full dowry, though it is usually not a large amount and only half is returnable if the woman is a non-virgin. The dowry exists to make a strong point to the woman – you have taken something for the right to your body – and it is part of the agreement.

"If the father or the guardian receives his daughter's dowry – this is not advisable – and fails to pass it on to her, then that would be treating the woman like merchandise sold by her father in the marriage. He is getting payment for her. It is the woman, not the guardian, who is entitled to the dowry."

After this explanation, there were no more questions about the dowry.

* * * * *

---

[35] Bahrul Uloom 216. (One *oukeya* = about 200 grams.)

# Witnessing and Announcement

Mustafa asked Seyyid Mohammed to talk about the issue of witnesses.

The Seyyid said, "What is meant by *'ishhad* in the marriage contract is that two men should stand as witnesses. Regarding this, Muslim scholars have different opinions. Some have said witnessing is obligatory. Others have said it is not *wajib* [obligatory], but *mustahabb* [recommended]. The first group based their ruling on the Prophet's (pbuh) *hadith*: **No marriage is without witnesses.** The others said witnessing is similar to the Prophet's (pbuh) *hadith*: **No prayer is accepted from the mosque's neighbor except that which is performed in the mosque.**"

At this moment, whispering among the students was heard. What astounded them was the disagreement among scholars when the meaning of the Prophet's (pbuh) *hadiths* was so clear. They did not quiet down till Mustafa asked for calm. One male student then had a question for Dr. Omar. **"With such disagreement, what argument is used by each side to support their ruling?"**

Dr. Omar was fully prepared. He said, "We will present some of the opinions of for each group. Most Shi'ites consider it recommended. The Sunnis say it is obligatory. Mohammed Hussein Az-Zahabi explains, 'According to the Hanafis, Shafi'is, and Hanbalis, witnessing is obligatory to render the marriage contract valid, based on the Prophet's (pbuh) *hadith*: **No marriage is without witnesses.** Imam Malik said, in a well-known opinion, the witnessing is not a requirement for validating the contract because the *Qur'an* does not make it a requirement for the marriage to occur and because the Prophetic *hadiths* are not explicit in requiring witnessing. The Shi'ites say witnessing is absolutely not a requirement of marriage because the *Qur'an* does not focus on it at all when talking about marriage. They also say the traditions regarding witnessing are interpreted as recommendations, or to be used in front of a judge if denial of the marriage occurs.' [36] Those who ruled that witnessing is obligatory based their opinion on a *hadith* mentioned by all five except An-Nisa'i, that, as in Al-Bukhari, Muslim, and Malik, some

---

[36] Mohammed Hussein Az-Zahabi. *Ash-Shari'ah Al-Islamiah* [*Islamic Laws*] (Cairo: Dar Al-Kutob Al-Hadithah, 1983) 69. See Document 3 at the back of this book.

of the Prophet's (pbuh) companions and their sons were married without witnesses, but just at a wedding party. Among those they mentioned: Abdullah Ibn Omar, Al-Hasan Ibn Ali, Abdullah Ibn Az-Zubair, and Salim Ibn Omar. They also said the Prophet (pbuh) married Safiah without witnesses and gave a dinner with dates and leafstalk, and then married Zainab and gave a dinner in which a small calf was served.[37]

"This matter is discussed rationally by Seyyid Izzuddin Bahrul Uloom, who focused on the evidence of the two groups. He considers witnessing to be one of the issues that triggered the dispute between Shi'ites and Sunnis. For Shi'ites, the marriage is valid without witnesses, but they do not forbid the presence of witnesses. They just do not see it as needed for the contract, while the scholars of other schools believe it to be needed."[38]

The same student stood, as though not completely satisfied, and addressed Seyyid Mohammed directly. He asked, **"What is the Shi'ah argument for ruling that witnesses are not compulsory in the contract?**

The Seyyid answered, "The Shi'ites concluded that witnessing was not compulsory in marriage after interpreting the verses of the *Qur'an*: **marry women of your choice, two, or three, or four, 4:3**, and **Marry those among you who are single, or the virtuous ones among your slaves, male or female, 24:32**. These verses do not imply a need for witnesses. If it were obligatory, it would have been mentioned. This contrasts with verses that say the dowry is an obligatory. Looking at history, we find the Prophet (pbuh) married many women and did not make it a requirement for witnesses to be present at the time of the marriage contracts. This was also done by the Imams of Ahlul Bayt and many companions of the Prophet (pbuh). There is no doubt that their deeds are reliable proof to be followed. The *Sunnah* represents the deeds of the Prophet (pbuh), his sayings, and his approval of the deeds of others."

Another male student then said, **"Dr. Omar, Seyyid Mohammed explained the Shi'ite opinion that witnessing is unnecessary, giving his proof from clear *Qur'anic* verses and from contracts made at the time of the Prophet (pbuh) and his companions. What is the case of those who say marriage requires witnessing?"**

---

[37] Ibrahim Fawzi, *Ahkamul Usrah fil Jahiliah wal-Islam* [*Family Law Before and After Islam*] (Beirut: Dar Al-Kalima, 1983) 54. See Document 4 at the back of this book.
[38] Bahrul Uloom 162.

Dr. Omar replied, "The Sunni scholars do not allow secret marriage[39] or its concealment. For the contract to be valid, witnesses must listen to the particulars of the contract so the marriage becomes known and unclear ancestry, should children be born, is prevented. Their opinion is based on believing marriage is a contract no less important than a contract for a loan or for compensation. The proof of requesting witnesses for a loan contract or some compensation contracts is the verse **call in two male witnesses from among you, but if two men cannot be found, then one man and two women who you judge fit to act as witnesses, so that if either of them commit an error the other will remind her, 2:282.** The marriage contract is even more important than other contracts that God has requested witnesses be present. To protect marriage from anyone denying its existence, the witnesses are obliged to announce it to other people, so this contract becomes connected to the honor and ancestry, and rulings that remain eternal are based on it."

Seyyid Mohammed now intervened so all opinions would be presented well and so the students would see the fine detail. He said, "Seyyid Bahrul Uloom – a Shi'ah scholar – replied to the proof Dr. Omar has presented by saying, 'True that the contract of marriage is not less important than the rest of the contracts, such as for purchases and loans, but the need for witnesses in these contracts cannot be made to apply to marriage, though the witnessing of marriage is even more important.'[40] This ruling is based on the verse **call in two male witnesses from among you, 2:282**, but to understand this verse we must read all of it. Allah says, **Oh, believers! When you contract a debt for a fixed period, put it in writing; let a scribe write it down for you with fairness; no scribe should refuse to write as God has taught him; therefore let him write; and let the debtor dictate, fearing God his Lord and not diminishing the sum he owes; if the debtor be an ignorant or feeble-minded person, or one who cannot dictate, let his guardian dictate for him in fairness; call in two male witnesses from among you, but if two men cannot be found, then one man and two women who you judge fit to act as witnesses, so that if either of them commit an error the other will remind her; witnesses must not refuse to give evidence if called on to do so; so do not fail to put your debts in writing, be they small or big, together with**

---

[39] *Misyar* is sometimes a secret marriage. See Document 5 at the back of this book.
[40] Bahrul Uloom (no page no.).

**the date of payment; this is more just in the sight of God; it ensures accuracy in testifying and is the best way to remove all doubt; but if the transaction in hand be a bargain concluded on the spot, it is no offence for you if you do not commit it to writing; see that witnesses are present when you barter with one another, and let no harm be done to either scribe or witness; if you harm them you will commit a transgression; have fear of God; God teaches you, and God has knowledge of all things. 2:282**

"We see the instruction to bring witnesses is found in this verse in three places:

- ❖ **when you contract a debt for a fixed period, put it in writing**
- ❖ **call in two male witnesses from among you**
- ❖ **see that witnesses are present when you barter with one another**

"However, the scholars understood the instruction in all these places to be a recommendation not an obligation, to the extent that Fakhr Ar-Razi said, in his commentary on this verse, that the *jomhoor* [majority] of scholars – he used the term *mujtahideen* [highest religious scholars] – understood it too. The proof of this is that the most people in all Muslim countries sell on credit without written agreements or witnesses. This is *Ijmaa'* opinion that all or almost all scholars agree on] that writing and witnessing are not needed for business. It is because declaring these things obligatory would make life very difficult for Muslims. The Prophet (pbuh) said, **I was sent with the easy *haneefiah*** [message]. Some said writing and witnessing were obligatory at the beginning and then were nullified by the verse **And if any one of you entrusts another with a pledge, let the trustee restore the pledge to its owner, 2:283**. Al-Taymi said: 'I asked Al-Hasan Al-Basri about it and he said: If he wishes, he may bring witnesses and, if he wishes, he may not; have you not heard Allah said: **And if any one of you entrusts another with a pledge...?**[41]

---

[41] Abu Abdullah Fakhr Eddine Ar-Razi, *At-Tafsir Al-Kabir* [*The Great Explanation*] (Beirut: Dar Ihya'a Al-Torath Al-Arabi, no year) 128.

"Therefore, the instruction to write and bring witnesses is interpreted as not obligatory, so one can apply it to marriage also as not obligatory."

Dr. Omar then continued, "I am presenting the arguments of scholars for cases where witnessing marriage contracts are considered obligatory, but it is not my opinion. Now I will continue with their second proof.

"The second proof is based on *hadiths*. Some are what the Messenger of Allah said: **Prostitutes marry without witness** [or explicit proof][42] and **No marriage is valid without a *waliyy* [guardian] and two reliable witnesses.**[43] In *Tuhfatul Al-Fuqaha*, Al-Samarqandi Al-Hanafi[44] cited different *hadiths* with the same meaning, told by the 11 companions of the Prophet (pbuh). He then discussed them and falsified them. Al-Shawkani[45] discussed them as well.[46]

"When we study these *hadiths*, we find the most important is **No marriage is valid without a guardian and two reliable witnesses**, which the *fuqaha'* [Shi'ite jurists] ruled to be a recommended rather than obligatory. This is similar to the Prophet's (pbuh) *hadith* **No prayer is accepted from the mosque's neighbor except that which is performed in the mosque.**

"It is the Maliki school, alone among the Sunni schools, which considers it required to make the marriage contract known and which rules that the point of the contract is to make it known rather than to include witnesses in the contract."

When Dr. Omar finished, Nasser asked to speak so as to arrive at the conclusion that he thought necessary about this argument. He stated, "From what has been said, we see the opinion of those who make obligatory witnessing of the marriage contract is not conclusive. They based their opinion on the *Qur'anic* verse relating to loans **Oh, believers! When you contract a debt for a fixed period, put it in writing, 2:282**. They compared bearing witness to

---

[42] Ahmed Ibn Al-Hussein Ibn Ali Al-Bayhaqi, *As-Sunan Al-Kubra* [*Greatest Laws*] vol. 7 (Hyderabad, India: Da'irat Al-Ma'aref Al-'Osmaniya, 1936) 252.
[43] 'Alaa Eddine Al-Samarqandi Al-Hanafi, *Tuhfatul Al-Fuqaha* [*Jewel of Fuqaha*] vol. 2 (Cairo: Al-Matba'a Al-'Amiriya, no year) 181.
[44] A Sunni who was one of the great Hanafi scholars; died in 333 AH (944 AD).
[45] A Sunni jurist who produced more than 100 works.
[46] Al-Shawkani 142.

marriage to witnessing terms of loans and other financial contracts. This is incorrect. Witnessing a financial contract is for proving it if denied, while witnessing a marriage is only to make the marriage known to people. This is what Dr. Ibrahim Fawzi proved in his book *Family Law Before and After Islam.* [47]

"As for those who argued based on **No marriage is valid without a guardian and two reliable witnesses**, it is a weak *hadith*. This matter – the presence of witnesses – has not been agreed on in the Sunni schools of thought. The three – Hanafis, Hanbalis, and Shafi'is – agreed witnesses must be present at the contract and, if two people did not witness when the particulars of the marriage contract procedure occurred, the marriage is void. The Malikis, by contrast, said the presence of two witnesses is essential, though they do not need to be present at the contract but at the marriage itself, meaning the wedding night when the husband and wife consummate the marriage. Their presence at the contract is only recommended. For more on this, refer to Al-Jaziri's book *Jurisprudence in the Four Sects*, volume 4, page 28. [48]

"This *hadith* does not mean the matter is one of obligation, since it is probable it may be recommended as a precaution against any dispute that may occur between the man and wife. The *qiyas* [comparison] with the loan case calls for this conclusion – that it is not obligatory – since some jurists said witnessing a loan is recommended.

"Then whoever makes witnessing of the marriage contract a requirement by comparing marriage to the loan case needs to submit three proofs:

❖ That making a comparison is valid, otherwise there would be no validity for comparison.
❖ That witnessing is necessary, regardless of whether it is compared to the loan case, since you must convince those who agree and those who disagree with you about the validity of comparing. Whoever believes comparison is a valid method in law can be convinced witnessing is essential. If you do not believe in comparison, you require other proof to claim

---

[47] Fawzi 85.
[48] Abdul Rahman Al-Jaziri, *Al-Fiqh Ala Al-Mathahib Al-Arba'ah* [*Jurisprudence in the Four Sects*], vol.4 (Beirut: Dar Al-Kutob Al-'Ilmiah, no year) 28. See Document 6 in the back of this book.

witnessing is needed for marriage contracts. Those who disbelieve witnessing is a marriage requirement, and say witnessing is merely recommended, do not have to present proof. The main view is that witnesses are not a requirement, so those who deny it is a requirement have the main view and are not obliged to prove it. Those whose belief is contrary to this main view are obliged to present proof.

❖ Third and most important, that witnessing loan contracts is obligatory. However, no scholar has said it is obligatory. It came as an advisory in the *Qur'an*, as we see in our daily lives. Every day, money is loaned between friends and within families without witnessing.

"We conclude loan contracts and marriage contracts are not comparable. To argue that marriages require witnesses because the *Qur'an* recommends witnesses for loans is like trying to build a house on water. It cannot be done."

Nasser looked at the audience, which was silent. When he found they did not want to comment on his speech, he knew they were looking for a discussion on a new topic.

* * * * *

## Guardianship and Competency

He continued by talking about *wilayah* [guardianship] of the girl, another element in the marriage contract. He said, "In marriage, guardianship of the girl gives the guardian the right to carry out the marriage contract with whomever he chooses on her behalf. The guardianship then means that of the father and the grandfather from the father's side. This is if the girl is *safihah* [irrational in her judgment and deeds]."

A female student spoke as if she feared an injustice under *Shari'ah* if the guardianship applied to responsible girls too. **"Does *Shari'ah* allow the girl who is *balighah* [mature] and *rashidah* [rational] to marry the boy who has chosen her, or whom she has chosen, without the consent of her guardian?"**

The Seyyid volunteered a response. "This question was raised with the Islamic jurists. Some Shi'ite jurists said no one, whoever he is, has guardianship – in marriage or in any other matter – over the girl who is *balighah* and *rashidah* (or over the boy who is the same). Each has control over his or her affairs. They are the only ones to decide on their marriage contract, and on whom they choose and when to marry. Such ruling does not need a proof, since it is a consequence of the main view and original concepts. Nonetheless, Ibn Abbas narrated that a girl went to the Prophet (pbuh) and said: **My father married me to his nephew, but I do not like it. He answered, 'Let what your father did become valid [that is, accept it].' She said, 'I have no desire for what he did.' He answered, 'Go and marry whom you want.' She said, 'I have no desire to go against what my father did. I wanted women to know fathers have no say in their daughters' matters.** [49] Based on this, a *balighah* and *rashidah* girl may decide whom to marry."

The same student had another question for the Seyyid. **"When does guardianship in the marriage contract become a necessity, and why?"**

The Seyyid replied, "Guardianship becomes a necessity for the boy or girl for three reasons: young age, insanity, or irrational thinking or behavior."

She now asked, **"What is the Islamic legal description of a *balighah* and *rashidah* girl who can marry whom she wants when she wants with no guardianship?"**

The Seyyid realized students today do not let anything rest – whether in the Sunni or the Shi'ite school – without quenching their thirst for information on vital issues. He said, "The Shi'ah jurists have an answer for your question, based on the sayings from the Imams of Ahlul Bayt. In one such saying, Zararah told that Imam Al-Baqir said, **If a woman is in control of herself – buys, sells, sets slaves free, bears witness, and gives from her money what she wants, she is allowed to marry if she wants without consent of her guardian. If she is not like that, she may not marry without consent of her guardian.** [50]

"Based on this, we understand, among the requirements of a woman's guardianship over herself, she should be *balighah* and

---

[49] Sabiq 90.
[50] *Wasa'il Ash-Shi'ah*, section 20, 285.

should have full control over her transactions, such as buying and selling, since, according to the prevailing ruling, transactions by those who have not reached *buloogh* [Islamic legal age of maturity] are invalid. Reaching this age is not enough, though. She should also know how to conduct herself. They apply a requirement that she should be *rashidah* and know what benefits her and how to defend against harm and corruption.[51]

"Zararah and Burayd also narrated that Imam Al-Baqir said, **A woman who is in control of herself is not irrational or under guardianship, [then] her marriage without a guardian is allowed.**[52] To explain this, let us go through what was relied on to permit marriage of girls without consent of their guardian:

- ❖ The main view that the marriage contract made by a girl without consent of her guardian is valid
- ❖ The general application of the *Qur'anic* verse **Believers, fulfill your obligations, 5:1,** that applies to such marriage if made without her guardian's consent
- ❖ The application of the *Qur'anic* verse ... **you shall not be blamed for what they may do for themselves lawfully, 2:240,** which applies to women who have not consummated the marriage
- ❖ The *hadiths* – and they are most important here[53] – are numerous. One is the *sahih* [authentic] *hadith* by Mansour Ibn Hazim that Imam Al-Baqir said, **Consent of the virgin and non-virgin is to be sought and no marriage made without their consent.**[54] Another is that Sa'd Ibn Muslim said that Imam Ja'far As-Sadiq said, **There is no problem with a virgin marrying, if she accepted without consent of her guardian.** [55]

"This is a summary of the opinion of the Shi'ah scholars."

---

[51] Though we focus on the girl being *balighah* and *rashidah*, this need also be present in the boy. If he is not *baligh*, his father or grandfather is his guardian; also if he is not *rashid* and has become *safih* [irrational], he must be placed under *hajr* [control] and his father or grandfather becomes his guardian.

[52] *Wasa'il Ash-Shi'ah*, section 20, 100.

[53] Ni'mah 70.

[54] *Wasa'il Ash-Shi'ah*, section 20, 271.

[55] Abu Ja'far At-Tusi, *At-Tahthib* [*The Discipline*], vol. 7 (Najaf, Iraq: Dar Al-Kutob Al-Islamiah, 1959) 254.

One of the male students stood and asked Dr. Omar: **"We have heard the Shi'ah opinion on the guardianship of the girl. What is the Sunni opinion?"**

Dr. Omar replied, "We can refer again to Dr. Ibrahim Fawzi's book, *Family Law Before and After Islam*. It says, 'The *Qur'an* does not state anything about the guardianship of women in their marriage. As for the *Sunnah*, there are a group of *hadiths* narrated from the Prophet (pbuh) that contradict one another. Some of the *hadiths* state the need for a guardian to agree on the woman's marriage. Without his consent, the marriage is void as the *hadith* narrated by Abu Musa Al-Ash'ari shows: **No marriage is valid without a guardian.** However, Al-Turmuthi said this *hadith* has *mukhtalafun 'alayh* [no agreement on accepting it].' [56]

"Another *hadith* narrated by Ayesha, the wife of the Prophet (pbuh), quotes the Prophet (pbuh): **If any woman marries without consent of her guardian, the marriage is void.** Ibn Shihab Az-Zohri, however, rejected this *hadith*. [57]

"Other *hadiths* narrated from the Prophet (pbuh) contradict the ones above. Three of these are **No guardian consent is to be sought for the widowed or divorced woman** and **The old unmarried woman has more right over herself than her guardian does** and **The widowed or divorced woman has her right, but the virgin's father gets asked for acceptance**.

"These contradicting *hadiths,* narrated from the Prophet (pbuh) and whose authenticity is disputed, led to different legal opinions on the guardianship of women. They can be consolidated into four main opinions.

"The first is held by the Shafi'is, Malikis, Hanbalis, and Zaidis. It does not allow the woman to go ahead with her marriage by herself or to pass authorityauthority" to someone who is not her guardian. If she marries without consent of her guardian, the marriage is void. The followers of this opinion say the guardianship of a virgin is an obligatory guardianship. Her father has the right to marry her to whomever he wants, whether she likes it or not, 'even if he married her off while drunk.' [58]

---

[56] Fawzi (no page no.).
[57] Al-Jaziri 46. The Hanafis rejected this *hadith* based on Az-Zohri's statement, when asked about it, that he did not know it. See Document 7 at the back of this book.
[58] Al-Jaziri 33. See Document 8 at the back of this book.

"The second opinion is that of Abu Hanifa and his student Abu Yousif and the Ithna'ashari Shi'ites. They say that guardianship of the woman is canceled when she reaches *buloogh*. Her marriage will not be subject to consent of the guardian, although consent is recommended. Ibn Rush Al-Hafeed believed there was no *Qur'anic* verse that prohibited a woman's marriage without consent of her guardian. Rather, it may be understood from some of its verses that her marriage is valid even if the guardian does not accept it: **If a man has renounced his wife and she has reached the end of her *'iddah* [waiting period], do not prevent her from remarrying her husband, 2:232.** It is narrated that Abu Hanifa had another opinion. The woman who has no father may marry any competent man. If she has a father, she may marry a competent man without his consent, but she may not marry a non-competent man without her father's consent.[59]

"The third opinion is the ideology of Mohammed, Abu Hanifa's student. He made the man's competence a requirement for the validity of a woman's marriage. If she marries a competent man, her marriage is considered correct, without need of the guardian's consent. However, if she marries a man who is not, her marriage depends on consent of her guardian. If he accepts it, the marriage is valid; otherwise, it is void. Both Syrian and Egyptian laws have implemented this school of thought.

"The fourth opinion is held by those who believe in joint guardianship. The woman *and* her guardian must agree before the marriage may be contracted. If the woman agrees to a marriage without her guardian's consent, or vice versa, the marriage is void. No differentiation is made between a virgin and a divorcée or widow." [60]

After Dr. Omar finished speaking, Mustafa said, "This is how the lecturers have summarized the opinions of Muslim scholars on guardianship of the girl. Some agree with others, while some differ. What Muslims nowadays practice differs from traditional family law practice concerning marriage, divorce, and inheritance. Interpretation of family law differs among the various Islamic schools of thought. Some people are trying to unify the views so they do not turn into disputes. Many secular laws [non-Divine laws] have been enacted that do not abide by family law to free people from its constraints.

---

[59]  Al-Jaziri 46. See Document 9 at the back of this book.
[60]  Fawzi 77.

"We see marriage as a great humanistic aim. Aware people will strive to make it an institution with its own moral, humane, educational, social, and sexual system. If we approach marriage as a short-lived adventure or as an empty desire without clear aims, striving for betterment would be unrealistic. We would reap only harsh, negative effects after entering the experience, and end up with regrets, problems, and difficulties that often cannot be overcome due to many obstacles. We men and women, as we enter the institution of marriage, should know our responsibilities and the roles that the regulations of this institution impose.

"Some enter the world of marriage as a way to run away from a reality full of pressures forced on them. They see marriage as a refuge. Others are drawn into it because it is the will of their parents. They therefore often quickly choose a partner. Later, the results may not be as expected. There are also others wanting to get away from their parents. They feel sufficiently qualified to have independent ambitions. They enter into marriage to find a new life, away from the do's and don'ts of the family. They are convinced they are capable of establishing themselves without other people's guidance or advice.

"Marriage is a realistic experiment requiring much deliberation, careful examination and testing, and avoidance of the temptation to rush to choose a partner. If the other person, male or female, does not complement the partner, then one will undoubtedly be a burden on the other and a disaster for their future life. This is because marriage, in all its human and sociological aspects, needs security, stability, and calm to provide a life full of confidence, harmony, and understanding. If this is not achieved, marriage will be a failed project far short of its essential humanistic aims. As the *Qur'an* tells us, **Among His signs is this: that He created for you wives among yourselves, that you may find repose in them, and He has put between you affection and mercy. Verily, in that are signs for a people who reflect. 30:21.**"

Mustafa thought his statement was vital. The audience found him to be an informed speaker. This was in part due to the years of knowledge he had acquired from his work at the university library. The statement he presented was designed to lead toward another element of marriage. He had experience in administrating at seminars and it gave him intuition. He knew when and whom to choose to speak or to give an opinion. He now looked to Dr. Afaf as the person to discuss *kafa'ah* [competence] as one of the foundations of marriage, especially as she had not yet contributed during this seminar. He sensed she had a lot to offer on the subject. He asked her, "How may all the goals I have mentioned be achieved through marriage?"

"To answer this question," she said, "we must be aware that marriage is not just an aim to satisfy sexual needs. It is not just a love of producing offspring, or even a means to prove oneself. Marriage is all these things and more, including a mental compatibility and spiritual tranquility between two people. To achieve this, the young man and woman must be competent. Competence means the man and woman are qualified to marry. It is illogical for a young man to imagine that, when he sees a beautiful woman and is dazzled by her beauty, she is his ideal partner. It is also incorrect for a woman to be attracted to a man because of his money, looks, or family. She would then believe that he will throw flowers under her feet and take her to the palace of her dreams. No, this is not competence! Competence means that the young man and woman understand the correct parameters of their choosing.

"If we take the Islamic meaning of competence, we find a group of great Sunni scholars – Al-Hasan Al-Basri, Sofyan Ath-Thawri, and Abul Hasan Al-Karkhi – see competence in marriage as linked to religious and moral parameters, ignoring competence based on ancestry. Their proof is found in the Prophet's (pbuh) saying: **If it is someone whose piety and manners meets your satisfaction, then accept his marriage proposal.**[61]

"Also, Ibn Hazim Al-Andalusi says all Muslims are brothers. The son of a black woman may marry the daughter of a Hashemite Caliph if he is religious and well mannered.[62]

"The Shi'ite scholars ignore the family or ancestry as a foundation of marriage, and consider religious piety to be the principle of competence. Seyyid Mohammed Hussein Fadlullah states, 'We have not found any Islamic basis for giving rulings that make marriage with persons from sects differing in color, race, or nationality *makrooh* [not recommended] provided they abide by true Islam and have the Islamic requirement of a believer-husband or a believer-wife.

[61] Al-Shawkani 145.
[62] Abdul Salam Al-Tarmaneeni, *Kitab Az-Zawaj 'Indal Arab* [*The Arab Marriage Book*] (Kuwait: National Council of Culture, Arts and Literature, August 1984) 177.

**There is no blame on a Muslim individual, but the blame is a *Jahiliah* [the era of ignorance before Islam] blame,** as Imam As-Sajjad has said.[63] One may not blame a man who marries a woman from another social class, even if some view her class to be lower, provided she has the merits of chastity, religion, and morals. The opposite view is *jahili* [ignorant], and the blame is *jahili* blame.'

"As far as general competence is concerned, *Shari'ah* considers Islam, and Islam alone, as the criterion of marital competence. It considers a Muslim man to be sufficiently qualified to marry a Muslim woman, and places no importance on family connections, ancestry, finances, or social status. A rich man may marry a poor woman and vice versa. A woman of noble family may marry a man with less noble ancestry, and so on.

"From this we know *Shari'ah* does not regard beauty, money, or family as important in rendering a Muslim man competent for a Muslim woman. Also, a Muslim man may marry a non-Muslim woman, though there is a problem for a Muslim woman marrying a non-Muslim man. As for attraction to beauty and other aspects of the body, this is up to the two people. Either they go ahead with the marriage according to their convictions about these characteristics, or they separate for psychological and emotional reasons."

At this point, a female student interrupted. **"Who is a competent man?"** she asked.

"The man of competence," answered Dr. Afaf, "is ready to take on responsibilities. The woman feels secure about building a life together with him and hopes to experience happiness in being married to him. He is the man who has acquired the characteristics summed up in the Prophet's (pbuh) *hadith* that I just mentioned: **If it is someone whose piety and manners meet your satisfaction, then accept his marriage proposal. If you do not, a *fitneh* [disturbance] and great corruption will take place.** The religious commitment in marriage preserves the woman's dignity, because this commitment is a moral process in which upbringing and education are mingled, proceeding from Allah's do's and don'ts. Through this commitment to marriage, the husband knows his exact responsibilities and obligations, will not oppress or be unjust, and will see in his life with his wife a rising hope renewed all the time. Also, good manners

---

[63] Fadlullah, *Kitab Al-Nikah* [*The Marriage Book*] Beirut: Dar Al-Malak, 1996) 26.

are essential to married life, and preserve it from the tensions that can destroy this life. The role of morality is not pure theory, but an action and a will – an action that strives to make the mind an arbiter in practicing the rights and obligations, and a will that holds onto the junctions of this life, tunes its beats, organizes its roles, and calms the emotional reactions with the sweetness of happiness and joy.

"The well-mannered husband sows good seeds in the family home so as to harvest – with his wife's cooperation – good fruit, protected by a happy atmosphere, even if the family life is sometimes brushed by difficulties and anxieties. The competent husband deserves married life when he comprehends that the marriage is a responsibility – a responsibility which consists of assuming certain roles in the educational, legal, and humanistic spheres of life."

When Dr. Afaf had finished, one of the male students stood and asked Seyyid Mohammed, **"What kind of woman is competent for the competent man?"**

The Seyyid replied, "Dr. Afaf mentioned some forms of a husband's competence. The woman qualified to enter marriage also has characteristics of competence. She is a virtuous woman who shares her husband's ambitions and hopes, wishes to live with him all his life, helps him through difficulties, and joins him in building their lives together. She hopes to see in their family a nucleus of a civilized, humane society to whose success she will contribute through her virtue, good manners, patience, and complete awareness of her humanistic and educational role."

After that, Dr. Omar volunteered, "All that has come out of this research is theoretical. To see this theory through to implementation, the upbringing-educational role must have its place. The proper upbringing of a family depends on the parents, who should prepare their children for marriage later. It also depends on the young man and woman because upbringing is the main assurance for the success of marital life, especially given that it is associated with the characteristics of their parents as a married couple, rather than as a mother and father. They transfer their marital experience onto their children so that the children may benefit from them by discovering the strengths and weaknesses in it, changing the weaknesses into strengths, and reinforcing the strengths with their own vitality and initiative.

"As a result, the couple will achieve social as well as religious success. We see in some experiences of marriage success at a religious level, but failure socially. The opposite is also true. There are those who succeed socially and fail on a religious level. It may be impossible to separate religious from social levels, since the socially successful may also be religiously successful. Their religious position may, however, not be complete if, for instance, the man treats his wife as Allah wishes him to but does not practice some *wajib* [obligatory] laws. The opposite is found in many devoted Muslims, who observe *Shari'ah*, even the *mustahabb* [recommended] laws, but in their marital life do not honor their religious obligations. From this, we can often explain the failure a couple may experience in their marital life. There must be a way to act on this theory, but this depends on the competence of the young man and woman. Without competence, we reap nothing but failed marriages."

Mustafa followed the discussion on competence with general comments on the state of society. "What we have discussed so far is various Islamic theories concerning marriage, which entails Islamic, social, and legal obligations. We talked about the elements of marriage and the differences in opinions about the contract, dowry, witnesses, and guardianship. We did that for a purpose that is firmly established in the depth of our souls. We cannot deny or hide it. The aim of these seminars is to show the vitality and ability of our Islamic system to build, free of complications, civilized and humanistic solutions for our youth and our society. Our goal is to find and present these solutions in an Islamically lawful, scientific, and clear way. These solutions will save young men and women from the dark tunnels that may hamper their abilities, suffocate their ambitions, and confiscate their dreams. These solutions center around the issues of marriage and sex.

"Our youth today, concerning marriage in particular, suffers from customs and traditions that are not sacred in any way. Society, through many of these customs and traditions, has made the laws take precedence over *Shari'ah*, perhaps under the banner of society's taboos, or due to having incorrect theories, or due to holding on to religious prohibitions. Many young men and women have felt crushed by prohibitions, whereas the domains of what is religiously allowed are as wide as the eye can see. These domains, diminished by secular law, have given way to unstable situations and mentalities that are burdened with customs and traditions rather than with religion. These modern mentalities have infiltrated the connective tissue of society and distorted reality to force oppression and ill-conceived upbringing on everyone. Anyone who tries to abandon these oppressive customs runs into confrontation and a prohibition mentality.

"Because the customs and traditions are more firmly established in this mentality than religion, and because many of our youth are governed by their desires and wish to get away from these customs, they try, both secretly and in public, to evade reality and take a path that destroys their morals, spirituality, and the zest for life within them.

"This is why we hope, through our seminars, to present a solution that will make our rising generation place *Shari'ah* and Allah's will before customs and traditions. Some of these traditions probably were needed during a certain era, but they have become fossilized and have failed to adapt to changing circumstances and thought."

* * * * *

## The Age of Maturity

"Now," said Mustafa, "we come to the final element of marriage: *buloogh*. Our Brother Nasser will inform us on the age of maturity and marriage."

Nasser began, "Marriage is a means to achieve our essential needs. The most important and notable of these is the need to satisfy emotional and sexual instincts and desires. This is what he or she receives from marriage and the connection with the other person. Because sex has a strong link to age, the question is posed forthrightly: at what age is a boy or girl qualified to enter the world of marriage? The scholarly opinions differ on the age of puberty. The Shafi'is say the minimum age is 15 years for boys and girls. The Malikis say it is 17 years of age for both. The Hanafis say it is 18 years of age for the boy and 17 for the girl. The minimum age of puberty for the Hanafis is 12 years for the boy and nine years for the girl.[64] This is what the Sunni scholars say. The Shi'ite scholars state the age of puberty is 15 years for the boy and nine years for the girl, but some believe the girl matures with puberty and not when she becomes nine.

---

[64] Fawzi 62.

"As a result of these legal opinions, family law in some Muslim countries has taken the rules of the Hanafis. This law states a boy may marry when he reaches 18 and a girl when she reaches 17. At these ages, they may enjoy the right to carry out the marriage contract by themselves. That is why Muslims of today have found that the marriage of young people too often has unhappy results. Family law in many Muslim countries has restricted marriage to those capable of reasoning, making decisions, and making decisions based on having either *buloogh* or *roshd* [responsible character] for both boys and girls.

"The Egyptian law number 56 of 1923 states a marriage may not occur if the girl is less than 16 years and the boy is less than 18 years. It is unacceptable for the marriage registrars to go through with the contract if they know the ages of the couple do not conform to the law. Syrian law, however, states in the Act 18: 'If a boy claims he has reached *buloogh* at 15 years of age and if the girl is at least 13 years of age and they wish to marry, then the judge should accept it – provided he is sure their claim is true and it seems probable from their physical appearance.' The United Nations resolution of November 17, 1967 mandated that all member countries ban the marriage of children and the engagement of young girls, something which may entail a change in the law by limiting the minimum age for marriage to 17 years for boys and girls." [65]

By this time, the seminar had passed the allocated time. Mustafa took the microphone to say, "My dear students, we must thank you and all the people who participated today. We hope to meet at the next seminar. Having already touched on many of the important issues of marriage, we want you to look closely at them and think deeply about solutions. Our question is: How may a young man and woman get truly acquainted so they will avoid entering a marriage that ends in divorce?

"We shall meet again and go further – next Thursday at 4 pm, God willing."

* * * * *

---

[65] Fawzi 62.

# CHAPTER FOUR
## Leaping into the Future

* * * * *

### Introducing The Leap

The days went by fast and the dates for the final exams approached. The seminars dominated discussion among the students and professors, even the administrators, despite needing to prepare for the exams. While most of them wondered what the next seminar would be about, the subject of "acquaintance" became the main conversation in the cafeteria and university courtyards at break-time. This came from understanding the subject's sensitivity and its effect on the future of every young man and woman.

Some students, especially those majoring in the social sciences, began reading religious and social research studies on marriage and the relationship between young men and women. These studies could serve as sources of information during the discussions, be compared with the lecturers' views, and help the students to form their own views and to decide whether they preferred the traditional and classic or the bold and modern.

On the appointed day of the fourth seminar, the lecture hall was packed with student from all departments of the university. Still more students were waiting at the entrance of the hall for extra seating to be provided. No one had expected that the numbers would be even greater than last time.

Those who came early, hoping to reserve seats, were surprised no seats were left, especially as the lecture hall had 170 seats. Nasser quickly arranged for more chairs to be provided.

At last, everyone had a seat, the atmosphere became calm, and silence fell over the hall. The students stared at the stage, as if feeling close to the lecturers in the seminar.

Mustafa opened the session, thanked everyone for the great attendance, and presented the results of the first three seminars. He said, "In the first seminar, we talked about divorce and its rate of increase. The figures painted a frightening picture of the breakup of the family. Also, divorce burdens society with the need to assist divorced women and their children. We listed the reasons for divorce and concluded the main reason was the couple's lack of acquaintance with each other before marriage. Entering marriage without knowing each other thoroughly means traveling on an uncharted path.

"At the second seminar, barriers to getting acquainted were discussed. Some believed getting acquainted could occur through friendship in a lawful and systematic way. Others thought that, during the engagement, many couples deal with this lawfully by reading the holy chapter *Al-Fatiha*. Others believed a permanent contract should be in the engagement to make the couple's relationship lawful. This would permit the couple to know each other very well. They assumed no lawful way to get acquainted in the Islamic world existed unless it was through a permanent contract, by which now they could get acquainted only after marriage. We did not reach the ideal solution we are seeking, one that does not put us in forbidden territory.

"We analyzed the various types of contracts, such as *'urfi* marriage, *misyar* marriage, and marriage with hidden intention to divorce, and found they were not solutions for acquaintance before permanent marriage. In these marriages, the two sides may discover everything about each other too late, after the woman has lost her virginity, gotten pregnant, and borne children. If the marriage is unhappy, the woman may be forced to leave the marital home and go to her parents' or relatives' homes and to the law court. Sometimes the woman is instead patient with oppression and accepts her reality, although she knows her decision to marry was wrong. Such acceptance causes society to lose a competent woman who would otherwise contribute to it because she does not challenge the injustice and misery that block her from achieving her ambitions.

"At the last seminar, the lecturers explained the meaning of lawful marriage and the elements that make it lawful – (1) the proposal, its acceptance, and the contract that embodies this acceptance, (2) specification of the dowry, (3) witnessing, (4) competence, (5) guardianship, and (6) age of maturity. They also presented in detail the differing views of Shi'ite and Sunni scholars on the fine points of which elements or not requirements."

As Mustafa finished his summation, he sensed Seyyid Mohammed had something important to say.

The Seyyid now said, "Before starting on a new topic, we must understand the meaning of *Shar'i* [lawful]. If we abide by it, we have obeyed Allah's command. If we violate it, we disobeyed Allah and his Messenger (pbuh). As we are talking about the relationship between a man and woman, we must look at the *hadith*: **No man and a woman get together without Satan becoming the third**. What is meant are unlawful private meetings without marriage. Applying the concept of *Shar'i* to this *hadith* turns it into the correct situation: 'No man and woman get together without Allah becoming the third.' What is now meant are lawful private meetings without marriage. That is why Allah says: **It is not for true believers – men or women – to make their choice in their affairs if God and His Messenger (pbuh) decree otherwise, 33:36**. What Allah and his Messenger (pbuh) order is always in man's interest so he will live happily and securely, while disobeying His command leads man to instability.

"I refer to this point because some people believe certain types of marriages – like *'urfi* and *misyar* – are lawful, and there is no doubt that they are. These same people also turn around and stand against *'urfi* and *misyar*, as if to say, 'These marriages are accepted by Allah, but I refuse them for myself!' If someone refuses them for himself, that is his business. It is not, however, his right to reject them for other people. Whoever does that does not mean to stand against Allah's laws and what the Messenger (pbuh) ordered. Rather, they cannot express their opinion correctly. They are subject to social influences and customs, many of which are against Allah's law and are hidden behind unclear ideas that aim to please society without thinking of what pleases Allah. It is Allah who sets the laws for people and who knows more than they do what is good and right and the way to salvation. From this, we understand the depth of the meaning of *Shar'i*, which is the system and foundation, the law, and the logic that Allah set up for people so they may choose what is best and distance themselves from what will drive them toward loss and the wrong path. Allah says: **This path of Mine is straight; follow it and do not follow other paths, for they lead you away from My way, 6:153.**"

The Seyyid sat back after his comments, and Nasser took charge. He said, "Dear Audience, we are discussing this because we hope to find a lawful way to help our society lessen the burden of marital problems. We aim to lower the rates of divorce. To do that, we must get acquainted before marriage and it must be within a lawful framework. A man and woman need to understand each other's character, tastes, and manners before committing to marriage. One person cannot gain this knowledge without getting close to the other, a closeness to be controlled within a lawful framework. The different types of marriage, such as permanent, *'urfi,* and *misyar,* are the most widespread lawful framework in our lives, but these lead to acquaintance after marriage.

"There is no bad person for marriage, only a bad choice in marriage. When a man and woman separate, it is not because one is bad or both are bad. It is because they made wrong choices. As proof of this, people who marry a second time may succeed in marriage. This is not a case of experience in marriage, but experience in choice. Some people marry four times and divorce four times. What does this mean? It is not experience in choice, but experience in marriage. The experience in choosing asks for maturity, knowledge, and examination from both parties – about their ambitions, their participation in each other's aims, their morals, and their type of personality, whether they are, for instance, nervous and tense or calm and easy-going. Can they adapt to each other's attributes? Their relationship is surrounded by their parents, relatives, and friends. Can they also adapt to these surroundings? The character traits deep inside a person, such as generosity, courage, and humanity, or meanness, weakness, and instability – do these traits agree with the other's personality? Dozens of questions like these are the right of both parties to ask when choosing a partner for marriage."

One male student said, **"It seems imprecise and exaggerating to claim there is no bad person for marriage. Can you please explain that?"**

Nasser replied, "You should not take what we say too literally. Now, what do I mean when talking about a bad choice? I mean the pillars that hold up the marital home. If a thief married a thief and they committed robbery together, a high probability exists that their marriage would continue. They are compatible and have the same desire to steal. However, if this same thief married a decent woman or if a decent man married a corrupt woman, their marriage would end in divorce because their choice is wrong. This is only an example. I am not encouraging the marriage of thieves. My point is that the correct choice assures the marriage continues."

A student now had a penetrating question. It was obvious the students had prepared for the seminars. Their questions showed a complete understanding of the issues. **"Which is more important: continuance of the marriage or happiness?"** she asked.

Nasser expected all varieties of ideas and opinions and he was ready for all types of questions – straightforward, deep, awkward, easy, hard. He replied, "Various schools of thought have raised many questions about this concept: 'Which is better: A happy and short marital life that may end in divorce or a long life and misery?' Two schools of thought came up with two different answers. Each school has its faults and its benefits.

"A happy marriage and one that continues for a long time may not be the same thing. The first occurs when both parties are happy with their lives. In the second, the marriage endures, but, as the days go by, the couple struggles to uphold what is left of their relationship. Life goes on despite all the problems because, if separation occurs, their options are limited and unclear. We are searching for a happy continuing marriage – even though there is no clear definition of a happy marriage. We say the thief is happy because his wife is a thief too. Righteous men and women should also be content because they have joint aims that bind them together.

"Continuing marriage may occur, despite its misery, for the sake of the children or the hope that circumstances will improve. We cannot go into the philosophy of this. What matters is how to make the right choice, by getting to know each other first, so the marriage will have a good chance to develop into a permanent and happy one."

Dr. Afaf wished to comment on Nasser's speech. "We agree on the importance and philosophy of choice," she said, "but the way we marry today still lacks true choice. This is true for a man when he marries by obeying the wishes of his mother. The mother thinks a woman suitable wife for him. After he marries, he finds she is not the wife he wanted. This is not choice, but accepting the wishes of others.

"A man and woman may love each other intensely. They marry, but it fails, because their choices were limited. When this man is asked how many other women he knew, he will say one or two. They may be his cousin or a classmate. The woman, too, admits that she accepted the first man who knocked on her door and she agreed right away, or that she rejected the first suitor and accepted the second. She thinks she has used her right to choose, but she has used her right to accept or reject. This is not choice."

Dr. Afaf used the logic employed by professors to explain ideas to students, but with a twist that challenged the traditions that force a son or daughter to marry or that limits the choices. She continued, "There will be no true choice unless we widen the margins of choice. The problem concerning the youth is that, when a boy or girl is recommended to one of them, they go ahead with marriage according to the appraisal of others. A boy or girl sometimes gives in to the parents and accepts marriage to whomever they think is suitable. This is where beauty, money, and status become essential in the acceptance of a young man or woman."

"By contrast, if I choose a man and my choice proves faulty and the marriage fails, then I would blame myself and not my parents or society. I chose wrongly at the beginning, even though conditions may have changed later that led to failure. I still must take responsibility for the bad result. And because it was my choice, I would have taken more time and made a bigger effort to try fixing the marriage, rather than run away from it and blame others, since it was my error. With freedom of choice, I would gain even from failure because my character would develop through assuming responsibility."

She paused and then said with emphasis. "We favor the increase of choices so that the right decision may be made." Silence spread over the hall, but it was an analytical silence. The students were acknowledging that Dr. Afaf had presented reality. The spirit of responsibility seemed to be growing inside them out of the new awareness that marriage is a responsibility and a lifetime of sharing.

Nasser broke the silence, and took the opportunity to follow the sequence of logical thoughts one after the other: "You agreed with our opinion in the other seminars that getting acquainted is essential in marriage. Every man and woman must search for a suitable partner because Allah does not create anyone without someone else to suit him. Therefore, we return to the question: How can we get to know each other?"

The students had answered this question in previous seminars. Their answers had mostly been related to the types of marriages, which did not solve the problem of acquaintance before marriage. Everyone was now waiting for a new idea, a solution not yet suggested.

Dr. Omar took over the discussion. "What I am about to say comes from a learned conviction based on Islam," he said. "I have come up with this idea after researching, studying, and discussing it, and putting aside my biases and ego. I searched for truth by keeping an open mind and remembering to satisfy God. An open mind does not surrender to passions, or get confused when analyzing and judging facts, or fear the obstacles to finding truth and the true path in life.

"I am a Sunni Muslim and proud of my Sunni background. I am also proud to be working with this team of Shi'ite lecturers. As a team, we are seeking a lawful way of getting to know one another before marriage. In this way, we hope to strengthen our family bonds and protect the family from the tensions, conflicts, and problems that cause divorce to increase. Divorce breaks up families and destroys children's hopes. Due to this disruption, individuals face difficult social situations that undermine society's stability. I stress that the social cost of divorce leads to moral, political, and economic loss.

"I have come to believe it is Islamically lawful to get away from the controlling influence of customs and traditions. Some of these customs have been considered sacred, but they have nothing to do with sanctity – only with what people have agreed on. They do not derive from Divine revelation or from a holy book, yet they have become social systems in which a person is condemned for failing to obey them. Therefore, I must mention the necessity to believe in Islam completely, not partially. If we believe completely, we will solve the problem we are addressing in our seminars, since Allah's law is the order and essence in every lawful human relationship. If we believe only in part, we will go around in a circle and surrender to the wishes of the community without considering Allah's order. We will miss the unified system that governs us all, and will instead be in various systems, with a range of opinions. This is how chaos begins because each person's temperament differs, **each party is happy with what they have. 30:32.**

"To not let customs and traditions take over and to not neglect Allah's *Shari'ah*, we are in need of a Leap."

Dr. Omar sat silently, seeing questions in the eyes of the audience. What kind of Leap is it? A Leap to where? A Leap how far?

"Throughout history," he said, "humankind has been responsible for many scientific discoveries and inventions. If science had stood still in the past, we would today not know the Information Age, the Internet, and scientific advancement in all fields. Humankind has succeeded, through thought and work, in mapping new frontiers and in forming hypotheses and conducting experiments to achieve revolutionary advances. It put science first, which led to the gigantic scientific leaps that brought great good to the world. When we are leaping here, we do not want to abandon Islam. We want our lives to be run by Islam, because we are convinced that Islam keeps us on the right path. Its law has protected people from many mental, moral, and social tragedies. It has also planned in detail their path in life, so they will not feel anxious and weak or become lost in life's agitation. What we are searching for now is within this framework: how we can get to know each other lawfully so this will lead to better marriages and families less likely to break up."

Dr. Omar saw the audience was impatient to hear about his Leap. He continued, "The Leap that I mentioned stems from Islam, through its laws, rules, and systems. With this Leap, we omit all customs and traditions incompatible with Islamic rules.

"First, The Leap is necessary because many customs block people's progress and ruin their lives. They do not offer awareness and do not allow the mind to think on its own and play a creative role in society. Second, we lecturers, who are of different Islamic schools of thought, took a big Leap. We leaped over our sects and returned to Islam's pure laws. Here we find a person who is Sunni and proud of it, and another who is Shi'ite and proud of it, and we are all Muslims. We differ in some ways, but we all believe in the fundamental concepts of Islam. The subject for which Brother Nasser brought us together took much of our time in discussions and debates. It drew us into the depths of our sectarian opinions and made us aware of our agreements and disagreements. Each one of us stated his or her views and convictions till we reached a consensus.

"After overcoming our inhibitions based on established customs and traditions and their rules, we can now present our ideas to you, within Islam's allowance of them, and their scientific solutions to every problem in life. I, the Sunni, addressed what does not make sense and seems to oppose *Shari'ah*, and the Shi'ites did the same. We reached positive and decisive results from which we identified the weakness that froze our society and produced sanctities not in keeping with *Shari'ah*. We must therefore make a Leap – a studied, lawful, and scientific Leap – so we land on ground that is unshakeable.

"Now we will place our research study into your hands. I must admit there are Leaps that our team have not yet been able to make, but we may succeed in making them in the future."

One male student was engrossed in noting down everything that was said, as to document the seminar in his way. The word "Leaps" caught his attention. He interrupted Dr. Omar to ask, **"What are the ideas that you all consider to be the future Leaps?"**

Seyyid Mohammed wanted to answer, hoping to let Dr. Omar continue with his main topic after he had explained what the future Leaps are. "At the moment," said the Seyyid, "we are researching several subjects. One is to what extent the wife has the right to block the husband from marrying another woman or, put another way, can she set conditions for whether her husband has the right to marry again with or without her consent, if the marriage has its faults? Another is whether determining to have sex is only the husband's right. Must the wife grant his wish if he tells her to come to bed, or is it a mutual decision? A third is whether *'ismah* [right to divorce] can it be granted to women. We are also examining the *khul'* divorce [the wife gives up her dowry so the husband will grant a divorce] and many other issues at the center of scholarly arguments.

"We have not yet established a permanent view on these subjects. Sometimes we lean one way, sometimes another. This team's work will not end with these seminars, but when we have reached a scientific and lawful decision on all these issues and when we have announced a solution for the most important issue – acquaintance before marriage. We are nearly finished, but not quite. This is what has led us to present the system to you – to ask for your questions, discuss it with you, and hear your views and objections."

When the Seyyid finished, Dr. Omar took charge again. As he started speaking, he was interrupted by a male student impatient at the long introduction to The Leap that the lecturers were delivering. **"What exactly is The Leap you referred to?"** he asked.

Dr. Omar smiled and said, "I am sorry but I must follow the order of my thoughts. Please excuse this lengthy explanation of the aim that we have cited."

He started again, "The *'urfi* and *misyar* marriages are lawful. Despite their lawfulness, some people reject them as they reject some customs and traditions. Sheikh Yousif Al-Qaradawi commented on this in an article in the magazine *Zahratul Khaleej*, July 22, 2000: 'I was once asked about *misyar* marriage. I replied confirming its lawfulness according to its elements and restraints. I could not believe the stir caused by my *fatwa* on *misyar* marriage in Qatar, the Gulf, and other Arab countries. I heard about it when I went to Morocco and other Islamic countries. This is what happens with any new idea. People differ in general until they reach a unified decision, or they remain with conflicting views. The conflicting opinions among the scholars and the details concerning the issues must not make a true believer anxious or annoyed – as long as the disagreement is based on interpreting proofs and factors that each side considers and not on following personal desires. The following of desires makes seeing correctly difficult and deflects people from the right path. **And who is in greater error than the man who is led by his desire without guidance from God? God does not guide the evildoers, 28:50**, and He also said, **And now We have set you on the right path; follow it, and do not yield to the desires of ignorant men; for they can in no way protect you from the wrath of God; the wrongdoers are patrons to each other; but the righteous have God Himself for their patron, 45:18-19**. True believers are hurt by opinions based on desires and by opinions that come from those whom the gracious Messenger (pbuh) described as **Ignorant leaders who, if asked, give rulings without knowledge; they have gone astray and led people astray.**

"'Differences based on interpreting proofs are good, essential, and a wide mercy. I gave detailed examples in my book *As-Sahwah Al-*

*Islamiah Bainal-Ikhtilaf Al-Mashroo' wal-Tafarruq Al-Methmoo* [*The Islamic Awakening Between Good Differences of Opinion and Bad Divisiveness*] of how people will continue disagreeing on many new ideas, as they differed on the old ideas. Some forbid and some allow, some make rules easier and some make rules more restrictive. My friends told me, 'You upset many women in Qatar who used to be on your side in everything. Should you not have ruled like these people, who won women's approval by standing against *misyar* marriage?' I said to them, 'If the scholar's concern is to win over some groups of people even if he displeases God, he will be wasting his effort and losing himself and his religion. People will never be satisfied anyway.' There is a saying: 'the satisfaction of people is an unachievable goal' and Allah proclaims: **Had the Truth followed their desires, the heavens, the earth, and all who dwell in them would have surely been corrupted, 23:71.**' [66]

"This is how Sheikh Al-Qaradawi leaped – over mistaken concepts – and issued his *fatwa* allowing *misyar* marriage. He feared none but God and ignored all speeches on forbidding *misyar*. He did this after proof had been established for him that *misyar* is lawful. He ruled it is allowed, regardless of people's agreement or anger, because the important thing is God's satisfaction. Sheikh Al-Qaradawi leaped past non-Islamic considerations and took the Islamic position that cares for the social classes needing such marriage to protect against succumbing to what is forbidden. Therefore, there must be a Leap."

Dr. Omar had finished clarifying his idea. All the lecturers were now convinced enough time had been spent on explaining the meaning of The Leap.

* * * * *

## The First Leap

Nasser quickly stepped in because he was the parent of the project. His concern was the audience's response to The Leap, as this audience was a sample of the model society. He said, "We may have burdened you, but what the lecturers were saying to introduce the subject of The Leap was necessary. The Leap is really two:

---

[66] *Zahratul Khaleej*, 22 July 2000: 65.

a foundation Leap and a secondary Leap. The foundation Leap relates to the morals of men and women. Morality is vital to building a stable society, where people feel confidence in themselves, have inner peace and a clear conscience, and walk on the path of virtue and righteousness. This should be the human path, where people interact with others through a spirituality containing virtue, so all feel safe from deception, lies, and other forms of immorality. Without moral values, our society would be filled with fear and lost to greed and selfishness. Relationships would become tense and conquered by deceit. Differences would turn into disputes and then into enmity, and end up in the courtroom."

After waiting for Nasser to pause, a male student called out, **"So, is this what you call The Leap?"**

"Yes," answered Nasser. "It is an essential Leap. Imagine a man marrying a woman. Imagine him wishing for her what he would never wish for his mother and sister. For example, he wishes them happiness and his wife sorrow. He will not let anyone hit, hurt, or abuse them, but he approves of disgracing and humiliating his wife. He may mock her or cheat her by giving her his word in marriage, but he is really only playing a game to pass the time and fulfill his whims and desires. This is deceit in all its meanings – to play with another's mind and to try to destroy another's hopes."

Here, Dr. Afaf interrupted assertively, as if the lecturers had agreed they were equally in charge and could step in whenever they felt it would benefit the discussion. She offered, "The aim of this Leap is to return us to our morals, to our inborn moral constitution, and to our spirit of humanity when interacting in our relationships, especially where it concerns marriage. Because marriage is a journey of a lifetime, we cannot deny this journey will meet with tensions and problems. To prevent these problems from overwhelming us, *Shari'ah* presents a clear foundation for handling these difficulties. The solution is not hitting, kicking out of the house, swearing, or shouting. It is cooperating by wishing for one another what you wish for yourselves. If cooperation cannot be achieved and unsolvable disputes result, *Shari'ah* has also created a vent to allow people to part on good terms, without one person violating the rights of the other."

To this, Seyyid Mohammed added, "We want The Leap to occur in the relationship between young men and women, and in our own relationships, so we may return to our roots. If the spirit of humanity and other moral values were present, we could control our relationships and not have rising divorce rates. Holding seminars to address the issue would not be needed. We know the issue's importance, but to some people it is unimportant. They give it little thought and put it at the bottom of their priorities. With ill feelings inside them, they push aside *Shari'ah* and morality, and so mold their relationships in wariness and fear.

"Therefore, as a first Leap, we need a moral Leap. It is essential for marriage."

* * * * *

## The Second Leap

There was a short pause as the audience seemed to be absorbing the lecturers' words. A female student was the first to break the silence. **"If this moral Leap is the first Leap, what is the second?"**

Nasser came forward. "The second Leap is the one that will solve our problem of acquaintance and set it in a lawful framework. It will make seeing each other easier for young men and women, without them being watched, and reduce commitments that burden them. They will be able to come and go freely. If they wish to separate, they may leave the relationship without hurting anyone's dignity, as the terms of the relationship will be lawful and clear. Now let us hear Dr. Omar."

With all the confidence of a person with a logical and systematic approach, Dr. Omar began, "Two seminars ago, when discussing marriage with hidden intention to divorce, one of the audience members asked about *mut'ah* marriage. We promised to speak about it later. This is now the second Leap that we introduce – *the lawful temporary contract*. And let us abandon the expression *mut'ah* marriage. This type of marriage is based on a span of time and its consequences. Our interest in this span of time is its importance in not requiring living expenses, witnesses, or a guardian's permission."

Dozens of students began to whisper, especially those who were there for the first time. They looked astonished, until Dr. Omar resumed, "We prefer and encourage people to get acquainted before marriage because of its importance to future success in marriage through fulfillment of emotional and sexual needs. No one can deny its importance in this and also in achieving maternal and paternal aspirations, insuring security, and providing spiritual tranquility. For this to be possible, one person must know everything about the other person. It is his and her right to know the other's personality, manners, and behavior, and also their intellectual ambitions, beauty, and other materialistic and spiritual traits – he or she may make an informed decision to accept or reject an offer. It takes time and privacy – and going together to parties, the movies, theater, and homes of parents and relatives – to study another person, especially seeing how they behave in social settings, and to discover their moral and emotional traits.

"Entering a marriage without knowing the partner is a Leap into the unknown. Each person jumps without knowing if the landing will be on weak or solid ground. For this acquaintance to occur, a lawful umbrella is needed to protect the two people from suspicion and abuse, which *Shari'ah* rejects. Some of you felt a lawful solution was getting acquainted through friendship or engagement without a contract. Others believed in *'urfi* and *misyar* marriage. We said they are permanent marriages, but agreed it was unclear as they are controlled by a man's temporary circumstances. Still it is difficult to end these marriages despite several ways defined by *Shari'ah* to do so based on material or emotional complaints. However, in Islam, we find a more preferable ideal way to get acquainted – by temporary contracts."

One male student was amazed by that expression and thought Dr. Omar wanted to avoid using the proper name. He called out without permission, **"You mean *mut'ah*?"**

Dr. Omar understood his thoughts and replied with a smile, "In theory it is *mut'ah* marriage, but we want to stop using those words. We must stress the principle of a temporary contract and its lawful elements. It is a legal bond between two people for a certain time period. If it ends, the two parties are not committed to the responsibilities that come with ending a permanent marriage – expenses and the negative effects of the divorce process. Also avoided are problems, tensions, and anger in the relationship between the two families that often result from a married couple's conflict.

"As we discovered in the previous seminars, the main cause of divorce is the lack of acquaintance. We also discovered – as a result of our team's profound discussions – that most of the problems in marriage are caused by the couple having made a permanent contract and by the difficulty of getting out of this contract if the marriage sours.

"Even with the lawful engagement we call *milcheh* [preliminary marriage with delayed sex], which means a contract was made, if one of the two decides to end the relationship before full marriage, obstacles will arise. If the engaged man wants to divorce and has not had sexual intercourse with the woman, he must give up half the dowry. Many engaged men refuse because they cannot afford it or because they feel they have already paid for too many of their fiancée's expenses. Then it becomes the parents' duty to pay the man half the dowry to cover gifts to his fiancée and other costs to get his agreement to divorce. How many courtrooms witness such cases?

"As for the fiancée, if she is having a bad experience and is seeing it will be impossible to live with her future husband, she can ask family to encourage him to divorce. If he refuses, she will be subject to psychological pressure and blackmail and will struggle with bitterness. If he accepts, she will be labeled a divorcée. We all know the injustice that accompanies that word, as it implies she is incompetent. New suitors may be deterred, and she may wait many years to recover from the emotional and social turmoil her engagement caused before finding a new opportunity to marry. In addition, during *milcheh*, the woman may have received her dowry from her fiancé and other gifts, but with time she may have learned her fiancé is not who she wants for a husband. If she asks for the divorce, she must return the entire dowry. Under such social and financial pressure and despite certain knowledge that she and her fiancé are incompatible, she may reluctantly decide to go through with the full marriage. The problems then emerge and grow in the marital home.

"What is the solution? The solution is in the term of the contracts. The Leap through Islam is one that we abide by as *Shari'ah* and as the order of life. We need this second Leap, which is linked directly – in morality and religion – to the essential first Leap. And we need to wish for others what we wish for ourselves. We should not oppress other people, take away their rights, or damage their dignity and humanity.

93

"Accepting the right of the two parties to make a temporary contract for getting acquainted with the intention of marrying permanently means the couple would bind themselves to a lawful relationship that would end at the end of the contract's term. They alone would be responsible for the length of the term. When the term ends, they may make another temporary contract if they need more time to assess each other, or they may get formally engaged or marry, or they may decide to separate. If they separate, the man would not have divorced the woman and she would not have become a divorcée or be labeled by any such word. Also, one party would not owe the other any money and arguing over this would be avoided. The main thing, however, that we aim to achieve with this is the start of a relationship of acquaintance without sexual activity."

An enthusiastic male student interrupted Dr. Omar and asked, **"If *mut'ah* marriage is a normal marriage based only on a time period, why is it not a sexual marriage?"**

Because Nasser saw the project as his own, he asked Dr. Omar's permission to give the reply. Nasser said, "We have returned to *mut'ah* once again, and this is not what we want. I urge you to forget it for now and concentrate only on temporary contracts."

**"Is *mut'ah* not a lawful marriage?"** another male student asked.

"It is correct," answered Nasser, "to say it is a marriage. It is not forbidden, Islamically speaking, to have sex within this contract. But, our aim in the beginning is not sex, for it is best that this happen later and within certain conditions. Our main aim is to achieve permanent marriage through acquaintance under a lawful temporary contract. When Dr. Omar will finish, we will explain of the details related to this issue. Our initial aim is for the young man and woman to get acquainted. When we think of a temporary contract, we should think of two people wanting to know more about each other, and not let our minds be distracted by sex. This is why we avoid calling it a marriage contract, even though it is definitely lawful marriage. To say marriage contract implies a sexual relationship, and we do not want to make sex the number one priority. What we need is acquaintance controlled by *Shari'ah* and the way we practice its laws.

"I hope my answer is not too long, but I must make an essential point. The legalization of *mut'ah* as a temporary contract has proved Islam's ability to solve social problems in all times and places. Though its

94

aim was temporary sexual gratification, sex is only one part of its legalization. The other important part is acquaintance between the two sexes. The social circumstances of the past did not require acquaintance. For the present and future, we need acquaintance. Also, many Islamic rules from the past and even from the present do not surface until a dire need arises.

"To understand this concept better, look at the story of the righteous man with the Prophet Moses (pbuh). We see from the sinking of the sailing boat and the building of the wall, to the killing of the child, that these events occurred in the past. But their benefits were saved for the future. Now the orphans will receive their treasure after building the wall. Now the tyrannical king cannot take away the rights of the poor. Now the parents will not suffer because they were mistreated by their son. And, not until now, did Muslims benefit from improved lifestyles due to commercial and financial transactions. This idea may also be applied to the sexual part of the temporary contracts that Muslims practiced in the past. Society built a wall over the sexual part, but the day has come when we need this treasure. To find it, we make a Leap over the wall. When using this legal temporary contract today, we need its principle of acquaintance and all that it implies – because acquaintance is the most important element in creating a happy and healthy future family. Now the idea has been brought into the light, we can talk about it later."

Nasser was content with his speech, and he left the rest to Dr. Omar, who added, "The second Leap is our acceptance of setting a time period in the contract. We called it 'second' because Shi'ites accept it totally, and Sunnis accept only half of it."

After Dr. Omar said this, someone asked him for clarification. Dr. Omar replied, "Some people accept the legality of the marriage with hidden intention to divorce, even when the man conceals that he will divorce after, for instance, finishing his studies abroad and returning to his country. Or, he divorces his wife only after new possibilities become available to him. Or he sends her the divorce papers without warning, not even by telephone or e-mail, as some have done through the Egyptian courts. This is in the Kuwaiti newspaper *Al-Qabas* in September 2002.[67] Is this not an issue of timing? It is, and a cruel one. This harms the woman who knew nothing of her husband's intentions, or what else he may do in the future. This may

---

[67] *Al-Qabas*, __ Sep. 2002 (no specific date): 20.

cause tremendous emotional damage, and may even destroy the children and their future. I am astonished by those scholars who accept setting a time period in the contracts without informing the woman, yet call it *haram* [forbidden] if the man were to declare his intention to her!

"Think with me and use your brains and your conscience. Is it not better that both parties enter into a contract with full knowledge of its duration, nature, conditions, and commitments, instead of into a foggy contract of no clarity? Is it not better, since they have accepted this kind of marriage with hidden intention to divorce, to accept a temporary contract that both parties know well, so the woman runs less risk of harm? Why do we accept this bad contract and reject the other? Some people accept allowing marriage with hidden intention to divorce because they argue that, the intention may change during the marriage to make it permanent. This is the same with a temporary contract. It may lead to permanent marriage if the couple decides make it so. There is no difference between these two types of temporary contracts, except that in marriage with hidden intention to divorce the husband knows when the marriage will end without the wife having the right to know. As for the other temporary contract, our second Leap, the two people would know all the details and rights. The girl would make her position clear to the young man during the contract's time period. Her obligations toward him during this term are lighter, such as not having to provide sex whenever he wants. She does not have to give him everything, and, if she does, then she would understand the relationship may not last forever. Because this time limit controls the relationship, she may decide to offer intimacy gradually.

"If we are two groups that derive from Islam and we both refer back to our own laws as the accurate ones, why do we deny some people the rights we claim for ourselves? Put aside all sectarianism and partisanships and think about this with awareness and logic."

Before Dr. Omar had finished, Seyyid Mohammed asked to comment. "If all our Sunni brothers will not agree with our system, then I ask the Shi'ites to believe in it because their sect accepts temporary marriage. According to their ideology, it is nothing new. The only new element of these temporary contracts is the method used to implement the contracts. We are also certain that correct application of this system will invite many of our Sunni brothers to make The Leap of consciousness and adopt our system."

Then Dr. Omar continued, "I have personally made this Leap and accepted the Shi'ite opinion because we Sunnis allow this, but in another way. Timing is important to us It saves us from falling into crises, and solves many problems. I also urge you not to link timing with *mut'ah* on the issue of acquaintance, because sex is present in *mut'ah* from the start. We do not want a marriage from the start, but instead a spiritual, pure, and honest acquaintance.

"Brother Nasser said the second Leap is linked with morality and religion during the process of acquaintance to permit finding a suitable partner for life. It is better socially to separate the words 'marriage' and 'timing.' We give it a lawful character, but without thinking of sex, so let us call it a contract that has a 100% Islamic term. However, there is a difference in acquaintance between the boy who asks the girl, Will you marry me?' and the boy who says, 'Do you accept a contract with me?' The first direct request leads to thoughts of sex and other rights, obligations, and responsibilities. The second request has limited conditions created by the lawful relationship between the two. We must insist on the word 'contract' and not cross Islam's lawful boundaries. When we say 'contract,' the two sides must question the conditions of this contract from the start. By these conditions, they enter into the relationship. They may soon decide to embrace the world of matrimony, to wait longer, or to separate, if they do not find compatibility.

"The Leap is needed. In it, we find a way of preventing many marital problems and crises. It is good for young men and women to enter into a relationship with clear conditions and specified aims. Scholars and lay people know this, but they do not implement it or give it much of a role in their lives. If the parents and young men and women could become convinced of the validity of this temporary contract, they would save society much strife, the harsh effects of which – destroying our homes and making families homeless – we are harvesting today. This results from entering into permanent marriage directly without one party studying their compatibility to the other.

"The aim of our research is a gracious one. We wish to see the family develop free of complications, and to reduce divorce rates, which are rising daily. Our steps in doing so stem from Islam, which we believe to be valid for every time and place, and capable with its legislation of harmonizing with the developments of the age – the age which will be founded on *Shari'ah* principles that embed in its laws the spirit of goodness and security for the individual and society."

When Dr. Omar finished his speech, silence fell over the hall. No one understood this silence. Did it result from accepting or rejecting Dr. Omar's speech or was it because the audience was contemplating it?

Mustafa whispered briefly with the other lecturers. They decided it was time to end the seminar, but they also had a surprise for the audience. "Dear friends," said Mustafa, "we thank you again for attending. To save your time and because the next seminar may clash with the coming final exams, we suggest now taking a half-hour break and returning as if we were starting a new seminar." When Mustafa paused to listen for objections, but did not hear any. He then stopped the seminar for a half hour.

* * * * *

## Analyzing The Leap

As the break began, the audience dispersed. Some headed toward the cafeteria for a drink. Others stayed in the lecture hall to keep their seats. They worried about losing their seats to late arrivals who were sitting on the floor along the aisles. The sound of animated discussions among groups of students filled the hall.

After the break was over and everyone had returned to their seats, Mustafa reconvened the seminar. He noticed some raised hands so he accepted a few questions.

The first question was from a female student in the first row. She was unfamiliar with the requirements of the temporary contract and wanted to be sure she understood them. Looking at the Seyyid, she asked, **"If I were to accept your argument and leap in the direction that Dr. Omar wants us to leap, after making sure this Leap is a lawful one, where do the requirements for the temporary contract and the permanent marriage agree and disagree, because we care about *Shari'ah* first and foremost?"**

"There is no difference except in the timing," said the Seyyid. "As for marriage and its elements, Muslim scholars have all agreed that marriage arises from the proposal and its acceptance, the wording of the contract, and the dowry, but they have some differences in opinion on witnessing and the announcement, the guardianship of the girl, and age. Some Sunni scholars believe the purpose of marriage is to bear and raise children and that is why they ruled the temporary contract is invalid."

One of the teachers in the audience was overcome with enthusiasm. He stood to express his objection to this interpretation of marriage. He said, **"Who claims marriage is permanent? If it is, why does Islam legalize divorce? Second, I have never – in all my studies during three decades – come across the idea that Islam makes childbearing and continuing the family line an obligation. It is the choice of the husband and wife. If there are *hadiths* with this meaning, they are a recommendation not an obligation. Otherwise, why is using contraceptives lawful?"**

Nasser was looking through his papers as the teacher was talking. When he found the page he was looking for, he asked Mustafa if he could interrupt the Seyyid's discussion. Mustafa granted this and Nasser said, "Concerning whether the aim of marriage is to bear children, I refer to page 15 of the book *Fiqh As-Sunnah*: 'The wife must be fertile. This is known by her healthy body and by comparison of her with her sisters and paternal and maternal aunts. **A man who got engaged to a barren woman said, 'Oh, Messenger of Allah (pbuh), I am engaged to a woman of status and beauty, but she cannot bear children.' The Messenger of Allah (pbuh) did not advise him marry her. 'Marry the wife who is loving and childbearing since I want to have you be more than other nations on Judgment Day,' he said.'** [68] If this *hadith* is correct, we see it as advice but not obligatory. Childbearing is not a requirement, because if it were, what would women who cannot have children do?"

The Seyyid continued his discussion on the marriage requirements that all Muslim clerics agree on: the proposal and the dowry. "First," he said, "we will explain the proposal, one of the two essential pillars for the contract to go forward. The proposal consists of the utterance of the marital agreement between the two parties and its acceptance. Though customs vary in the Islamic world, in the

---

[68] Sabiq 15.

Middle East the woman speaks first. She or her proxy utters *ijab* [the words of the agreement], and the man or his proxy utters *qubool* [its acceptance]. *Ijab* expresses her wish to establish a marital relationship under certain conditions, including receiving a dowry of a particular amount, and *qubool* expresses his satisfaction with her wish. The two parties have now stated they intend to enter into marriage. The words must be clear, and a gesture of acceptance is not enough. It is most important for one party to know what the other wants, including when the marriage should occur. Since wishes are often kept private, they need to be unveiled in the utterances to show the desire to marry.

"The second pillar, the dowry, is an indisputable issue. We reviewed its legal aspects in our third seminar and do not need to spend more time on this.

"We move on to witnessing of the marriage contract, one of the elements disagreed on by Muslim clerics. We detailed in the third seminar the views of the Shi'ites, who find it unnecessary, and the Sunnis, who differ among themselves on the issue. The Sunnis who believe it required fear that one of the couple may deny the marriage later. Seyyid Sabiq says, 'Some scholars believe witnesses are not needed, like the Shi'ites, Abdul Rahman Ibn Mehdi, Yazeed Ibn Haroon, Ibn Al-Munthir, and Dawood, and Ibn Omar and Ibn Az-Zubair have married without them. Ibn Al-Munthir said, 'There is no established *hadith* on the issue of witnesses,' and Yazeed Ibn Haroon said, 'Allah commanded witnessing in trading transactions, not marriage.' [69]

"Most Sunni scholars have stated no marriage contract shall be established without proof and without the presence of witnesses during the contract signing. If the two parties ask the witnesses to keep the marriage secret, the marriage would still be valid. However, Imam Malik and his followers stated that witnessing the marriage is not obligatory. [70]

"The details of witnessing are also an important issue. It is a *Sunnah* for the witnesses to be just people, meaning righteous people, yet disagreement exists over this too. 'The Shafi'is said, 'Witnesses must be just.' [71] However, some Hanafis believe justness is not a requirement and marriage may be established even with witnessing

---

[69] Sabiq 39.
[70] Sabiq 38. See Document 10 at the back of this book.
[71] Sabiq 40.

by corrupt people. They say: 'Provided the couple believes it was acceptable for the marriage contract to be made, it is valid even though witnessed by drunkards – if they acknowledge that their witnessing will validate the contract, even if they may not remember the contract after sobering up.'" [72]

Part of the audience looked puzzled. One male student interrupted Seyyid Mohammed to raise an objection. He said, **"If witnesses are necessary during the contract-making with the clear aim of safeguarding the marriage from denial by one or both of the parties, or safeguarding a child's ancestry from denial, how could a corrupt man be allowed to be a witness? His corruption might permit him to sell his conscience and morals and deny his witnessing. And how can a drunkard who does not know what is happening around him be a witness?"**

The Seyyid's approach was logical and he did not react hastily. He replied calmly, "We respect all legal opinions and may find good reasons for their validity. Scholars come to their rulings after *ijtihad* [intellectual process for reaching a *fatwa*] and these rulings represent a legal Islamic conviction. The Leap we ask of our Sunni brothers here is not the most important Leap, only a normal Leap. It is the transfer of allegiance from one scholar to another, not a Leap from one sect or ideology to another. It is a change from one place to another within the sect. Muslims may adopt the scholar's ruling that convinces them from different schools of thought within the same sect, and so not worry about the issue of witnessing."

One of the teachers now had a comment. **"If we accept not having witnesses for a temporary contract, we assume your reason is that the couple should get acquainted modestly, not publicly, and that the acquaintance is not for sexual gratification. But witnesses are still needed for a permanent contract to safeguard marriage and children."**

The teacher's comment pleased the Seyyid. It gave him the chance to confront a problem that he was afraid many in the audience faced: the mistaken belief that Shi'ites opposed witnesses for marriage. The Seyyid said simply, "We do not object to witnesses. In this team's opinion, witnessing is good, but it should be the couple's decision."

---

[72] Al-Jaziri. 21. See Document 11 at the back of this book.

It was now Dr. Omar's turn. "I did not leap to this only through *Shari'ah*. I examined and discussed witnessing with the other lecturers. I found that Imam Malik and the students of his school of thought made a decision that agreed with *Shari'ah*. Malik reached his result through deep legal investigation. Who can deny he was a scholar? When he issued a *fatwa* allowing the absence of witnesses, it was based on law. From this, we know we are saying nothing new. If we give up witnessing, we will make people happy. Happiness appears when we do not complicate issues are in harmony with *Shari'ah*.

"There are issues that lose their meaning with time. In the past, society was closed. Today's open-mindedness was not present. A young man and woman who had made a contract were forbidden from going out together. Their lawful contract was known only to family and close friends, and not to the general society. Today, if a contract is made, even a temporary one, there is no way to deny it. The girl who has entered into a contract of six months, for instance, can drive with the young man in a car, go on a trip with him, and invite him to her parents' house. Society is the biggest witness to their contract, providing they respect the lawful relationship, when they are seen together at school, in the street, or at home. As we want the relationship to be present also at home, we need witnesses. But, instead of bringing two witnesses, let us give them the freedom to date under the eyes of everyone. All society would witness their relationship, as it is lawful and cannot be suspect. Suspicion is a disease that settles in some people's souls. Islam has confronted and fought it. If we ask for formal witnessing, to get rid of suspicion, it is as if we are nurturing the disease. But, by openly admitting a relationship's lawfulness, we fight suspicion by tearing out its roots.

"Another part of this depends on the times we live in. Science has made astonishing discoveries that we may now use to serve religion by safeguarding people's rights and enforcing their duties. If we fear men may deny their children, science has a solution. A DNA test can determine paternity with unarguable scientific precision. In the past, a child's ancestry might or might not become known after he was born, but today science can positively identify the child's ancestry when still in the womb.

"To prevent wrong interpretations, we respect all Muslim scholars. Their thoughts on some issues have been correct in conforming to their time. They laid down a foundation from which we may proceed to new lawful decisions, so that we are not stuck in a situation where a law was laid down for special circumstances. If a scholar or cleric remained fixed on the jurisprudence of others before him, we would never benefit from his own jurisprudence or doctrine or studies. Life develops, and so do the orders that stem from *Shari'ah* to serve humankind. This happens from within *Shari'ah*, not from outside it, because the system we have faith in is Islamic. Even the interpretation of the *Qur'an* is not confined to one interpretation. They depend on the interpreter and his knowledge of law – and this is his right. If he is incorrect, Allah rewards him once – for trying to interpret a question concerning law. If he is correct, he is rewarded twice – for trying and for succeeding in finding the right interpretation.

"As life develops, *Shari'ah* gives its order to every new phase. Humankind today makes many Leaps. Many subjects that we feared to talk about in the past, such as if the earth is round or flat and if the Earth revolves around sun or the sun around the Earth, have today become routine subjects for discussion because *Shari'ah* has an answer for every question. Otherwise, how could we say Islam is correct for every time and place?

"I am sure scholars had this feeling and conviction in the past, but traditions and social pressures prevented their thoughts from breathing clean air and giving new ideas a place in society. Still, many open-minded religious people did break certain constraints and refuse to surrender to a social atmosphere controlled by stifling customs and traditions. If they had stopped from and courageously putting forward their new ideas, we would not have them today. We will not dwell on this in today's seminar, but I ask this: How many modern scientific methods that some scholars once forbad are now acceptable today? In addition, the clerics in the past did not give *fatwas* regarding many issues, such political elections, because they were not relevant at that time.

"We must all keep in mind that Allah has graced humankind with science. He wants people to develop, for he does not sanctify backwardness. He wants to build a life and make it breathe with the acquisition of knowledge. When God gives people this knowledge, it is for their happiness, their goodness, and their peace of mind. It is not to hinder their progress by denying them the benefit of the resources that He has bestowed on this world. In this, religion was made easier, not harder, to follow. Its ease is found in science and in the knowledge of those who do not contradict *Shari'ah*, as seen in the removal of obstacles to proving or disproving a child's ancestry.

"Let me make an analogy using a large retail store in a Western country. One of its policies was, without asking questions, to permit the return of all goods. One day a man asked an employee to refund on an item that he claimed to have bought a few days before. He had no receipt for the purchase and that type of item was not even sold in the store. The employee refused, but the customer insisted. Finally, the employee contacted the company's president. The president said, 'Ask him the price and give him that amount. We will not change a successful system because of one person.' The president did not want to compromise the company's reputation because one person was maybe taking advantage of their policy. If this person was sent away dissatisfied, he might have spread bad rumors about the company.

"In the same way, why should we fear a few deceitful people who deny their wives or their children, to wipe out a system that Allah created for man's happiness?

"Time flies, life develops, the understanding of science and technology increases, and whoever denies this be at the back of the caravan. This assumes the caravan does not leave them stranded in the desert. We have seen the retreat of Islam's strength in the face of great ideological attack. Do not be deceived by the entry of more people into Islam, because a greater number of people are leaving Islam, not formally but by their lack of commitment, way of life, ethics, and interaction with others. They are not connected to Islam except in name only as they are imitating Western lifestyles. They embrace new ways without reflection and live far removed from Islam's spirituality and realism."

When Dr. Omar finished, a shy female student asked, **"Do other elements of marriage, like the announcement, need a Leap?"**

"The announcement does not need a Leap," Seyyid Mohammed answered. The announcement of marriage is lawfully recommended, generally speaking. Sheikh Al-Qaradawi says about *misyar* marriage: 'The Malikis' custom of requiring the witnesses to keep the marriage a secret would make the marriage unlawful, but only if the witnesses were asked to keep it a secret during the contract-making. However,

if secrecy was asked for after the contract-making, then it was lawful.'
[73] As for the Hanafis, they recommend announcing the marriage by
beating drums or raising flags.' [74]

"From this, we believe what makes the announcement important
to people is similar to the issue of witnessing. It is psychological,
mostly about anxiety and curiosity. Many people have an urge to
know everything happening around them, but why do they need to
know the exact nature of the relationship between a young man and
woman walking in the street? Are they married or not? It is none
of their business, especially as this curiosity is a kind of spying on
people that God has forbidden. As for the beating of drums, we
see that only as an expression of happiness and not as a way to
announce marriage and stop suspicion. Should we give those people
who did not hear the drums the right to be suspicious? This is the
case for announcing the marriage. It does not require leaps, only the
transfer of allegiance from one scholar to another or from one legal
ruling to another within the same school of thought.

"We will go to a more sensitive issue: the guardianship of the girl.
It is a subject of many scholarly debates. During our third seminar,
we explained the differences among scholars on whether *Shari'ah*
allows a mature young man and woman who have chosen each
other to marry without her guardian's approval.

"The Shi'ites believe guardianship ceases after puberty. The Sunni
scholars are divided. The Shafi'i, Maliki, and Hanbali , school of
thought forbids a girl to make contract for herself or anyone else. If
she marries without her guardian's consent, the marriage would be
considered void. Abu Hanifa's and his student Abu Yousif's school
of thought suggests the girl's guardianship ceases at puberty. 'As
for the mature girl, whether a virgin or not, she cannot be forced into
marriage, and her guardian cannot stop her from marrying. Rather,
she may marry whomever she likes, providing he is competent.' [75]

"Our team spent much time studying the issue of the girl's
guardianship. We concluded this guardianship was given only to
the father, based on a reality in society that the girl should submit
to her father's authority, not disobey him, and always carry out his

---

[73]  *Zahratul Khaleej*, 5 August 2000: 23.
[74]  Al-Jaziri 13.
[75]  Al-Jaziri 34. See Document 12 at the back of this book.

orders and wishes because he is the one who looks after her. This guardianship applies only to girls. Society allows boys to marry on their own, but forbids girls to do so. If we accept the guardianship of girls and not boys, it is our duty to present evidence to prove the correctness of this opinion, but we cannot. When the issue is examined from a realistic perspective, we find no difference between the two in this respect or between the two sexes, humanistically, in any related respect. Boys may work and earn a salary; so may girls. Boys may have studied and have a degree; so may girls. Boys may, therefore, not be financially or mentally superior to girls. Another matter is Allah's justice. He does not differentiate between men and women, except for their physical features. Even in this, men are not superior to women. If a 17 year old girl marries a 25 year old man, she must be able to assume the responsibilities of running a household, raising children, and handling other duties. But, the wife who has a career like her husband does must also carry out her domestic responsibilities. If he works in one profession, she works in two: the housework and her career. If adept, she can succeed in both.

"We conclude the *'aqilah* and *rashidah* [responsible and rational] girl is capable of getting married on her own. As for the social considerations, we must overlook them if the girl chooses a competent young man capable of assuming marital responsibilities."

Dr. Omar now commented on what the Seyyid had said. "Allah has blessed me with two daughters. I love them dearly and do not want to be disobeyed. But I do not think it rational to use my repressive authority if they do choose two righteous, competent young men for marriage. You all know the bad outcome that occurs when fathers practice oppression and injustice on their daughters by marrying them to men whom they do not want. This is done under the principle of the father's guardianship over the girl, which does not make justness of the guardian a requirement, since 'corruption does not invalidate the ability of marrying off.' [76]

"Some people hold on to the opinion that scholars 'have agreed marriage is valid even if carried out as a joke. Should a father say, "I give you my daughter in marriage,' and the man says, 'I accept,' the marriage is considered valid even if they are both laughing.' [77]

---

[76]  Sabiq 87. See Document 13 at the back of this book.
[77]  Al-Jaziri 27. See Document 14 at the back of this book.

What kind of choice is it when such a guardian, joking and laughing, marries his daughter to this man, and she must build a life with him without having a say?"

Dr. Afaf did not want to lose the opportunity to give her opinion. "Such behavior is a conspiracy against women! It crushes their humanity. This is what traditions have done, not *Shari'ah*, which has no hand in it. If we return to the texts of the Prophet's (pbuh) life, we find the story we presented earlier as evidence that a competent, mature girl needs no guardian. For those who did not attend that seminar, Ibn Abbas tells a story about a girl who went to the Prophet (pbuh) and said: **My father married me to his nephew, but I do not like it. He answered, 'Let what your father did become valid [that is, accept it].' She said, 'I have no desire for what he did.' He answered, 'Go and marry whom you want.' She said, 'I have no desire to go against what my father did. I wanted women to know fathers have no say in their daughters' matters.** [78]

"There are men who do not want a woman to raise her head. They want her to submit to repression and make other people's wishes and desires come true. She must do nothing but be submissive and obedient. She should be under her father's control, as he pulls her by the ear to her husband, who will pull the other ear! This husband continues to take the same road that her father had taken, in upsetting, repressing, and controlling her. This repression is nothing except concealment of the man's vices, failure to meet his responsibilities, and selfishness.

"Do not take my words as a generalization accusing all fathers and all men. Many fathers are kind, open-minded, and committed to their daughters' happiness. They look on their daughters with humanity before looking at their parental authority. They put pleasing Allah before following customs and traditions."

After this, a female student reminded the lecturers, **"Is a leap needed for the dowry?"**

Nasser said, "Before answering this, I want to repeat what has been said before about witnessing and announcement because it is very important. Sunnis do not need to leap because they can transfer from one scholar's opinion to another within the same sect. Shi'ites

---

[78] Sabiq 90.

do not need to leap because those two issues are not obligatory in their sect.  Now, about the dowry. It is one of the requirements of marriage that the different schools of thought agree on, so no leap is needed.

"Also, concerning the age of marriage, we will not look at the opinions specifying the ages 15, 17, or 18 years. The team defines maturity as the girl who can buy and sell items, who can choose her field of study, who is eligible for a driver's license, who is given a work permit, who can join the military, who is eligible to vote in political elections. She is competent and responsible, and society admits her competence. This is the standard from which we get our proof that the girl has matured mentally and widened her awareness, can differentiate between good and bad, knows where her priorities lie, and has sexual maturity. She therefore deserves freedom of choice because this is Allah's norm – that humans reproduce, learn, and work, and, when they reach a certain stage, naturally they are responsible for themselves. A girl who has these characteristics of responsibility, awareness, and intelligence is free to marry on her own. This too needs no leap.

"As for the exceptions, if we want to prove that a girl, when reaching this stage, is still incompetent or irresponsible, we need evidence for it. Scholars have said, when a girl lacks competence, she needs her guardian's permission to marry. This is fair. However, if the guardian is immoral and corrupt and does not care about her needs, she must take her case to a civil judge, or an Islamic judge or authority.

The lecturers were now nearly ready to begin explaining the nature of lawful acquaintance, its principles, and the ways it avoids leading straight into permanent marriage. Rather, it gives freedom of choice to the young man and woman, allowing them to make an informed decision to accept or reject an offer and wait for a better opportunity.

Nasser spoke first. "Before we begin, I must refer to the importance of the lawful system in our lives. When we talk about a lawful contract and a lawful marriage, *Shari'ah* inspires us. It is a Divine order that Allah imposed on humankind. Allah ordered us to commit to this duty because it ensures people's personal interest and goodness. The Creator of humankind is more knowing than people are in matters that concern His creation. This system – like any system – has commands and prohibitions. When people accept this system from the *Qur'an* and the *Sunnah*, and tackle any issue, while keeping in mind and observing the Islamic system, they have in effect entered the Islamic system that they have committed themselves to. We understand from the word 'lawful' that we believe in Allah, who has laid down a system for every time and place in our lives. This system covers everything in human relationships, trade, prayers, marriages, and other issues encountered on this clear path.

"This system has 'fixed' and 'not-fixed' features. The fixed ones may not be altered in any way, whereas the non-fixed ones may change within the system's framework, though not externally. They surrender to progress from time's passage and, ultimately, change our needs and requirements. If we apply this rule to marriage, what do we find?

"When a young man and woman venture to marry, they must apply the system of lawful relationships to their marriage. If the man asks for the woman's hand in marriage and if she accepts his proposal, or if she asks for his hand [astonishment appeared on some faces in the audience, as if they had never heard of this before] and he accepts, this means they have agreed to use the lawful system, as no marriage may be contracted without the approval of both parties. This is natural and obvious. The pillars of the lawful system are (1) the proposal, its acceptance, and the contract that embodies this acceptance, (2) specification of the dowry, (3) witnessing, (4) competence, (5) guardianship, and (6) age of maturity. The main pillars are the proposal and the dowry. The couple must commit to all the rights and obligations and accept the system completely, without exceptions."

One male student stood and asked Nasser, **"You talked about fixed and non-fixed features. Can you please explain what they are?"**

Nasser said, "The utterance of the vows – the proposal stating the agreement on conditions and its acceptance – is a fixed feature that cannot be changed under any circumstances. The requirement of a dowry is also a fixed feature, but its amount is flexible. It is the woman's duty to decide on the amount. She may ask for a dowry appropriate to her status and social rank, and that might be a great amount. Or, she may prefer a handful of wheat [a small amount] and, if it is beneath her status and rank, no one may deny her this right. Also, no one may force a man to accept or reject it. His acceptance means he is ready for marriage. His rejection implies that he wants to await another opportunity. It is recommended that the dowry be small, but the woman is still free to set the amount.

"As for the guardian and witnesses, past society was different from today. The father did not allow his daughter to go out and she could not marry whomever she wished. This society limited her potential and education. She became satisfied with oppression and confinement. She accepted her father's authority because it was he who fed her, clothed her, and fulfilled all her other needs. Today, she is out in public and that gives her knowledge and awareness of the world. She spends as much out of the house as her brothers do. If we acknowledge her dependability and maturity, and if we set aside the scholars' opinions agreeing with guardianship, then why do we need this guardianship when effectively this guardianship no longer exists? It does not mean the girl rebels against her guardian. She should observe Islamic manners and listen to the advice of her guardian, especially if he is a righteous man and is experienced and aware of the reality of the world. However, if her personal interest clashes with her father's wishes, she may disregard her father's opinion, provided she is convincing and polite.

"Regarding witnesses, without returning to the scholarly debate over whether they are needed, if we feared the possibility of a man denying a marriage or a child, mostly this denial is imaginary. Science has solved the question of paternity with the DNA test. Yes, if the couple married in a forest with no one else there and the man later denied it, this would occur only if he had little faith. However, with normal marriage between men and women who come from well-known families and live within society, how can a man deny his marriage or child? This is why we see guardianship and witnessing as non-fixed.

"For age of maturity and competency, we may also alter opinion according to new circumstances. Society used to marry off the girl at puberty, whereas now she marries when she reaches full sexual and emotional maturity. This goes for competency too. In the past, social rank, family, and tribal background were considered. A man of low social rank could never marry a woman of high rank, and vice versa, whereas now, that has changed. Society no longer focuses on status and background, but considers education, knowledge, religion, and upbringing. These are the new assets for marriage. We changed according to changing circumstances. We understand the reality of the new way and it does not clash with Islam's lawful system."

Seyyid Mohammed now wanted to add his thoughts to Nasser's discussion of the system to be sure the concept was complete and had no gaps. "Nasser portrayed a clear truth," he began. "Now let me review the reasons for the great need for this system.

"First, when two people enter into marriage, they have entered a system that specifies responsibilities, rights, and obligations. They must set conditions that do not contradict the system.

"Second, if they have a dispute, they must return to the laws of this system, which can solve any problems between them.

"Third, the system's general laws are consistent for all generations and time periods, and they may be adapted without touching any of the set laws. Because Islam has given us the space to move by allowing us to change the non-fixed features, we can do so by exchanging the customs with a new system. The world today moves by a system. Without it, all would be chaos. Rights would be lost and effort would be wasted. Consider the ISO standards – the International Standards Organization. It specializes in labor, administration, trade, industrialization, and others matters organized by systematic responsibilities, rights, and obligations, with special features that governments and companies commit to and avoid violating its conditions, as a delay in any of its features results in a delay in all its features. We cannot follow some of the features and leave the rest behind. Rather, we must be completely constrained by them until we attain complete results, without any deficiency.

"Here is an example. If you went to a company governed by the ISO system and you asked for a product, you may be given the product – abiding by the system – in two days. If you went 20 times more, you get the product in two days every time. No disruption takes place with the delivery because this system is fully committed to carrying out all specified steps, starting with an employee welcoming you as a guest and showing you to the waiting room, and moving to writing the invoice, accepting payment, and loading the merchandise onto its transport vehicle. The ISO system means you record every step of work and link it with the system. Its main motto is: 'Say what you do. Document it. Do what you say. Prove it. Improve it.' If you have been granted this quality certificate, the work, in all its details and particulars, must be worthy of being related to the system, and free of confusion and mistakes. The system is transparent, and no one opposes it. We all believe in the ISO system, just like whoever believes in a system for his trade or profession should also believe in a system for his home, marriage, and society. We agree that the system is the right path of life and the road to professional success. Based on this, when we adopt a system for temporary marriage to foster acquaintance before marriage, it is from our conviction of the necessity of this Islamically lawful system."

The students seemed receptive to the presentation of these ideas. The positive atmosphere in the hall gave Nasser encouragement.

* * * * *

## The Five Stages of Acquaintance

Nasser began to present the specifics of the new system. "After much research and debate and after acquiring a full understanding of *Shari'ah* and all the rules, we, the team, arrived at a system of people-introduction that makes entering into and getting out of acquaintance easy, and so avoids or reduces to a minimum the negative effects of separation. The system sets clear conditions and responsibilities. Let us speak first about relationships, which are controlled by stages. Before that, I mention what the relationship should be between one human being with another. If you see a woman in the street, you wish for her the good that you wish for yourself, your sister, or your mother based on: **Like for your brother what you like for yourself**. Your treatment of her should be according to the Islamic way, as dictated by the religion.

"Our system of acquaintance has five stages. The first is the introductory stage – the Islamically-permitted mixing between sexes that occurs in public. There is no doubt that society's members are open one to another, as we mix at work, at the market, at school and university, and in various public places. This means many individuals get introduced to others as a result of shared circumstances. This makes it possible for them to draw an initial idea about each other. When we say mixing, we mean the Islamically-permitted mixing between a man and a woman that does not involve being alone together or touching or looking with *reeba* [wrongful intent]."

A female student said, **"We know mixing between men and women is forbidden."**

"This is true," responded Nasser, "only if the Islamic constraints, some of which we have mentioned, are not observed. Mixing between men and women is not forbidden unless it crosses the Islamic boundaries. In normal situations when mixing occurs responsibly, free of suggestion of sexual provocation and idle leisure, it is not forbidden. If it leads to suspect situations, then mixing becomes forbidden.

"Here, we must point out that, when a young man and woman are *khalwah* [alone out of view from other people], it implies a covert agreement between them that being alone may allow feelings and desires to emerge, and that their sitting with each other will not be like that of a brother and sister. Based on this, being alone is not in itself bad. What is bad is what it can lead to, what Islam does not allow.

"We say mixing should not lead to deviation, but must be Islamically-correct and must occur only within the framework of work, learning, or general situations of everyday life. From this, the young man and woman will start to get to know each other, even if just in an initial way. This type of mixing is not forbidden by the legal scholars, but what some scholars rule is a precaution – not a prohibition – to shut the door to prevent *sadd bab ath-thara'ia'* [bad results from happening].

"Second comes the stage of acquaintance. This is where the two have noticed each other and find a mutual attraction or interest. They then enter into a temporary contract that carries a condition in the way that they treat each other as human beings: he treats her as he would his sister, and she treats him as she would her brother. We have named this stage *feeqah*!" [79]

The moment Nasser said *feeqah*, there was an uproar. Some people started laughing loudly, others laughed more shyly, and some began whispering. Mustafa almost lost his temper as he tried to control the situation. Dr. Omar signaled to him not to intervene, but rather to give them time to react. At last, it grew quieter and a female student

---

[79] The word segment "panion" derived from *rafeeqah* [companion].

asked, **"Should they treat each other as sister and brother or as a legal couple?"**

Nasser replied, "When a boy asks a girl to be his *feeqah* [some started laughing again, but Nasser did not stop], this means he should treat her like a sister. He may see her without a *hijab* [headscarf] and sit with her alone, without hurting her feelings with talk that carries sexual implication. As he cannot see his sister except within the parameters that Islam has allowed him to see her, the same applies to his treatment of this girl. He is allowed to kiss her on her cheeks, but not the mouth. He may put his hand on her shoulder, but not more. What we want from the 'panionship', and what we emphasize, is the relationship must stay within the limits of Islamically-permitted friendship, with no sexual pressure and with no duties and responsibilities. The girl leaves this relationship without the boy having seen private part of her body. When the relationship ends at the contract term's expiration, neither is held to obligations or promises.

"The third stage we call *meeqah*[80] [laughter started, though not as loud as before] and it is more advanced than the 'panionship' stage. If the two have discovered each other's psychological, moral, and humanistic traits, they can move a step farther in their relationship. This allows them some of what is permitted between husbands and wives, provided that the girl's virginity is not compromised. No act requiring an *'iddah* [period of abstention between marriages or contracts] is allowed.

"The fourth stage is *seeqah*, which is when the relationship between the two becomes like that of a husband and wife. We know that society is governed more by succumbing to the pressures of traditions than by living up to the concepts of Islam. Be sure that society – though it may take 50 years – will be convinced of these two fundamental points: first, that *seeqah* is an Islamically lawful relationship and, second, that it is natural for women to fulfill their sexual needs, where appropriate, before marriage. A wide sector will have been established in society by women who recognize that they need not give up their Islamic right to this.

---

[80] Part of the word *'ameeqah* [deeper].

The stages that Nasser listed moved one female student to raise a logical question. She asked, **"What is the wide sector you just mentioned?"**

Nasser replied, "The wide sector are the women who do not look forward to permanent marriage because of special circumstances, such as the wish to complete education, inability to beget children, or full-time attention to study and research required by scientific careers. If they find themselves unable to resist the urge for sex, they may enter into the lawful *seeqah* and so be protected from resorting to forbidden acts. This stage is also very important for spinsters, divorcées, or widows."

The moment Nasser had finished answering, another questioner asked about the fifth stage in The Leap to lawful acquaintance. Nasser told him, "It is the permanent marriage that occurs after acquaintance and if the two people agree to accept this. They decide according to their convictions. From this, we find any young man or woman who wants to marry must take the route of lawful acquaintance that begins with the type of acquaintance that does not need privacy or lead to suspicious looks. This leads them to *feeqah*. We encourage this stage to continue as long as is needed to get thoroughly acquainted. If they are compatible, they will move along to *meeqah*. This stage should take a relatively long time and the girl should remain a virgin. Also, depending on their compatibility, they then move to permanent marriage."

This caught the attention of one of the university professors. He asked Nasser, **"Why did you skip *seeqah* in taking a couple from *meeqah* to permanent marriage?"**

Nasser replied, "It is not because I forgot: It is because the girl who is still a virgin in the stages of acquaintance does not need to enter *seeqah*, and she must remain in *feeqah* and *meeqah*."

**"What about the spinsters and the divorcées?"** a female student wanted to know.

Nasser answered, "They may choose, though we advise them to enter *feeqah* and *meeqah* in the hope that Allah will help them to find the state of permanent marriage. The non-virgin should also respect the virtues of modesty and awareness to prevent her from rushing into a sexual relationship at the start. She make sure of the man's character first, and consequently of relationship's solidity. If a child is born, is the man competent and able to carry out his responsibilities? If he is capable of doing so morally, he may not have the financial or emotional resources to support a child."

Time was running run out. The seminar had covered much ground, but the audience still wished to continue. This was clear because they remained in their seats. Mustafa let a male student ask a question on the dictionary meaning of *feeqah* and *meeqah*.

The Seyyid answered, "These words are not in the dictionary, but there is no objection to creating new words for new ideas. These ideas are vital as they deal with the most important aspect of our lives – the family. Our team created new words to give new meaning to an old subject, though this was new research in both its basis and its objectives. To satisfy your curiosity, we can clarify the meanings in this way. Any relationship between two people begins with companionship; you escort someone to the door, just as he would escort you, whether you know him well or not so well. So that the boy does not say that the girl is his girlfriend and people get the wrong idea about their relationship, we removed the *ra* from *rafeeqah* [companion] to make *feeqah*. For the phase when the relationship becomes deeper and more intense, we removed the *'a* from *'ameeqah* [deeper] to create *meeqah*.

"*Seeqah* is well known and commonly used. There is no need to explain it. We propose these terms to make it easier for young men and women to comprehend the idea of the system. They can choose to use them or not to use them. The words are there to symbolize the meanings. In summary, this is system that The Leap brings us to, and the ideas are now in your hands."

After this, a male student said, "Many of us are not convinced by what you have presented. We have questions and want to hear your answers. You should not rush to end the seminar."

Nasser replied, "Because it is so late and we have already had a double seminar, we must postpone answering more questions tonight. We can continue the search for the answers next week."

Mustafa intervened with a suggestion. "To save time and also because some people are shy about speaking in public, think about our subject during the next week and write down questions that come to mind. You may hand them in and we will answer as many as possible during the next seminar, which will also be our last one. We will, of course, still be taking oral questions. And we hope to see you all next week."

A male student said, "We could bring forward the appointment and not delay it until next week. We could meet on Saturday, before the exam days come closer." Voices from the audience were heard murmuring their assent.

Mustafa reviewed this quickly with the team and noted that he expected the discussion would be wide-ranging. The lecturers had no objections, so he asked the audience, "What do the professors and students say about meeting next Saturday morning at nine o'clock?"

Everyone agreed.

* * * * *

# CHAPTER FIVE
## The Light on the Path

* * * * *

**Temporary Contracts and the Need for Conditions**

Early Saturday morning, the students, teachers, and guests from outside the university stood outside the door of the lecture hall. They had come eagerly because the previous seminar had filled them with questions. They also wanted to get seats to avoid having to stand or sit in the aisles. This is exactly what happened to some after the doors were opened at 8:30. Although extra seats were provided, they were not enough. Many people stood or sat cross-legged on the floor. When the lecturers arrived and took their seats, the groups that were standing were still talking among themselves. They stopped when Mustafa asked everyone to be silent.

After welcoming the entire audience, he announced, "The discussion today will be scientific. We aim to serve our society, which today suffers from many problems. The most crucial problem is the struggles and decline of the family. During the last seminar, to address the problem, we offered a solution in the shape of a social system, and explained its features. We now open the seminar to discussion. Please tell us what you think and ask the lecturers your questions."

After this short introduction, a professor had the first question. **"When talking about your system, you seemed uncomfortable to call it a *mut'ah* marriage. You preferred temporary marriage.**

**Since *mut'ah* marriage is widely used in jurisprudence, what is the reason for not using this expression? Was it to get away from thinking of sexual acts, which do not occur in *feeqah*? However, they are present in *meeqah*, since you suggested that some though not all sexual acts were allowed, and complete sexual intercourse is permitted in *seeqah*, if the couple wishes. Why persist with the expression temporary marriage?"**

Nasser wished to reply. "I must give an introduction to this answer. Some scholars have no problem that the word *nikah* may be used for both intercourse and the marriage contract, especially within the language of religious doctrine. *Nikah* is the direct meaning of the contract, but is used metaphorically for intercourse. It is said *nikah* does not seem in the *Qur'an* to mean sexual intercourse except in the verse **...until she has *tan-kah* [wedded] another man, 2:230.** [81] This relates to the concept of *muhallil* [intermediate husband] that applies when the husband and wife have divorced on three separate occasions, usually because one or both are quick-tempered, and they want to marry a fourth time. To do so, the wife must wait through the *'iddah* [abstention from marriage for three menstrual periods], marry another man, then divorce him, and wait through another *'iddah* of three mentrual periods and before remarrying her first husband. Couples like these often remarried for the sake of their children. [82]

"What confirms *nikah* means the contract is the verse: **If you *nakahtoum* [marry] believing women and divorce them before the marriage is consummated, you are not required to observe an *'iddah*, 33:49.** Here, *nikah* does not mean sexual intercourse. The meaning is clear and evident – if you make a contract with a woman without having had sexual intercourse and then divorce, an *'iddah* is not needed. The woman may marry another man right after her divorce.

---

[81] Yousif Ibn Ahmed Al-Bahrany, *Al-Hada'iq An-Nadirah* [*Fresh Gardens*], vol. 23 (Beirut: Dar Al-Adwa', 1993) 20.

[82] This practice belonged more to the past than to the present. The husband was more often the divorcer. If he did this three times, the idea is that he should not be able to get his wife back automatically. The wife must first marry a *muhallil*. If this new husband treats her better than her first husband did, she could decide not to divorce him. This is one more example of how Islam provides solutions for all problematic situations.

"This helps to explain that our system of acquaintance is a lawful contract. It does not necessarily mean having sex in the early stages. We believe in progressive gradual stages of acquaintance to allow the couple time to study each other's mentality, capabilities, and readiness for creating and committing to a permanent contract.

"The word 'contract'; applies not only *mut'ah* marriage, but also to permanent marriage. All we have done is add the word 'temporary' because this contract is for a limited time. Its philosophy is based on timing. The relationship ends when the term, or time, ends. If the couple wishes, they may renew it.

"We do insist on the word 'contract.' It is because of our changing times. Every era forces itself on us, whether we like it or not. Today we live in an era of increasing social problems and complicated marital life. This was not so in the past, as the husband agreed with the girl's father on many marital issues without the girl's say in the decision. The father received the dowry in advance from the husband, and the husband moved his wife into his marital home, which he shared with his mother, father, brothers, and sisters. His wife had no freedom to refuse. She was also forced to do household chores and serve everyone as though it were her duty – and problems arose from this.

"Today it is different. The girl may be a university graduate and is working. She is now as productive as the boy. She knows her rights, obligations, and the limits of her responsibilities. What she accepted in the past, now her mentality and education do not allow her to. Our insistence that the word 'contract' means we instill in two people that marriage is a mutual agreement. Whatever they agree on, they must implement and commit to. Therefore, marriage is a contract. When the couple gets stuck in a conflict and if one tries to take more than is his or her right, they must return to the terms of the agreement and ask is this right present in the contract? Because we believe marriage is a contract and a pact, we wish the word 'contract' to mean universally all these things, so that, even in permanent marriage, people may search for the essence of this contract and its conditions. Our advice to whoever wishes to marry is to specify the conditions and not leave the marriage document blank where conditions should be written down. If they are convinced there should be more conditions, they must add them even if they do not expect conflict to occur. They may later return to the place that specifies the terms as a solution when they do face unanticipated problems.

"This is what happens in society, and individuals and organizations do this in their contracts, with trade and work. It applies even to membership in a social club or sports club. The page listing the terms and conditions notes legal points that explain and clarify the nature of the relationship and the agreement between the two parties. An important element that should not be omitted in any agreement is the part entitled 'notes' in which the individual may add a condition suitable to his personal circumstances and that will complete his vision and aims. [83]

"So, yes, we approve of the word 'contract.' The word's narrow definition does not mean as much as its connotations – the philosophy of the word, its hopes and aims, the place it points us to, and the way it offers correct solutions and appropriate ground to stand on when someone abandons their responsibilities without considering the interests, rights, and feelings of others. We must believe in the philosophy that the word 'contract' is based on, so that we do not submit to unclear agreements and the dominance of repressive customs and traditions. Today, if we want to marry, we sometimes put secondary priorities ahead of the more necessary ones. We agree on where the wedding party will take place, the type of sweets, food, and drink, the price of the hotel, and the number of invited guests. The couple's families need only one day to decide these issues. We forget to agree on what truly is important, the essentials that are in the heart of the contract. I ask the whole audience: how many couples do you know who have agreed on all the matters about which conflicts occur? What means are available to get us out of these conflicts with the least amount of loss or with no loss?"

The professor who had asked the question was writing down the main ideas in Nasser's answer. He stood once again and asked Nasser, **"Can you talk about essential conditions that belong in a marriage contract?"**

Nasser answered, "For example, in the case of divorce, who takes the children? Because scholars' opinions differ on who has the right to raise the children in the early years of their lives, this leads

---

[83] See Checklist for Permanent Marriage Contract at the back of this book.

to family arguments that last for years. What kind of upbringing should they have after the divorce to shelter them from hatred and spitefulness? Whose right is it to take the apartment and the car? Also, the woman's dowry is a significant amount of money. Does it remain the same amount after 20 or 30 years of marriage as in the first years of marriage?

"As for covering the expenses, why must a judge specify it? We may or may not be satisfied with the court's ruling. Where are the conditions in the marriage contract that specify the exact amount? If the conditions are established, this may prevent the man from rushing into divorce or stop the woman from requesting divorce or even from setting out in this direction if the *'ismah* [right to divorce] is in her hands. Therefore, specifying the conditions are a priority and a necessity."

A female student, who was also putting her efforts into jotting down these details, asked Nasser, **"Are there other principles?"**

"Yes," said Nasser, "there are many. One is the woman's right to complete her education or to continue in her profession. Another is whether the couple will live with his parents or in an independent home. Another is whether the husband will give her an allowance of five or 10 percent of his salary to be put in the bank. This will reduce the size of the dowry. When he gives her this freely, problems will be less severe after divorce. If the marriage is successful, this money will be a family investment. If the husband were unable to work, the wife's savings could help them. Also, when the wife has this money, she will not burden her husband with requests for clothing or other personal items.

"There is an important point concerning conditions that I will now introduce. In the event of divorce, the parents often fight each other by using their children. For example, in marriage, the civil authorities give the guardianship rights to the father, until the children reach 18 or 21, depending on the country. He also is in charge of their finances and has the right to hold their civil papers and passports. When a divorce occurs with the children under their mother's care, the law prohibits her from being financially in control of them with money she has saved in the bank and from obtaining passports if she finds it beneficial to travel abroad with them. To not let conflict occur over these issues after divorce, the woman must make it a condition in the marriage contract, or subsequently, that whoever has custody of the children after a divorce should also have complete authority over them. Although the guardianship of the father is one of the fixed rules, it will then become one of the non-fixed rules because the father is sharing or relinquishing his guardianship rights with the mother in the best interests of their children.

"Here is where the vital role of the parents, society, and organizations lies in directing and managing these sensitive issues. The young man and woman will not be able to form the foundation from which they can proceed in their relationship without the benefit of the awareness and open-mindedness resulting from experience gained by the older generation. How many problems and disputes would we lift off our society, our children, and even ourselves if we improve our child-rearing and make decisions wholeheartedly and with open minds, especially if we derive all our answers from *Shari'ah*? Let the limits and terms and conditions be laid down, and let them be characterized with clarity and vision. *Shari'ah* is always at the service of people as it is made up of fixed and non-fixed features. The agreements will consider the fixed *Shari'ah* rules and must commit to the non-fixed rules that do no conflict with the general *Shari'ah* framework.

"Our attachment to the word 'contract' stems from a set conviction. We want to open up a wide horizon in front of the eyes of those wishing to marry. We want to convince them that the contract consists of practical steps toward what they hope will be the cause of their life's happiness and the stability of their feelings. The main question we present to them is: Do you know the conditions of your contract? Second: Have you considered the possibility of encountering problems and the lawful means to help you overcome them? Third: Have you written down the conditions that you agree on and kept in mind that Allah will watch if you observe these conditions?

"We turn to *Shari'ah* with our differences and problems. This lightens the load on civil judges and courts in handing down rulings and setting rules that do not oppose *Shari'ah*. Before we send someone from his family and from her family to discuss a problem and judge a situation and before all efforts are wasted, let us have the rulings ready in the conditions, and take responsibility for them in front of Allah and human society.

"I also refer to our system and its gradation through the *feeqah* and *meeqah* stages. The time period of each stage should be long enough to give the two people an opportunity not just to get acquainted, but also, if they are finding themselves compatible, to define and agree on the terms for the next stage. It is especially important when the next stage involves building a permanent marital life together.

"Happiness depends on this."

\* \* \* \* \*

## The Philosophy of Timing

There were no questions for Nasser and the focus shifted to another lecturer.

One male student, whose facial features and dialect revealed a North African origin, now asked Dr. Omar, **"You are a Sunni who has accepted the timing in the contract that the Shi'ites believe in. Also, through your studies you have found the Sunnis have accepted half the timing concept, which is marriage with hidden intention to divorce. If the Shi'ite will become free from the temporary contract after its time limit ends, will the man in the marriage with hidden intention to divorce also be free from any relationship after he divorces his wife without her knowing his intentions?"**

Dr. Omar understood and replied, "The responsibilities after divorce in a permanent marriage and after separation in a temporary one do not change. In the permanent marriage, if the wife gets divorced, she inherits nothing from her marriage and she gets no allowance. Her allowance is only for her children. This goes for the temporary one also. What is forbidden in the permanent is also forbidden in the temporary."

**"Can you explain this subject more?"** asked the same student.

Dr. Omar replied, "After divorce in the permanent marriage or at the end of the time period in the temporary one, and after she finishes her *'iddah*, the woman becomes forbidden to her husband as though he were a stranger. Even if they had been married for 50 years and he knew everything about her, he may not now kiss, hug, or see one strand of her hair after divorce. If they are parents, the child is theirs in both contracts. They must raise the child by lawful and humanistic agreement to ensure the child develops a balanced personality and mental stability.

"The temporary contract and marriage with hidden intention to divorce have an essential difference: clarity in the relationship between the two people. In the temporary contract, the relationship is transparent and there is a clear picture of everything within the lawful framework. The woman knows the path she is on, and where the steps of her journey will end. Marriage with hidden intention to divorce is deficient of transparency. This transparency stands for justice and clarity. Society is the pillar of the world. This is why civilized entities make its continuity and stability a priority, but no society will succeed if its social and economic principles are not based on clarity. Imagine not having transparency in human issues, especially in marriage, an institution that expresses the highest form of humanity. This means the absence of clarity and the concealment of truth, disregarding ethics that Allah has commanded. Organizations collapse and countries fall apart from the absence of transparency. Therefore, how can we build a family when there is a lack of clarity? To portray this difference we say: when we swap the words 'temporary marriage' with the *feeqah* and *meeqah* contract, as Brother Nasser said, the words indirectly convey a certain action and a certain relationship and goal."

The North African student was still thinking and wanting the details to be clarified. He asked, **"When does the indirect conveying of the idea you speak of occur?"**

"If a stranger knocks on my door, I open the door and say, 'Come in, you are welcome.' The words 'come in, you are welcome' to a stranger convey the necessity to abide by the normal manners and etiquette for a visitor. He would naturally feel he is a stranger in the house, but would be reassured of the host's approval before he takes the first step and enters. He will also know what is expected of the host, which is also defined by social codes and manners.

"When he enters the visitors' room, he enters with respect, conforming to the manners of entering another person's house. He cannot use the bathroom without asking for permission. He cannot go to the kitchen and eat or drink water until he gets permission from the host, even if he is hungry or thirsty. He knows he has no right to enter the bedrooms, use the telephone, rummage through belongings, or do anything that contradicts etiquette and good manners. His rights are restricted to sitting in the visitors' room, after the words 'come in, you are welcome' are spoken.

"If he overstepped what is religiously and socially accepted – if it happened to close my eyes and he took that opportunity to rummage through my private possessions – he would not be acting as a guest. Or if he went into the bedrooms or used the bathroom and threw the towels on the floor or messed up my children's belongings. After discovering this, I would not allow him to re-enter my house. I know his manners. He is unfit to be a guest.

"If a close friend visits me, I say, 'Come in, my house is your house.' He enters the visitors' room straight away. If there were no religious issues for my wife, he could use the bathroom without asking for permission. He could open the refrigerator if he wanted food or drink. He could use the telephone. If he wanted to rest, he could do so without entering a bedroom. He would do all these things based on 'my house is your house.' If we added the connotation of the words 'come in' to *feeqah* and *meeqah*, what would we find? The words 'come in' would stand for the contract, and entering of the house would mean what the woman allows in her relationship with the man.

"The meaning of 'come in' would depend on the contract type and its conditions. *Feeqah* means that the boy would act toward the girl as if she was his sister, with the right to hold her hand, kiss her forehead, and see her hair. This is what he is allowed to do when entering her house, as he is limited to the visitors' room. After getting permission, he is free to enter the kitchen. In *meeqah*, the relationship develops more. He may see her body but without doing complete sexual acts. This is what 'my house is your house' means, but 'my bedroom' is private and I don't want anyone to share it with me. In *seeqah*, sexual intercourse is allowed, if the couple wishes. It is unconditional: one may use all the 'rooms' and 'household objects' because the homeowner is making them available to the other person. He or she does not feel awkward at the other person's house when a lawful system is in place.

"By the freedom and restrictions that I give the guest, and my understanding of the way he enjoys the privileges without overstepping the boundaries, I get a picture of his manners and soul. I have the choice to gradually give him the right to use the whole house. The house stands for the person's body, the words 'come in' stand for the temporary contract, and *feeqah, meeqah,* or *seeqah* shows us the depth of the guest's right to use the house. 'Come in' comes with limitations, as does the temporary contract in its progress through *feeqah* and *meeqah* to *seeqah.*"

"Here is a real example. A contractor and his crew of four workers were installing a new kitchen in my neighbor's house. After lunch, one of the workers disappeared. The others could not find the missing man and they resumed work without him. An hour later they heard the lady of the house scream from an upstairs room. They rushed upstairs and found she had been startled at finding the missing man asleep in her bed.

"When this homeowner said, "come in," to the workers, it meant they could go into the kitchen to do their work and probably, with her permission, use the bathroom. It did not mean anyone could enter her bedroom and use her bed for a nap. The boss fired his worker for violating that principle. It was, however, permissible for the others to go into her bedroom when they heard a scream because their motive was to help her."

The North African student began to be convinced, but a female student now raised her hand to speak. **"Is the aim of the temporary contract in *feeqah* and *meeqah* to get to know the other person in depth, commit yourself to him, and feel compatible with him?"**

Dr. Omar was pleased. "Exactly," he said, "that is the correct meaning. When I gave the house example, I did it with a purpose. Is the person I have let into my house worthy of being a guest? Will he respect its rules of etiquette? If I permit him to sit only in the visitors' room and he deceives me by prying into my private possessions, will I let him into my house again? If he asked to go to the bathroom and used my toothbrush, can I tolerate such a person? The way he behaves in my house will clearly reveal his personality. When a girl agrees to *feeqah*, she will study the boy, watch all his actions, and judge if she is compatible with his conduct. She then chooses to move on to *meeqah*, or leave the relationship after the term expires because she is unable to live with a boy who oversteps the boundaries placed on their relationship, because their personalities clash, or because he is not the man of her life. What goes for the girl goes equally for the boy."

One male student now asked, **"Does not what you have just explained bring us back to the conditions of their relationship before entering this contract?"**

Dr. Omar said, "We again stress the need for conditions. They are the essence of any relationship that binds two people together. Our aim in advocating conditions is to protect the girl first and foremost. She has the right to set the conditions she wants, provided that they do not contradict *Shari'ah*. In *feeqah*, she may impose limits that the boy must respect. If he abides by them, she will know he respects his promise and his acceptance of the conditions. Also, in *meeqah*, when the girl feels assured of the boy's manners, his compassion, and his piety, she can progress to the stage of permanent marriage, having taken sufficient time in the previous stage. This is why we do not find it necessary for a virgin to enter *seeqah*.

"When I make a contract with a woman for permanent marriage and secretly intend to divorce her, the woman acts as though our marriage is permanent and builds her hopes, ambitions, and future on our relationship. She will give me her life, her secrets, and her future. When I divorce her, her dignity will be wounded. She will be full of regret and disappointment, and may distrust all men for a long time. Her financial future will be in jeopardy, especially if children are present and she is left responsible for them. However, when she enters *meeqah* in the temporary contract, she knows the possible outcome and gets a clear view of her relationship with the man. When she accepts *feeqah* for a period of time, she is not forced to submit to the man's wishes, give him complete authority, or confess the secrets of her heart and soul and put these in his hands. If the man walks one step, she is not obliged to walk 10 steps. She may make two steps as a moral gesture. But, if she made 10 and he took her emotions and gentleness for granted, she must blame herself because she should have been careful. She should have understood the penalties and been strong and firm in her steps, not easy or weak.

"We stress what the words convey. If the contract is for *feeqah*, the woman should offer the rights appropriate to that stage and not step over its limits, so she has no regrets. If the contract moves into *meeqah*, she must be even more careful. She needs awareness and knowledge because, if she does not accept this man as a husband [or he does not want her as a wife], this stage could separate a happy life from and a miserable one.

"The difference between marriage with hidden intention to divorce and temporary marriage is that the woman in the former is deceived and will be shocked one day when the divorce papers arrive, whereas, in the latter, she is in a transparent relationship that she studies at every stage. The decision is in her hands. She may continue if her mind and heart are reassured, or withdraw before it is too late for anything but lamentation and regret."

A professor in the audience was unconvinced. He wanted proof of Dr. Omar's belief in temporary marriage. He asked, **"Do you feel the honorable Shi'ite lecturers, through your long discussions and numerous meetings over the years, have influenced your thoughts and judgment and attracted you to their ideas?"**

Dr. Omar replied, "Thank you for the opportunity to clear up an important issue. Our meetings made evident the need to eliminate sectarianism, and so allow new ideas to arise built on *Shari'ah* and on logic. This is my scientific program, on which I have spent great effort and years of my life. I have thoroughly researched my ideas and believe in them completely. I accepted an idea that I did not believe in before without inherited sectarian thoughts and only when I became convinced of its value in the long run.

"I return to a time when Brother Nasser came to discuss his ideas with me and invited me to be one of the team. I was unsure at the beginning and wondered if Nasser wanted indirectly to convince me to promote *mut'ah* marriage. After thinking it over, especially after approaching it scientifically and realistically and after having serious discussions, I saw Nasser was approaching me directly. His ideas and research were serious, and it was worth entering the experiment. I joined the team without being completely convinced, but for the experience. I was used to scientific research and intrigued by this search for new ideas. I was driven deep into ideas that took me back to the era of *Shari'ah* at the time of the Prophet (pbuh). I researched these ideas, and discussed their history and their soundness. Then I discovered how to apply them to the family – the family too often torn apart by tension and conflict to the extent that its members lose hope. I saw a large beam of light illuminating a path in front of our young men and women on which they could walk righteously, correctly, safely, and with strength.

"Also, the deep philosophy of my life is that Allah is the truth. I think of everything that aids me in reaching Allah as a bridge to Him, especially when it does not involve clinging to fancies, fanaticism, and favoritism. This is essential for scientific research. Whoever worships Allah with clear awareness and understanding does the same. One of the greatest problems that hinders our awareness is that we practice certain acts and accept various theories in the belief they are from the soul of religion, when they are really handed-down beliefs. They may have no connection to the truth, even if they are not myths and ideas that are strange to our beliefs, or they take advantage of naïve minds. They become implanted in the conscience as if they are one of the sacraments. I will not tackle the nature of these beliefs and folklore because it does not concern our seminars.

"What convinced me was not based on Sunnis vs. Shi'ites, or that these people opposed and others agreed with certain ideas. It was that our conclusions stemmed from the depth of Islam and its social system and reflected on the family unit. What distinguishes our work is that we present a new lawful type of system – *feeqah* and *meeqah* – that serves everyone, even if they are unconvinced of its importance to their future marriages, in the hope of creating families surrounded by happiness and illuminated by mercy and love.

"The key is the timing, which is taken from Islam. The Shi'ite school of thought has applied it, while some Sunni schools of thought reject it. My acceptance of the issue of timing is not a victory for one school of thought over another. It is a victory for all of Islam, because we all drink from the same flowing river. Every time you drink from it, it increases in vitality and goodness and remains flowing forever. This great river is for all Muslims, for all humankind. Did not Allah send Mohammed (pbuh) as a mercy for all people? This river is the salvation that branches out into many tributaries from which all other rivers stem. They all flow out to nurture the land with fertility. When you drink from one of these tributaries, you are taking from one spring and also returning to the source. The river Islam and it flows until Judgment Day; its tributaries are the legal rulings of the scholars. Whichever one you take from, you will have taken from Islam itself.

"When you are committed to opinions from the Shafi'i school of thought, you are not supporting this school of thought but rather Islam as a belief. If you take a belief from the Shi'ites or Hanafis or any others who do not oppose Islam as a religion, doctrine, and system, you are supporting the religion itself. This is a logical concept that Sunni scholars followed when they proved it with their scholarly principles: they left Muslims free to follow any scholar.[84] I took from the Shi'ites the issue of timing in the temporary contract because the timing has its own extremely important philosophy. Timing is crucial in many aspects of our lives. In agreements reached between two people, between a company and an economics expert, between a university and a cultural adviser, or between two nations, a clause specifies the period of this agreement for a year or two or five – for logical reasons. This time limit allows for judging the agreement's success. If all goes well, these agreements and contracts may automatically be renewed. If one party wants to withdraw before the contract's expiration, a clause states the conditions for allowing the withdrawal.

"We lay out clear conditions in our business dealings, but we do not systematize our social interactions by creating agreements with time limits and by specifying the responsibilities of each person during the length of the agreement. Let us say a boy makes a contract with a girl for *feeqah*. If he expresses love, she should know this not long-term love. It covers only a period of acquaintance in which the two people are unsure of their suitability for each other. This is the importance of timing. The problem nowadays is that we have not mastered the art of emotional competence as some have mastered physical fitness. When a girl hears 'I love you' from a boy, her heart melts and she gives in without limits when she should be acting in response to this love within the principles of acquaintance for a period of, say, one month. If *meeqah* was for one year, she should not give all her soul, her time, and her responsibilities without limits when, during this time, she should give only what is enough to determine whether she is a good choice to be his wife and he will be a good enough husband.

"By timing, we mean getting to know each other gradually and studying of the possibility of succeeding in permanent marriage. Having the chance to do this comforts us and lifts a burden from us. It clarifies all these issues and saves us from entering the unknown, as we do not know what life has in store for us.

---

[84] Al-Jaziri 303. See Document 15 at the back of this book.

"The sensitivity and importance of the issue force us to address it from all sides so the explanation is comprehensive. Therefore, I finish my remarks on the philosophy of timing with this point: the word 'timing' suggests that the relationship between two people does not reach complete union – their meetings are not continuous and there is no permanency. When I time the relationship, it means something is missing in the relationship. This missing factor is necessary because I am unsure of the other person's character, and unsure if we fit for each other or have similar ambitions. The timing of *feeqah* and *meeqah* confirms the relationship is incomplete, as it is at the acquaintance stage. When the couple finds they are capable of taking on life's obligations and responsibilities for starting a family, they will move on to the permanent relationship with clarity. The timing specifies the responsibilities of commitment to this permanence that is not the beginning or the end of feelings. Emotions do not open or close in one day and night, nor are they limited to a time that ends with the end of the duration. Emotions are not connected to marriage, for marriage is a responsibility, a movement with firm steps, and a commitment to duties.

"We must understand the issue correctly. We do not mean, if a boy and girl make a contract for a month, they must fall in love with each other for a month. Rather, they should commit to the responsibilities of this contract and know where these responsibilities begin and end.

"Another vital issue on timing is the pause or a separation between the contract's end and the time before a new contract may be made. The pause may last minutes, hours, days, or weeks. It is valuable because it allows breathing room for reflecting on and evaluating the previous relationship and contract terms. We may decide to enter a new contract with or without changes or to withdraw entirely from the relationship. This pause without a contract allows more realistic analysis because it is not subject to the influence and pressure of the contract's obligations and commitments.

"This has been a summary of the philosophy of timing and the benefits of timing in the lawful contract. Also shown were the benefits of our entire new system of acquaintance, which adheres to the jurisprudence of the Shi'ite school of thought and, except for the timing, to that of the Sunni school of thought. All Sunnis should adopt the timing because of its advantages.

Nasser Rida

"I hope I have convinced the colleague who asked the question and satisfied his love of knowledge.

"I end with the story of a teacher who took a piece of white paper and put a black spot on it. He asked his students: 'What do you see on the paper? They all answered that they saw a black spot. The teacher said, 'Praise Allah! I blocked your sight from all the white of the paper. Your eyes saw only a black spot that does not compare to the size of the white: it is no more than one to a thousand!'

"Let us, ladies and gentlemen, not seek the negativity of the black that is hardly visible, but work to comprehend all this white, which is full of radiance. We will never regret it."

* * * * *

## A Question of Witnesses

The audience took a minute to absorb Dr. Omar's speech. Then the female student who had been concerned about priorities joined the discussion again by asking Seyyid Mohammed, **"Do we need witnesses in *feeqah* and *meeqah*?"**

"Why witnesses?" the Seyyid replied. "Who has heard of a married couple going to a judge to solve a dispute and he asks them where the witnesses are for their marriage? This does not happen or rarely happens. The disputes between married couples occur inside four walls where there are no witnesses and no father or mother to hear them. They cannot witness them. When a quarrel begins, it starts in the marital home and not in the families' homes, but it can quickly travel to the families' homes. It begins at home, and who starts it? We do not know. If a problem starts between a husband and wife over a glass of water, who would know if the woman fulfilled her husband's request quickly or delayed in bringing him a drink? Who would know if the water in the glass was hot or cold, and if the quarrel started because of that?

"Having witnesses in the past may have made sense, but is their presence necessary today? During our previous seminars, we proved they are not needed during the marriage contract-making and we proved it through Islamic sources, both Shi'ite and Sunni. The benefit of having witnesses in our system for *feeqah* and *meeqah* is questionable.

134

"Let us talk about the woman in the temporary contract and her need for witnesses to her contract with the man. In this contract, if the man mistreats her and she becomes convinced he is the wrong person for her, she does not need a crowd of witnesses to see his actions. She need not to bring one of her relatives and one of his to act as mediators in the dispute. She need not stand in front of a judge to complain about her husband's ill-treatment of her. This is because she has entered a temporary contract, in the stage of *feeqah*. With the end of the time period, this man will immediately leave her life and she becomes forbidden to him if the contract is not renewed. She will have a clear picture of the kind of man he is and will be better able to avoid others of the same mentality and personality. She will know that men of this specific type are incompetent, and are often not ready for permanent marriage."

A female student standing in one of the aisles asked, **"What if the time period of the contract is long and the girl cannot leave the contract quickly?"**

Seyyid Mohammed replied, "The woman must be aware of her role in the temporary marriage contract and her ability to be in harmony with the man, including the possibility of his bad points surfacing before the good. She must put her self-interest first. She must be clear about everything when entering a temporary relationship, where her rights and duties lie and how wide and far-reaching they are. She must consider that, before anything else, the relationship is temporary test period. She should not surrender all her emotions and heart to the man, lest she end up a hostage to his desires and actions. When she enters *feeqah*, the period must be controlled by an essential consideration, her awareness that events may happen that are incompatible with her nature and personality. So, she specifies a time period that is reasonable and short. If she feels the man lacks the assets she deserves, she will be kept safe by the time she set at the start, and will leave the relationship at the end of the specified time. We warn against entering into long contracts. They may not be in the interest of either side, especially at the start of an acquaintance."

The North African student participated again. **"What if she becomes pregnant? She needs witnesses if the man denies it."**

Seyyid Mohammed: "Not all men deny it. Most register their marriage contracts when a child is on the way. We hear of those who resist registering, but not of those who register. In *feeqah* and *meeqah,* there are no complete sexual acts and pregnancy does not occur. Even if it did, a DNA test will prove the child's paternity. However, preventing problems is best. The woman must know her responsibilities under this contract and so avoid creating problems for herself and slipping into situations she does not wish to be in. The woman's awareness of the system gives her the ability to refuse to accept any breach of the contract by the man, such as a revocation of his promises or commitments.

"The reason for bringing witnesses will vanish when the two parties know their roles. We are not compelled to have witnesses, especially for *feeqah* and *meeqah*. We do not oppose bringing witnesses if one of the parties has a reasonable need for it."

The North African student, not totally convinced, asked, **"Why do we need no witnesses?"**

Seyyid Mohammed said, "If a boy and girl were meeting at a public place to get acquainted and they made the temporary contract *feeqah*, why do they need witnesses? The need for witnesses is only for a lawful contract, which places a relationship in the lawful framework that will keep it safe so that neither can succumb to committing a sin or violate the other person's rights. If they reached *meeqah*, or *seeqah*, and if the girl did get pregnant, then a year or two or three would have passed since the start of their relationship. All society, including parents, friends, and neighbors, would know their relationship was lawful.

"Let us for a moment accept the argument for witnesses. Whenever a young man and woman want to get acquainted under a lawful contract, and the time period may be short, they would discover their intentions and their wishes concerning permanent marriage, to what extent their thoughts and personalities coincide, and whether they suit each other for building a life together. What is the need for witnesses in their relationship? If it is to protect themselves from the eyes and tongues of society and from suspicion, then we ask: What have others to do with the relationship between two people, especially as they are bound together by a lawful contract? If we give society the right in that, then we would have given it the right to interfere in the personal affairs of others with no lawful justification. The infringement on the rights of the two would be all the greater if the couple's actions did not violate public order and did not conflict with the law and or *Shari'ah*. If we want witnesses to banish suspicion from the relationship, this would mean embracing negative ideas verging on mental illness and would give people an excuse to be curious and spy. Islam rejects this totally.

"If the girl feels witnesses protect her, let her have witnesses – but without arguing over the types of witnesses. The security guard of a building and a grocer may be witnesses, because God does not specify an identity or social status. Let the witnesses be their classmates at university for *feeqah* of one week's duration between two students, and let their colleagues wish them joy in the hope that their lawful relationship flourishes and develops into a permanent marriage with children. The insistence on witnesses confirms submission to society's curiosity. In marriage, we request witnesses to attend the wedding and to authenticate it. In divorce, we do not request witnesses. Why? If we see a necessity for their presence at marriage, let them attend, but let it be to witness the adherence to the agreements, conditions, and promises made in case of divorce settlement, like the alimony and the visiting times to see the children and so on.

"The forming of some relationships between the two sexes occurs without witnesses or a contract of lawful status. Let us not deceive ourselves and fixate on superficial matters. People meet and become friends. They join other friends in sharing special occasions together, like birthdays and graduation parties. We never ask them to have witnesses in their relationships. Why should we ask it from a young man and woman, when their relationship is set within a lawful framework and with clear limits and agreements, that they use witnesses and registry officials?

"What is demanded from us is to protect ourselves and society, and to rid our souls of doubt, suspicion, and false accusations. We should not hold a couple responsible in a way that makes them yield to society's intrusive notions. Rather, they are under the watchful eyes of Allah and his constant supervision. The eyes of God do not sleep. When the eyes of society sleep and every human being at the end of the day lies in his bed and sleeps, Allah alone remains awake, observing. He will one day ask those who entered lawful contracts, what did you agree on? Where did you go wrong? And when were you correct? How did you carry out these conditions? And how did you violate them? Only Allah knows the truth about that, whereas we humans fool each other and do what we want. We may steal, drive past red traffic lights, deceive police officers, cheat others, violate people's rights, and use witnesses and the law in our own interests.

"With Allah, it is different: **The day when every soul will come pleading for itself; when every soul will be repaid for its deeds; none shall be wronged, 16:111.**"

✱ ✱ ✱ ✱ ✱

## Announcement and Guardianship

The audience seemed ready to move a step farther in discussing the elements of marriage. A male student stood and asked, **"Why are most families so meticulous about planning the wedding? Is it for the purpose of announcing it?"**

Nasser had the reply. "Yes, it is to make it known. Why?"

The student said, "So people should know this person married that person."

"That meaning is superficial," said Nasser. "The purpose of the wedding is social. People rejoice that the couple has established a lawful marital relationship built on agreements and conditions. The wedding occurs so happiness flows into their hearts because they agreed to complete life's journey together and to create a happy family that will become a joyful and righteous nucleus for society. This is the true philosophy of marriage, not playing drums and flutes so that people will know this person married that person.

"Certain ideas must be corrected to firmly establish Islam in the souls of future generations. It is wrong to consider witnessing and announcing marriage as ways to legalize what are forbidden. The acceptance and agreement and the dowry are all the requirements in the contract's wording that open the lawful path in front of the couple who wishes to build a life together. Even if we assume witnessing and announcing are needed during the contract, the necessity would stem from a requirement that witnesses must attest to all the agreements during the contract-making. These agreements reflect the conditions of both the young man and woman, such as completion of their education, value of the dowry, and specifics concerned with the marital home. These agreements are vows, documents, and contracts sworn to before Allah, who says, **Believers, fulfill your obligations, 5:1**, and **Those who keep faith with God do not break their pledge, 13:20**, and **Keep your promises; you are accountable for all you promise, 17:34.** "

A female student asked Dr. Afaf, **"My question is not related to the allowed and forbidden, but linked to social considerations. You oppose a father's guardianship over a mature girl. The Hanafis agree with this opinion. But, because society is so sensitive to the father's role as the head of the household, should the daughter get his permission for the contract so as not to hurt his manhood in the eyes of society?"**

Dr. Afaf said, "We raise this question, as though we legalize society's wrongdoings and find from all wrongs a right and from all sins a truth. Who has the right to accuse this father of not having male pride? From what lawful basis has this sprang? *Shari'ah* does not encourage this, and does not allow us to impinge on our dignity and people's honor. Here, I add to what the Seyyid said on witnesses. If a man and woman are talking in the road, must we prove they are married? Is it to dampen the flames of society's curiosity? Prying should be forbidden. It is unrealistic to allow doubt and suspicion and to make them lawful. If so, we should also be allowing envy, backbiting, slander, and all kinds of dangerous mental illnesses. Who among us would be content with that?

"Any reason that strives to paint a negative picture of the two people on the road is unfounded and illogical. What makes us doubt they are man and wife? Why do we make our doubts our law and give them the trait of being allowed? If we do not eradicate this, we make forbidden sins lawful. This applies to the father who is presumed to have his manhood, humanity, and honor impugned. Who gave anyone the right to question this father's manhood? Who gave anyone the authority to interfere with what his daughter is doing? Society, with all the people in it, do not have the right to interfere if the girl has done nothing to damage her dignity or to reflect badly on society.

"This girl is protected by her headscarf or by her honor even without a headscarf. So, who has the lawful arrogance to impugn her dignity and accuse her father of not having male pride? Even if she was walking alone in the road in the middle of the night, no one has the right to do that. Yet, if she was walking in an indecent way and without decorum, even in daytime and even with her parents and siblings, she must be prohibited from acting in such a way to protect public order and to respect morality and protect honor.

"Our society's legitimization of what is wrong will delay the development of awareness and put it in direct contact with backwardness. Development will dim and eventually wither. We will be unable to leave this dilemma unless we give people freedom within themselves and fill them with moral, humanistic, and civilized order and law.

"What right has society to interfere with the relationship between two people, and to say this relationship will cause psychological and moral harm? Society pays for its mistakes, and suspicion will weaken its structure and tear it apart. The relationship of young men and women within *feeqah* and *meeqah* leaves no room for suspicion and holds an even greater benefit – it offers them permanent marriage after enough time has been spent studying each other and after all kinds of behavioral and moral interactions have occurred. It is a system capable of greatly reducing the pressures that infect today's marital life.

"Let us think beyond the present place and moment. Let us think of a nation's future reality for we are all responsible for its joy and stability.

"We come to a strange distinction – present with the Sunnis and the Shi'ites. When the *thayyib* [non-virgin woman] wants to marry, even if she is 15 years old, her guardian's consent is not needed. The virgin, however, even if more than 30 years of age, must obtain her guardian's consent. This idea is strange because we connect the father's permission with providing protection for his daughter. He sometimes knows better than an inexperienced girl where her interests lie. How can a girl who marries at 15 and divorces a few months later, remarry immediately after her *'iddah* without returning to her father by guidance? What is her knowledge of life? What is her ability to discover where her interests lie in a new marriage? Has she become more mature after becoming a *thayyib*? And yet a virgin who is mature and aware – and because of her age and life experiences is competent to separate good and bad and know her best interests lie in avoiding corruption – is not allowed to determine the suitability of a man.

"This irony proves that insisting on the guardian's permission in marriage is more a social than a religious issue. It is as if society, when giving a *thayyib* the right to choose her husband when she is 15 years old because she has become *rashidah* yet denying a 30 year-old woman the same right, is acting as the father giving the husband permission to marry his daughter for defloration! This is unrelated to maturity or protection."

* * * * *

## Emotion and Sex

It was surprising, though maybe not, that it took this long for the discussion to turn toward "affection." Now, one of the male students asked, **"What is the role of affection between the young man and woman in *feeqah* and *meeqah*?"**

Pleased at this question, Nasser rushed to answer. "Affection is not limited to a young man and woman. It is present between two friends, a parent and child, a teacher and students. It fills people with true and caring feelings and causes them to wish joy to everyone around them, just as if having hate in yourself causes you to hate others. Affection comes from impulses in the brain, which sends messages that help us plan in building a sound relationship and in providing a good environment between people. It is far from scheming and deceiving, and close to good will and noble human sense.

"A Muslim scholar once said, 'Islam does not stop a boy from being attracted to a girl in any way that affects the attraction we undergo when in love, just as it does not prohibit a girl from becoming attracted to a boy, as long as the attraction stems from righteous motives that do not stray into immorality. The attraction must lead to a lawful relationship, rather than develop in a different direction and turn toward thinking about unlawful behavior. Islam rejects thinking that transforms itself into deviant practice, but does not object to emotions that reach lawful results. Islam has tried to protect against the strength of these emotions so the couple does not stray down the wrong path. That is why Islam has laid down restraints at all levels of the relationship.' [85]

---

[85] Fadlullah, *Te'emmulat Islamiah hawl Al-Mar'ah* [*Islamic Philosophy of the Woman*] (Beirut: Dar Al-Malak, 1997) 60-61.

"Affection is essential to life. Often, affection needs a reciprocal good emotion in another person to find hope in it and bear its problems and pain – and that join it in rejoicing and sorrow. One must know how to plant affection in another person, and how to search for suitable land for its growth, to permit the first signs of love to flower inside it. If you do not succeed in placing your affection in the other person's heart, you will not receive back the same good emotion and will have wasted your time. This is why *feeqah* and *meeqah* are important. They mean acquaintance first, and a study of the person who will reciprocate your feelings and be your refuge. The other person must take care of your feelings in the hope of establishing a shared life with you. Searching for this person needs introductions and steps, and these introductions and following steps are *feeqah* and *meeqah*, which specify the features of the journey that we move along with the person whose hopes and ambitions we believe are compatible to our own."

A male student asked, **"To what extent will young people will adopt your ideas? Will they try your system in the hope of building a happy family? Do you count on time playing a role?"**

Nasser replied, "We are sure – and so are you – that young people are convinced of the need for acquaintance before marriage. They do it now, but wrongly, and not awaiting a signal from us to encourage it. For them, the matter is not open to discussion. So acquaintance occurs through channels that lack lawfulness and the right controls.

"We here all agreed that acquaintance before marriage is essential. We estimate almost 70% of divorces are caused by a lack of getting acquainted before marriage.

"To reduce the divorce rate, we have presented *feeqah* and *meeqah* with the aim of creating the right framework and the best method to facilitate acquaintance between the two parties. You and many young people in our society feel a need for this acquaintance. We have not held these seminars to advise you on nutrition, but rather to direct you to the type of food that produces the vital energies in human beings, reflects positively on their mental and physical faculties, and results in safety, stamina, and strength.

"Young people today are aware, and their awareness has shown them the importance of acquaintance before marriage. Our concern is that this acquaintance takes the lawful path. Young men and women now get acquainted in parks, gardens, cinemas, and parties, and some do not know of a lawful path for this acquaintance. This is why problems result and why *Shari'ah* is violated in its concepts and its laws.

"This kind of youth goes out to get to know another, even if the lawful guidelines are unclear. However, there are young men and women who are committed to their religion, but who have shut the doors on themselves and not taken any path, including the allowable one. They see others getting acquainted and living their lives, and they resent it. They falsely think the doors are shut. This causes regret and sorrow, especially for girls who see colleagues and friends living their lives while they sit home and wait for the husband of destiny. There is no husband of destiny without making effort and depending on Allah. We do not want girls to envy those building relationships on acquaintance that violates God's laws.

"We want a switch: the girl who befriends a boy with the aim of getting acquainted with a lawful contract will now be respected by the friend dating a boy with no a lawful contract. The first returns home comfortable in mind and conscience, with no doubts in her heart. The other is open to regrets and guilt, struggles within herself, and questions whether she is doing right or wrong. Whoever commits forbidden acts must feel guilty, if not in a religious sense then in a social sense, because they know within themselves that they have committed a social wrong. The first girl need not lie to her family, while the second girl must invent dozens of false tales. Young men and women who get acquainted under the eyes of God are those who stand before God at prayer times. The others live in an unstable world full of contradictions and torments of conscience.

"Goodness lies within our youth. They are the hope for building a promising future. They have great capabilities and productive power. When we succeed in touching their minds and feelings, then straightforwardness, nobility, and firmness will become their slogans in life. We will soon see our young men and women take each step of acquaintance within our lawful framework and so fulfill their hopes and ambitions.

"We, the team, bet our system will be implemented very quickly in Western countries, where more than 20 million Muslims live. They are more ready to apply this system than are the Muslims in the East.

Nasser Rida

The social atmosphere in the West makes freedom of the individual a priority. Each person acts according to what best suits him or her. We also bet Western Christians, when they see Muslims implement this system successfully, will start adopting it with a few changes to fit their religious beliefs. Even if they do not adopt it, they will recognize a system that firmly organizes instinctive human desires while respecting people and their humanity.

"Our system's path, even though not full of thorns, is not spread with flowers and fragrant herbs. But, the other paths that people take today are full of thorns and problems. Even if we meet hills and mountains, the paths taken by others descend into deep valleys that stifle hope. In our system, the young man and woman hold a compass guiding them to a goal with focus, protection, and awareness. Our path and the other paths differ greatly. Our system will one day be implanted in the hearts, minds, and conscience of youth."

A male student said, **"In meeqah, the relationship between a young man and woman develops more. He may see her without her hijab and kiss her mouth. The sexual stage in meeqah and feeqah is different, even if meeqah does not allow the full sexual act, given your stress on retaining the girl's virginity. What if a mistake happens? In a moment of weakness, a girl loses her virginity. How would she face society, a society that sees her as a 'match' – without benefit once struck and lit?"**

Dr. Omar replied, "People who compare a non-virgin to a match insult women and their dignity. Only a jahili mentality [of the ignorant, pre-Islam era] compares a girl to a match. The Prophet (pbuh) married divorced women and widows who were non-virgins.

"Our team has not reached a clear philosophy on virginity. We asked doctors and psychologists about the reason for the hymen, and we surveyed girls and even married women about their feelings on virginity and on what the hymen means to them. Is it similar to what pregnant women feel when carrying a fetus in their womb? The answer was no. From a physiological perspective, the virgin does not feel her body has the membrane. It is like the eardrum, which no one feels. But Allah created everything for a reason. The benefit of the membrane relates to the rights of women, for her rights differ whether or not she is a virgin. Also, keep in mind that we do not know everything. The membrane may have been created for more reasons than we have yet discovered."

144

A female student at the back of the hall had not yet participated in the discussions. She had been a listener, jotting notes in a pad. She now objected to the last remark as though it devalued her. **"How do the rights of a virgin and a non-virgin differ?"** she asked.

"They differ," said Nasser, "on the dowry or marriage settlement. A divorced virgin gets half the dowry, while the non-virgin gets the full dowry. Regarding her expenses or maintenance, the virgin receives no maintenance during the permanent marriage while she remains in her parents' home before moving into the marital home. If the husband makes it a condition that the girl must be virgin and she is not, he can sever the contract. There are other matters, but they do not concern us in this seminar.

"I stress what Dr. Omar said, that physiologically the hymen's function is unimportant, but psychologically it has a role.

"Whoever has the opinion that affirms the importance of the hymen supports *feeqah* and *meeqah*. We believe this represents the Islamic system in the issue of acquaintance and subsequent marriage. The hymen's presence is required in *feeqah* since the girl's treatment by the boy remains precisely within the bounds of the treatment of a sister. What *Shari'ah* allows him to see of his sister's body is what he may see of the girl's body with whom has a temporary contract for *feeqah*. The same is true for *meeqah*, which is an advanced stage of long enough time to allow the couple to know each other psychologically and physically and to have understood the extent of their harmony and compatibility for possibly becoming a husband and wife in the future, while preserving the hymen.

"Apart from the legal Islamic position, the hymen is a psychological more than a physical matter. It is unimportant, even for the man – just the moment he penetrates, without feeling anything in most cases. Ask the husbands: how many felt its presence on the first night?

"There is also a common illusion that married couples find pleasure on the first night. On the contrary, pleasure does not begin on the first night, or in the first month, but after time has passed, which might be long. It begins when full physical and psychological knowledge and emotion have developed between the two, after they have gained experience with each other and know the places of pleasure, and

145

when they experience the spiritual closeness associated with love, and the physical merging that gives them total pleasure. It is untrue that a man feels complete sexual pleasure with a wife whom he hardly knows, with a stranger regarding feelings and personality, especially as her enmity may be aroused and she may resist defloration on the wedding night. The rituals removing the prohibition of defloration – and the contract, and the acceptance of the father as proxy and the cleric writing the contract – are formalities aimed at preparing the woman psychologically, but she still may not be ready. She may act unconsciously to protect her sense of wholeness. She may think her parents forced her into marriage and she has no choice over losing her virginity. This may fuel her enmity and result in frigidity.' [86]

"Psychologists have also said, '...a boy may prefer to stay unmarried rather than deflower a girl, and a girl may fear defloration and become terrified about the wedding night, and be struck by insomnia, anxiety, and intense tension,' [87] and sorrow despite the general atmosphere of joy on the wedding night.

"We do not want to generalize. These are only examples of what may happen on a wedding night. These examples illustrate the need to prepare for marriage, and this preparation is the lawful acquaintance that prevents young men and women from entering a strange world that may harm them when they are seeking happiness in a new life.

"As society, in its customs and traditions, views the loss of virginity negatively, the girl – and the boy – should take precautions in *meeqah* and avoid anything to cause her to lose her virginity. As mentioned in the question, if she did lose her virginity due to weakness, as long as the contract is lawful and the couple has agreed to move from *meeqah* to *seeqah*, it is their business alone. Society has no right to tarnish their relationship, especially if they have respected their promises, conditions, and vows and all the consequences of these. If they fulfill their religious responsibility, which preserves the girl's dignity and the boy's humanity, and if it results in a child, they must give the child all the maternal and paternal rights. If the agreement

[86] Abdul Men'em Al-Hafani, *Al-Mawsu'a An-Nafsiyah Al-Jinsiyah* [*Encyclopedia of Personality and Sex*] (Cairo: Madbouly Library, 1992) 428+.
[87] Al-Hafani 428+.

between them was lawful and Allah and his Messenger (pbuh) were the witnesses, society and parents have no right to object or slander them."

Questions full of awareness continued to arise. A female student stood and asked, **"Despite the hymen's lack of great importance, as you have explained, you stress the importance of protecting it in *meeqah*. Why?"**

Nasser replied, "If they preserved their promises and vows and their relationship was under the eyes of God, the choice is theirs. We created these stages for philosophical and psychological reasons. Each has a system, limits, and considerations. If the girl agreed with the boy to *feeqah*, but he wants to violate the agreement and move to *meeqah* or *seeqah* with violence or material seduction, the girl should know he is incapable of taking on responsibilities. He does not respect his promises and cannot be trusted, so how can he be her husband? If she had awareness and took precautions, realized his schemes and wrong actions, and was able to confront and stop him, she would be able to pull out safely and not renew her contract before she regrets such a relationship."

The same student wondered, **"What if she did not have that awareness?"**

"Girls should study our system closely,' advised Nasser. "If they decide to follow it, the path is clear. They should be aware of the material and non-material seductions that men normally use. They should not be fooled by false promises and false hopes, and not give in to illusions without care for their future. Many girls possess awareness, knowledge of reality, and responsibility. But, if a girl closes her eyes to the reality of a boy who cannot keep his promises and who violates the conditions he accepted in the relationship, neglects her role in the relationship, and marries him despite his lack of virtues, she is to blame. His attitude revealed his true personality, but she overlooked it and accepted it.

"This is not exclusive to the girl. The boy, as well, when he enters a relationship gradually, must discover the girl's true intentions. Her goal may be to get his money or status, and to get him into a permanent marriage for only her own interest, without intention of building a proper marital home and a family governed by stability and happiness.

147

"We need not look at this in a bleak or pessimistic way. We have full confidence in the many young men and women who were raised with morals and virtues and who respect their promises, vows, and agreements. Many people take great care with the dignity and honor of others. They do not stab them in the back, but 'place them on their eyelids', so to speak, by respecting their privacy and appreciating their humanity. Our system is not a fancy-dress party, where a lottery is held and you accept what is handed out. Not at all. Our system brings people into the areas of light where others may be seen with all clarity. In our system, the girl dates her colleague from work, a neighbor, a relative, a family friend, or a brother's colleague, not someone she met in the street. She is dating him for a purpose – to study the possibility of building a family. This is one of the noblest goals. The probabilities of deception or cunning between people who are open to one another are low, especially if they are individuals who are connected by relationships, friendships, and brotherhood, and who have come from homes that gave them good morals and perfected in them the spirit of goodness and responsibility.

"These young men and women are in the first stage of life. They have purity and are not yet affected by political problems or religious, sectarian, or tribal malice. Their feelings are still pure. The problems we mentioned are with those who have traveled a distance on the road of life and gone astray on crooked paths. Our system is not for them, but for those who are at the beginning of the road.

"Our system is comprehensive, but it starts in the home, with good upbringing. If a bad situation arises, we should not blame the system but those who misuse or abuse the system. Our system is built on morals and it preserves morals. Only morals can help implement the system with full correctness and realism."

\* \* \* \* \*

## Age and Parents

Nasser had finished, well satisfied with the students' liveliness. A new male student now asked, **"What is the appropriate age to enter *feeqah*?"**

Seyyid Mohammed was ready. "Specifying maturity and puberty and identifying when both parties are allowed to go to court to marry are disputed among the Islamic schools of thought. They argue over whether the age is 15, 17, 18, or when sexual maturity occurs.

"These same opinions also differ regarding the permanent marriage contract and the possibility of registering and documenting it in the Islamic court. This does not concern our system because registration in court is not required. It is a temporary contract that may become permanent if the couple so agrees after a long acquaintance. They may then document their marriage at the official registration office. The contract, as a matter of principle, whether permanent or temporary, is 100% lawful – if it follows all the requirements, even if not documented or registered in court.

"In our long discussions, some preferred 18 as the best age for *feeqah*, while others said 21 was more suitable. If we go back to the scholars' opinions, some allow the girl who is *balighah* [mature] and *rashidah* [rational] to enter the contract without her guardian's permission. However, other scholars said, despite reaching puberty and being responsible, she needs her father's permission to marry. We have discussed these opinions from a legal angle at a previous seminar. If we connect *feeqah* with age, no criterion exists to say this girl has become *rashidah*, and no written test exists in which the young man and woman answer questions to tell if they are responsible even if they are 18 or 21. Any 15 year old may pass such a test theoretically, but who would guarantee their success in practice? [88]

"Another point is that we cannot give the guardian sole right to specify the *roshd* [responsible character] of the girl. If we link *roshd* with age, who can say for sure that her father is a *rashid* [rational] person and can certify his daughter's *roshd*? We may doubt the father's *roshd*, so he must present proof that he is *rashid*. The father who is cruel to his children, who does not observe his duties toward them, who rebukes his wife and tarnishes her dignity, or who applies pressures that hurt the whole of the family, is he *rashid*? We might not say 'No,' but who could say, 'Yes'? Who could prove either one?

"If the matter is linked to age, differences in opinions will occur. Only civilized society, adhering to laws that do not contradict *Shari'ah,* can specify. When society gives young men and women driver's licenses

---

[88] Ni'mah 71.

at 18 years of age, and so allows them to drive among thousands of people in the street, it is admitting their competence and *roshd*. Some of us saw this and adopted 18 as the age of maturity. Others, although not against driving at 18, believe the youth have not yet matured enough to know all life's complexities, where their interests lie, and the consequences of their behavior. These others point to countries where the right to vote in elections does not begin till 21.

"We surveyed many sectors of our society with a questionnaire. It showed society leaning toward the first opinion. Where 18 year olds have voting rights, governments in those countries acknowledge the reality of today's advanced cultural, political, and social awareness and say the youth know whom to choose to represent them. Young men and women at this age are competent enough to enter the university, and know what specialty they want and whether it conforms to their scientific leanings. We therefore conclude the age of 18 is reasonable for *feeqah*. Some non-Divine systems do not give all rights to 18 year olds, but our system is Divine. We are compelled to follow *Shari'ah*. Why change a Divine law that takes care of the most important need in young men and women's lives?

"If this age is not accepted at the present, after 20 years society will accept it as reality based on research and experience, and will see it is best."

One student raised her hand. **"When their feelings for the opposite sex have started to emerge, cannot 15 or 16 year olds enter *feeqah*?"**

Seyyid Mohammed replied, "We do not object. A girl may enter *feeqah*, especially if sexual maturity in evident – as may a boy – under the observation, guidance, and care of responsible parents who understand their children's circumstances and view their emotional needs and sincere feelings with awareness and wisdom. At this age, teenagers need their parents more than at any other time to guide them in the right direction, so they may grow up free from complications, trained to carry out their responsibilities, sure of every step they make. This happens only when a good father and equally committed mother are present to guide their children to the shores of safety. The father's guardianship is needed at this age. We reiterate that the father must be balanced, wise, and observant of *Shari'ah*. At 18, a girl may enter the contract herself."

Here, a female student in the first row asked Dr. Afaf, **"How should the parents train a girl for *roshd* status, so, when she becomes 18, she is *rashidah*?"**

"The father and the mother's role to prepare the girl," said Dr. Afaf, "is one of their greatest obligations and responsibilities. They will not have a girl characterized by composure and poise, beautified by modesty and good manners, and armed with religion and morality, if they do not raise her well. They must educate her, and give her a brain from their brains and an eye from their eyes, till she grows to see her life in an objective way. This will come only from correct care and safe direction. This is what she needs to make rational, open-minded decisions. This will affect all her actions, including her behavior in *feeqah* and *meeqah*. When parents clarify the sublime goals of these stages, the girl will fully grasp their meaning and lawfulness, and will appreciate the wide horizons and clarity that they offer and that should reflect positively on her future. She will know how to limit the relationship with the boy, and will not need to learn it from friends who may know less.

"The parents must also raise her on virtue, morality, and religion. Then, when she reaches the age of 18, she will make rational decisions, specifically concerning her marital future, by understanding the importance of our system in specifying her choices.

"Our responsibilities toward our dear children are great – in sharing their hopes and showing them where awareness may light the correct path before their eyes. This is not present in *feeqah* and *meeqah* only, but also when specifying the traits of their friends. We do not accept or refuse building a friendship without getting acquainted, usually gradually, and without having safe foundations and clear principles for building it on a firm land.

"We parents must also open our hearts, minds, and understanding so our children feel there is a caring heart to take refuge in, a rational mind from whose experience to learn, and an understanding that welcomes and protects them from catastrophes. We must teach them to seek refuge in us with their problems for there to be mutual trust, and not to run away from problems because of our own worries and problems. We must not leave raising them to the streets, society, and friends. The mother a security guard to the girl if she is not her daughter's loyal friend, and the father is a jailer to the girl if he is not a merciful and just ruler. Let us – here I address first myself and then the parents among us in this hall – open to them hearts and minds that look on the most diverse, pure, and noble experiences, so our children become our friends. They can tell us their worries, difficulties, and secrets and have a safety rope to hold when facing troubles.

"Our duty is to direct the boy who has a relationship with a girl to respect her privacy, keep her secrets, protect her dignity, and treat her like a sister. We must plant these morals in the boy's mind because these youth are our hope. The same goes for the girl, who must observe the lawful concepts of *feeqah* and *meeqah*. We totally refute what girls do in Western societies. A girl did not leave the house 100 years ago in the West without her mother's permission, but today the mother accepts her daughter's independence and reminds her to carry contraceptives because she knows the girl sleeps with her boyfriend.

"We hope to generate a conviction in the correctness of our philosophy for relationships and acquaintance, and to one day reach a point where the parent asks the daughter: Did you make a lawful contract with your boyfriend? Have you acted within Allah's boundaries? Was your trip to the park, the seaside, or somewhere private bound by a lawful contract that will protect you on Judgment Day as it does in this life?

"We stress education is crucial to our system. The team is sure that applying this system will make parents more serious about education. They will more carefully guide their children in the right direction, especially seeing to it that their son protects another family's daughter, looks after her dignity as if she were his sister, and makes their relationship positive. Consequently, the parents will be protecting their own daughters through the spread of this education and morality. It will destroy society's wrong idea that 'the boy is carrying his vice,' – that is, that boys, but not girls, are allowed to have vices – as the boy will know his responsibility toward girls. This cannot be achieved without our system, which drives parents to put the utmost effort into correct upbringing.

"These are the parents' lawful obligations. Neglecting this will make us wake one day to a lost generation, wasting its energy and abilities, without goals. If we shut our eyes to Islamic and humanistic truths, it will hurt our performance as parents. Nowadays some wives allow their husbands to commit adultery and go to underground places, but do not allow them a second marriage, even if a pressing reason exists. This has occurred only because some individuals have lost awareness of what is Islamically lawful.

"When we see some of our sons and daughters, in their relationships, are not setting lawful boundaries and when we hide our heads in the sand like ostriches do, we turn our backs on the danger that will one day storm into our comfort and stability and will throw us into the unknown ocean. This will happen if we remove from our thoughts and reality *Shari'ah* ruling that draws up the most correct code for releasing people from the fortresses of anxiety and taking them to the light and the joy of living."

* * * * *

## Clarifying the Words

The students were totally absorbed in the discussion. Many hands were being raised at once. Mustafa called on a male student who changed the subject. **"You said the parents' are responsible for clarifying *feeqah* and *meeqah* for their children. Why do you use these strange names? They may agree on the limits of this relationship without mentioning the terms in your system. Is it not enough for a boy to say to a girl: will you marry me? He means I love you and I hope you love me, so let us together make a home and have children. She may say yes or no. So why these names?"**

"Good question," said Nasser. "When a boy asks a girl out for dinner, for example, the request has many uncertainties. Some are: Will she come to pick him up from his house or will he come to hers? If the boy goes to her house, is he not obliged to say, for instance: 'I will pick you up at seven o'clock in the evening. I will wait at the gate outside. I will press the car horn once. You will walk 30 steps from the house door, then get into the car and put on the seat belt. I will start the car and drive at 40 mph. I will stop in front of the restaurant, get out of the car, and open the door for you. I will park in the car park, and we will enter the restaurant and choose a romantic place to sit. We will order dinner and then eat and talk.'

"Is it reasonable for a boy to tell a girl these details before their date? Of course not. When he suggests going out for dinner and she accepts, it means he will pick her up from her house, she will go to his house, or they will set a time to meet at the restaurant without one picking up the other. The one phrase 'go out with me' replaces the details.

"We come to the terminology of the temporary contract. When a boy and girl agree to *feeqah*, the girl is not obliged to say, 'I will go out with you, but not sleep with you. You may not say anything that compromises the image of chastity or touch my breast. You have the right only to greet me by handshake, to kiss my forehead, or do whatever seems suitable in the first stage.' If they did this, their meeting may end before they had finished talking!"

The audience laughed and Nasser continued. "We must promote *feeqah* and *meeqah* and their conditions so boys and girls will be fully aware of all rights and obligations, and what our system involves: vows and commitments, its limits and its nature, and where it starts and ends. It is the responsibility of society and of the family to explain the concept to make it clear and familiar.

"When we ask a student 'what stage have you reached in your studies?' and he says, 'university,' we automatically comprehend the university stage differs from the primary, intermediate, and secondary stages in curriculum, study hours, teacher expertise, and building structure. One word reveals meaning, conditions, and what is entailed.

"When we say *feeqah* and *meeqah*, we know they mean, after the lawful introductory relationship of mixing, the primary and secondary temporary relationships. This idea will become a clear system for any couple wishing to marry and create a family.

"It is the same for the word *misyar*. When we hear it, we automatically understand the wife has given up her right that her husband should stay at her house. She has also given up her allowance, and, depending on his circumstances, has given him the freedom to transfer money to her whenever he likes, when he goes back home and when she is waiting for him to return to her in a year or so. She may also forego the wedding, the party, or whatever is associated with the customs of this marriage. All this applies to *'urfi* marriage, with minor differences, for these marriages are permanent. Every time we take away one of the non-fixed features of the permanent marriage, though not the proposal and its acceptance or the dowry, a permanent marriage still remains.

"Today, when we say 'permanent marriage,' and we pull away the word 'permanent' because of the timing, it becomes *seeqah*. When we specify the relationship as *seeqah*, but remove the one feature of sexual intercourse, it becomes *meeqah*. When we completely remove sexual acts and are left with emotion only, it becomes *feeqah*. This is with the consideration of compatibility and the gradation from one stage to another, and the conviction of the couple in this transfer, as they have the freedom – if their personalities agree – to specify the relationship, depending on their agreement on the conditions. We cannot disallow the boy and girl to kiss on the mouth in *feeqah*, if they both agree on it. We do not want to force one uniform way on everyone. We aim to specify the clothing, and individuals may specify their measurements of comfort."

The female student in the front row interrupted. **"Please clarify their options more."**

Nasser answered, "For example, a girl enters *feeqah* with the condition that she will not remove her headscarf on that day in particular. This may be for a specific reason – she may be having a bad hair day. But, on another day, she may show her hair, as now she is mentally prepared and comfortable. This may positively affect on the boy because, when they like each other, it will provide them with the comfort of lawfulness.

"The system, therefore, is flexible, cares for the mind and body, and provides opportunities for deepening a relationship. This corresponds to the aim of any two people to achieve stability and happiness. Had this been applied years ago, we would not now feel the need to change. These terms would have become essential fixed features that would be understood immediately when heard.

"The main elements of the marriage contract, despite their many details, all branch out from one word: agreement. It is the agreement of the two people. For the agreement to occur, the couple must see each other and the families must meet. These are the usual circumstances. The agreement of the two is essential and is summed up by the word 'acceptance.' The contract is void if one party does not agree, because going forward in that case would cancel out the basic human right of freedom. The agreement protects this right, and the terms of the contract will make it a lawful relationship. This also applies to the dowry. That the woman specifies the dowry is a basic principle. If we deny her this right, it would be – from a human view – a kind of slavery for her, and – from a legal view – the contract is invalid without it. This Divine system will exist till Judgment Day; whereas the non-fixed features that do not contradict the system may change with time.

"*Feeqah* and *meeqah* are two of the non-fixed features that come from the depths of the marriage system itself. They will serve us for generations."

* * * * *

## A System for Everyone

A student spoke as if her question related to her personal situation. Solemnly she asked, **"*Feeqah* and *meeqah* are an introduction to permanent marriage and suitable for virgins. *Seeqah* is a lawful solution for widows, divorcées, and spinsters. As some of these women are non-virgins, is it in their interest to also apply *feeqah* and *meeqah* to them?"**

Seyyid Mohammed answered, "We advise virgins to prolong *feeqah* and *meeqah* to allow enough time to determine the suitability of the match. We want the boy to do so too.

"Before entering *seeqah,* a non-virgin and a man have no obligation to enter *feeqah* and *meeqah*. We encourage it, but do not require it. Our opinion does not limit their freedom to choose. We believe it important to get acquainted and enter relationships gradually. Although their arrangement is temporary, it does not negate the contract's main goal to determine compatibility for permanent marriage. This goal is achieved through the gradation of the stages.

"*Seeqah* is a temporary lawful contract in which the couple engages in complete sexual acts if they wish. They must know the relationship's limits and accept its consequences. If a child is born, a relationship, even from afar, remains between the two with the child as its axis. The child will need to be cared for. Many questions arise from both sides."

The same student asked, **"What are these questions?"**

Seyyid Mohammed replied, "Here are three. Is the father ready to care for the child himself and do his private circumstances allow it? If the father were to hand parental custody to the mother, is he sure their child is safe with her and she is a competent mother? Also, is the mother sure the father will assume his legal obligations to register the birth in his name and provide the child with the full financial protection against need?

"The couple may not – in morals, behavior, education, or religious observance – suit each other for permanent marriage. However, what if pregnancy occurred through accident, deception, improper seduction, or force, and the marriage was registered as permanent because of social reasons? Could a woman who had been tricked live with a deceptive man, especially if she was not truly willing to be tied to such a person?"

**"What is the solution?"** the same student wanted to know.

Seyyid Mohammed replied, "The man must make sure this woman is competent to raise a child. He must know where 'to cultivate' for Allah says, **Women are your fields 2:223**. This means marriage is cultivation requiring suitable land. Is the man ready to ensure water is available, ready to prepare the earth, and ready to endure sleepless nights of worry over whether his plants will grow? If the requirements for good cultivation are not provided, but he nevertheless goes forward, he has planted his crop on a rock. His hopes will be dashed and his wishes not come true."

The questioner's neighbor asked, **"This is directed to men. What about women?"**

In his customary quiet way, Seyyid Mohammed answered, "Even if had this not been asked, I was about to direct a response to women. I remind women this contract is an awesome responsibility. Agreement with it means she accepts a man under terms given by the Prophet's (pbuh) *hadith*, **If a man, whose religious observance and morals satisfy you, comes [to propose to your daughter], give him [your daughter] in marriage.** She should accept someone who will share the responsibility with her, armed with virtuousness, humanity, and religion.

"This great responsibility is why we encourage the non-virgin to enter *feeqah* and *meeqah* before *seeqah*. The time may stretch to six months or need only two days. It depends on her trust in the man and the man's trust in her. It also depends on prior acquaintance: are they recently acquainted or have they known each other for years? *Feeqah* and *meeqah* may last a short time before entering *seeqah* provided the acquaintance has been studied thoroughly, planning and caution are exercised to avoid bad outcomes, and an understanding exists that the relationship may end even though sexual intercourse has occurred if signs of problems arise to make permanent marriage undesirable.

"We do not recommend that non-virgins jump from *feeqah* to *seeqah* and skip *meeqah*. However, *meeqah*, practically speaking, may be shorter for non-virgins than for virgins.

"The normal approach to our system is to start with *feeqah*. It gives the woman the most choices for proceeding to a further stage if all goes well or for ending the relationship with the more comfort than doing so at a later stage. This contrasts with today's reality, where women are encouraged to jump directly into permanent marriage without a realistic chance to get acquainted. If she discovers incompatibility after marriage, the only options are to bear it or seek divorce."

A professor said, **"We understand *seeqah* is practical and lawful for divorced people. The woman may make a temporary contract with a man whose morals and mentality are unknown to her. What if she makes a contract with her former husband?"**

"This question comes at a suitable moment," said Nasser. "Imagine a man and woman married for a long time with children. They do not get along and find divorce is the best solution. Divorce occurs according to the *Qur'anic* principle **...or separate with kindness, 2:229.** The husband, wife, and children each get what was rightfully theirs. The divorce agreement is that the children live under the wife's care. The woman becomes 35 or 40 years old. Her chances to remarry are slim, or she may not want to. However, in response to sexual desires, she may approach her former husband, even if he is married. If he still loves and respects her, they may make a temporary contract. This has great benefit. She is addressing her needs, and the children will be happier to see their father entering the house than a stranger. They may also go out together with their children, as the relationship is lawful. It reflects well on everyone. Allah's mercy is in the temporary contract for its philosophy enables us to solve many problems."

A female student contributed by asking, **"Is *feeqah* really necessary for the girl if she already knows something about the mentality of the other person and he shares her feelings, especially if he is a relative or family friend?"**

Seyyid Mohammed replied, "We are specifying stages governed by a specific system. We are not tailoring one-size-fits-all clothing. Every human being may choose the most suitable size. We still encourage *feeqah* as a start, even if they are cousins or family friends. The girl may be familiar with the boy's manners and traits and like him, but she is not compelled to nurture feelings toward him because they are neighbors or classmates. Yet she may want to use *feeqah* to study him more thoroughly through a new perspective to understand more deeply her ability to live with him as a husband. Cousins sometimes need time to accept each other sexually because they may view themselves almost as siblings. It is better in our system for relatives and friends to enter *feeqah* first and then *meeqah*, when they may step beyond the limits of *feeqah*.

"The *feeqah* and *meeqah* constraints are not fixed. They cannot be because the fixed ones are set in *Shari'ah*. We have no authority to make anything lawful, only, after extensive study, to suggest boundaries suitable for our system. It is not forbidden for the couple to kiss on the mouth in *feeqah*, so they are not obliged to go on to *meeqah*. In that way, the girl remains in *feeqah*, while granting the boy a privilege from *meeqah* and continuing to preserve the rest of her sexual privacy.

"We must trust the youth to aware of their responsibilities and promises. We must give them the right to add what they feel is suitable to the stages because it is their business to know what is best for themselves. They alone can determine what affects their interests. We cannot hold them accountable for anything except what contravenes Allah's law. It remains for the girl to get to know the boy's hidden characteristics."

The voice of a female student was heard. **"What are these hidden characteristics?"**

Seyyid Mohammed said, "The girl's delusions about the boy's love may conceal his traits. He may show jealousy, yet conceal his suspicion about her behavior and normal actions. He may seem protective, yet really be greedy for her money or other material or immaterial gain.

"How can she differentiate between love and suspicion, between protectiveness and greed? Through being together, following up, and studying the person, she can see differences over time and discover all these things in the stages before permanent marriage. The girl is face to face with the boy's private issues and personality, from the general ones to the most intricate details, from the smell of his sweat to his way of thinking and his mind's horizons. She will learn his likes and dislikes, and possibly that he hates what she loves. She may discover compatibility. We do not know. *Feeqah* is especially important because it has the least intense emotion, and emotion may cloud judgment – especially too much emotion too soon.

"From *feeqah*, she will determine his future directions. If they marry, will he let her leave the house, will he turn her parents into enemies, will she be a servant to his parents, will he break up all her friendships, will he allow her to keep studying or be religiously observant, and will he make a good father?"

A male student stood and objected, saying, **"This is an exaggeration!"**

Seyyid Mohammed replied, "Let us call it an exaggeration, but, still, an aware girl can discover much about a boy's private life in these stages. What she discovers will lead to her informed decision whether to choose this boy for a husband. We recommend entering all the stages to maximize the chances of making a sound choice and to minimize the chance of encountering failure. Having choices makes life easier."

* * * * *

## A Woman's Reputation

A male student now brought up a distinction in how society treats males and females. He asked, **"How can you convince society about a girl's right to try feeqah and meeqah with many different boys without tarnishing her reputation?"**

Dr. Omar came forward. "Before the psychology of this, a lawful consequence results from an awesome responsibility toward God.

Because this lawful consequence underlines the lawfulness of the relationship, we have adopted our system. If believed *Shari'ah* forbade it, we would have avoided the study from the start.

"*Feeqah* and *meeqah* are lawful relationships, and from here our ideas have been launched. We must consider that the young man and woman, when entering a relationship of this sort, are protected by a lawful framework. No one may deny it, or touch their reputation and dignity. Whatever they do in these stages within the conditions relating to the aim of permanent marriage is lawful and governed by Allah's supervision.

"Now let us consider the girl's position. If she were to know five boys in school or in her neighborhood, she will be able to make a temporary lawful contract for *feeqah* and *meeqah* with only one of them. She will get to know him, but she does not want to fool around and waste time. When she talks to the others, she will talk to them about studies or social or general issues. With the special boy, she will talk in private about issues that form the basis of the lawful contract.

"Her concentration and thoughts will be focused on him and no one else. When she makes a contract with a boy for a period of time, she cannot make a contract with another at the same time. The second contract would be void.

"When the contract term ends, or when *'iddah* is over for a non-virgin, she has the right to enter another lawful relationship. This is a normal. Who can forbid her if she felt the first boy was unsuitable, or the second or the third? Who can object if her choice falls on the fourth, having done all this under lawful contracts that had terms, conditions, and rules and involved no religious contravention? If her reputation gets tarnished, we must ask: Do we follow the narrow-mindedness of society or what Allah made lawful?

"A girl has the right to be in one relationship at any one time with one boy. However, *Shari'ah* gives a boy the right to make a contract with more than one girl at a time. We do not see society getting uneasy about a boy's many relationships, and there is no disgrace. The only real disgrace is what violates *Shari'ah*. This applies to all young men and women, and this should live deep inside us all. We must reject any idea of inferiority of the girl, and that her disgrace is much worse than a boy's is. The boy who enters into contracts secretly with more than one girl at a time will be discovered, and the girl who entered into a contract with him, in the hope of marriage, will leave him if this situation displeases her.

"As for a girl's numerous relationships under lawful acquaintance, we must view this positively. Here, we see the importance of the boy's awareness."

One of the teachers asked, **"How does this relate to awareness?"**

Dr. Omar responded, "When the boy chooses to marry a girl who has known four or five boys in previous *feeqah* and *meeqah* relationships, he must see the cup as half full, not half empty. The realism tells the boy: do not see it as negative that she has known four or five others before you – this is the half empty cup. Rather, see that she is selective, discerning, and careful, that she has chosen you from among all these, and honored you with her choice. She saw in you the qualities that make a good husband, one who would protect her and who has traits of competency, and humanity that the others lacked – this is the half full cup. When the boy puts *Shari'ah* and intellectual truth before the fancies of the ego and selfishness, he will wish for others what he wishes for himself.

"We must put *Shari'ah* in all our life's issues, and take it all, not only some of it. It cannot be divided. *Shari'ah* has given the boy wide horizons that allow him to get to know a girl through a lawful contract who he hopes will become the mother of his children, and it has given the same right to the girl.

"The positive effects the boy experiences while choosing a suitable girl to share his hopes and ambitions will prevent him from his breaking off the relationship because of a detail that does not change anything, such as knowing the girl may have had a lawful acquaintance before he entered her life. He will recognize that a person's freedom, within the limits of lawful fundamentals, cannot be confiscated or be subjected to ill judgment."

A seated male attendant, who was not a student or a teacher, said, **"The curious or nosy boy will insist on knowing the girl's history."**

Dr. Omar was firm. "That is his problem and no one else's. If his mental inadequacy causes his suspicion, he needs treatment. Should we accept his right to nosiness, we make bad mental attitudes lawful and we may be confirming our prejudices too if we establish such mental illness is health and does not need a remedy. To the boy who persists in discovering a girl's past, we say, a boy has no right to insist on knowing a girl's past, as it is not the girl's right to know his past. Only certain aspects of the past life are open to question, such as if either was married before, if either has children, or if the girl is a virgin. This they may know before starting a new life. The boy has no right to discuss the girl's lawful relationships, unless they both agree on knowing this about each other.

"Our system must change souls to respect women. A man has to respect himself to respect women. Islam's attitude is **Like for your brother what you like for yourself and hate for him what you hate for yourself.**

"The mind and religion make us respect the privacy of others. It does not allow us to transgress its sanctity under any circumstances. In doing so, we wound our capacity to prove our humanity and rationality."

A male student interrupted to ask, **"Under your system, it seems, as in the West, every boy has his girl, and every girl has her boy. They can move to a new relationship every month or two. What do you say?"**

Nasser rushed to answer. "This comparison is incorrect. The girl in the West may build a relationship with two or more men at one time and outside any religious framework. We must not generalize and judge them. Some are like our girls and will have only one relationship. Yes, if they leave a relationship and enter another, they do not care about a an *'iddah,* as we are vigilant about. This is not in their social customs. In our system, the girl, whether or not a virgin, may not tie herself to another person lawfully till after completion of her temporary contract or of *'iddah.*

"Our system is in the heart of the truth. It is not backward, nor lacks values and allows just anything. It gives women choices. They may exchange a young man for another, but within the system itself, not from outside it. When a woman leaves a relationship at the end of temporary contract or gets divorced in a permanent contract and is still a virgin, she may marry whomever she wants directly. Allah said, **If you marry believing women and divorce them before the**

marriage is consummated, you are not required to observe an
*'iddah,* **33:49**. This supports *feeqah* and *meeqah*. The non-virgin
must wait for two menstrual periods after the temporary marriage
contract, and for three menstrual periods after the permanent
one. This is conveyed in Allah's verse **Divorced women must
wait [keeping themselves from men] three menstrual cycles,
2:228.**

The same student asked, **"How does the first verse you mentioned
support *feeqah* and *meeqah*?"**

"The content of the blessed verse is clear," said Nasser. "It means
that, if a woman makes a contract with a man and they do not
have sexual intercourse, she may after leaving him enter directly
into another relationship. This removes negativity from the woman,
safeguards her reputation, and confirms, after leaving this contract,
she may search for another suitable man.

"We also assume we are talking about an honorable girl who has
been brought up on chastity and dignity. She understands religious
rules, and has set out in life fully aware of her humanistic and lawful
role. She does nothing but what satisfies Allah, and stays far away
from what displeases Him. She is armed with education that has
molded her principles, and she knows where to find the places full
of light."

A female student had a question for Dr. Omar: **"You mentioned
your system requires two leaps – one essential, that is the
moral, and a second, that is a system of gradual stages of
acquaintance – to achieve successful marriage. Is the first leap
not enough?"**

"No," said Dr. Omar. "Neither the first leap nor the second leap alone
can make marriage succeed. The two leaps complete each other,
and the absence of either will wreck the essential features of the
system. The proof is in the marriages between cousins. A proportion
of the youth marry their cousins. Relatives usually treat each other
with manners, kindness, and mercy due to their close relationship.
However, many cousins divorce. Manners are not enough to achieve
successful marriage, even if a right is exercised in the choice of
marriage partner. People may think cousins do not need the gradual
steps in the relationships up to permanent marriage, because *feeqah*
and *meeqah* may take a long time and their family ties allow them

to paint a clear picture of each other, at least of traits that are not hidden. Nevertheless, these stages are needed to give them time to absorb the coming change in their relationship and to assist in their journey toward reaching a happy marriage.

"Marriages between relatives are falling apart, so imagine what may occur when two strangers marry without all the benefits of our system. We therefore need both leaps: the combination of morals with the stages of acquaintance to lead us into the light."

\* \* \* \* \*

## Knocking on the Door

A member of the audience asked, **"Are we to understand that, as you give the boy the right to step forward, with the aim of getting to know a girl in the hope of marrying her, and to knock on her door, you give the same right to the girl?"**

Dr. Afaf answered said, "Peace be upon you, Khadija, wife of the Messenger of Allah. Peace be upon this virtuous woman who comprehended, by great awareness through practical experience with him, that he would be an excellent husband and father to her children. She showed her true feelings despite their difference in wealth and age, and announced her desire to him to achieve the cherished hope of her heart. She was the one who knocked on the door to his honorable heart, and she received what she sought and what she deserved.

"Why do customs still control some of the most educated and aware among us? Why do we follow social situations that may have no lawful obligation? Why does the boy knock on the door, as if it was his exclusive right and not the girl's right too? No *Qur'anic* scripture or correct Prophetic *hadith* forbids this. We submitted to tastes formed by habits that are not encouraged in any way by the logic of Islam, the civilized religion."

A male student, thinking this would damage Islamic society, asked, **"You give young men and women the right to enter into numerous contracts and build many relationships of acquaintance with ease. Will this not propagate moral decline in Islamic society?"**

"This judgment is hasty," said Nasser, "and lacks precision and relevance for one simple reason: our encouragement of acquaintance in relationships, even when they are numerous, presents no lawful problem because they are all under Allah's eyes and supervision. The acquaintance is founded on lawful contracts having principles, constraints, and responsibilities.

"These acquaintance relationships are Islamically lawful, so we treat the truth unjustly by describing them as relationships leading to moral decline. When we stress the word 'lawful,' we put the relationship in a moral and humanistic framework. We have in all the seminars shown the lawfulness of our system. If all the evidence we have presented has not convinced you of its lawfulness, it is your right to remain doubtful. It is not your right to stop others from being convinced.

When we invite you to a lawful system of acquaintance that aims to achieve a permanent secure marriage, are we inviting you to sin? When we say in *feeqah* a boy must treat a girl the same as he treats his sister, are we encouraging moral corruption? In *meeqah* and *seeqah*, when we call for conditions in the relationship, are we calling for moral decline?

"Moral decline occurs by transgressing on honor and dignity, when there are no lawful connection and religious deterrent. If we are conscientious about the necessity and obligatory position of lawful ties in the relationship between the couple, this represents the peak of morality and the fear of Allah.

"When a boy and girl get to know each other, acquaintance occurs through an Islamic contract, within one or two months or one or two years, for the noble goal of building a family in the future. It must be in the highest moral category, where you see relationships with discipline, integrity, and correct behavior.

"Our system abides by religion. Any lawful fault, any complacency, in fulfilling the conditions of the relationship offends the other person and also offends Allah's law. It is because this contract has Allah as supervisor and witness. He will ask us one day, when we stand between His hands, if we fulfilled all our promises.

"Overreacting prevents the eyes from seeing clearly and leads to hasty conclusions. The question that the honorable student asked reflects the outlook of the upside-down pyramid. Why? Because when our team calls for marriage, we are trying to reduce the divorce rates through our system and push the specter of divorce away from families. The woman is usually the greater victim in divorce, especially when assuming responsibility for raising the children. She then has three roles: provider, mother, and father. To prevent this from happening, our system calls for marriage in which the couple knows each other well before entering marriage and has a chance to make an informed decision when choosing a lifelong partner. This gives the marriage a greater chance of success. We are calling for cohesiveness and stability, not chaos and disarray. We are calling for religion and its true practice. We are calling for a reverse in moral decline by proposing a system that will attract youth away from forming unlawful relationships and will stop the disintegration of families by lowering the divorce rate.

"Society opposes and attacks the logical and rational way, and accepts the wrong way and theorizes about it. An example of this is the unjust judgment that the last question cast on our system. Our answer is: before marriage, let people enter into lawful contracts that protect against sin and its deep pits, which tarnish morality, honor, and virtue."

A teacher asked, **"Do you allow your daughters to knock on doors?"**

Dr. Afaf wanted to handle this question. "It is not about allowing, but about encouraging our daughters and other people's daughters. The girl we encourage to enter this system is one, we hope, who will study her steps carefully and protect herself by reticence. We do not mean being unsociable or retreating into the darkness of the self, but practicing openness to the outside from deep within feelings of responsibility and caution and understanding the benefit and harm in everything she encounters.

"We let a girl knock on the door of whatever education, occupation, or specialization she desires. She has a right to choose her career. Similarly, we should let her knock on the door of lawful acquaintance. The act does not lack honor or dignity. When a girl finds a boy that she likes for his religion, manners, personality, and profession, why cannot she knock on the door of his heart with courtesy, morals, and good intentions?

"Islamic history has many examples. Khadija opened the door in this way. The *Qur'an* tells us about Prophet Shu'aib's (pbuh) daughters, who were helped by the Prophet Moses (pbuh) to draw water, despite the great crowd around the well. They told their father what he had done with good intent. I will quote Seyyid Izzuddin Bahrul Uloom on this incident from his book *Marriage in the Qur'an and Sunnah*. He says, '...he is, therefore, the man that women look for, so where is the objection for one of the daughters to propose to him? Certainly, she turned to her father to say, **Father, take this man into your service; men who are strong and honest are the best you can hire, 28:26.'** [89]

"Why would a father object when his daughter had found the man of her dreams? Both men are prophets and both are well advanced on the path that takes them to Allah and guides people to the heavenly righteous teachings, one of which is the law of family and marriage. It is the most beloved lawful teaching for Allah.

"Shu'aib (pbuh) replies to the request of the proposing daughter by going forth to greet the guest and saying: **I want to give you one of my two daughters in marriage if you stay eight years in my service; but, if you wish, you may stay 10; I shall not deal harshly with you; God willing, you shall find me an upright man, 28:27.**

"The caring father answers his daughter's call, and, without it being a burden, the father is led to tie with a contract two hearts that wanted to be together to build a home. With all simplicity and without introductions, Shu'aib (pbuh) faced his guest to say, **I want to give you one of my two daughters in marriage**. Moses agreed to this proposal, they married, and so the story ends – a story of the woman suggesting marriage, not, as usual, the man.

"At the time of the honorable Prophet (pbuh) and under the auspices of Islam, the woman who removed the mask of fear from her face and publicly chose her life partner was encouraged by the bearer of the Message, the Islamic legislator.

"The *hadith* says, **A woman from Ansar [Muslims of Medina] came to the Prophet (pbuh) and entered the house of Hafsa**

---

[89] Bahrul Uloom 143+..

[a wife of the Prophet (pbuh)]. **The woman was well-dressed and her hair was combed. She said, 'Oh, Messenger of Allah (pbuh), a woman does not ask a man to marry her. I have had no husband for a long time, and I have no son. Do you need a wife? For I am here, I am offering myself to you if you accept me.' Mohammed said good words to her and prayed for her, then said, 'Oh, you Ansari woman! May Allah reward you, you the Ansar, for your men have supported me, and I have desired your women – or your women have desired me. You may go now, may Allah have mercy on you; Allah will reward you with Paradise because you wanted me and for your presentation of love of me and joy for me; my answer will come to you, God willing.' Then the verse was revealed, and any believing woman who gives herself to you [the Prophet (pbuh)], and whom the Prophet (pbuh) wishes to take in marriage, this only for you [the Prophet (pbuh)] and not for the believers. 33:50.**

"Another *hadith* is narrated by Imam Al-Baqir. **A woman came to the Prophet (pbuh) and said: Marry me off. He said, Who would like to marry this woman? A man stood and said, Me, oh, Messenger of Allah. The Prophet (pbuh) said, What do you give her? He said, I have nothing. The Prophet (pbuh) said, Do you know some *Qur'an*? He said, Yes. The Prophet (pbuh) said, I have married her off to you for what you know of the *Qur'an*.**[90]

"The Prophet (pbuh) did not refuse her or get angry. He did not say a woman must be proposed to and she herself should not propose, especially in front of people. Instead, he presented the woman's request publicly. The woman had the right to ask for a husband.

"As for reticence and what a woman is supposed to be like, these views should not prevent women from entering fully into life and charting a course. She may put her hand in whoever's hand she wants, if he carries the required attributes.

"*Shari'ah* accepted and made lawful these events in Islamic history. We have no other law, parallel to Allah's law. He created people, and then established a system for their lives so they might find happiness and security. He knows best what benefits and harms people.

---

[90]  Abu Ja'far Al-Kulainy, *Al-Kafi* [*All-Encompassing*], vol. 5 (Beirut: Dar At-Ta'aruf, 1995) 568.

"Society finds excuses for young men and women who sit in cafés and public places, not for the purpose of marriage. Society does not burden itself to search for lawful alternatives to this. And, by limiting her ability to search for a suitable partner, society withholds the woman's natural, lawful right to preserve her honor and hold on to her dignity.

"Let our role model be Khadija – a woman who looked for a partner and saw in Mohammed (pbuh), not only his Prophethood, but also the husband and future father of her children."

* * * * *

## The Temperature Rises

After Dr. Afaf's answer, a male student erupted with hostility toward the entire project. He was agitated and yelled his questions. **"How can you allow your daughters go out with boys in this way? Where is your gallantry as fathers and mothers? How can you sell them for this cheap price?"**

Seyyid Mohammed answered him. "The real question is not how can we allow it, but how do you allow your daughter to be married without going through such a system?

"Are we selling our daughters for a cheap price, as you are saying? Perhaps that question is better asked of the father who marries his daughter to the first man who knocks on his door, and probably they will not see each other before the wedding night. Does it not seem like this father wants to be rid of his daughter? He deceives himself if satisfied with asking the suitor a few questions. This is only 'decoration' for the process of marriage. How many girls marry in this way, or are forced to do so, and have lives turned from then on into intolerable hell? We do not sell our daughters for a cheap price, but rather value them highly if we give them freedom protected by *Shari'ah*. We allow the girl to go out and get acquainted in hope of marriage, by using a lawful system we are proud of. We allow her to find out before it is too late whether the boy will interfere with her joy of living and if their marriage is likely to be a problem added onto the many problems of our society."

The same student still looked upset, though he was no longer shouting. **"If your system benefits people, our scholars and**

170

**forefathers would have taken it up years ago and motivated people to use it. I see no benefit in presenting it today."**

Dr. Omar wished to reply. "Our system and all the problems that appear before and after marriage were not hidden from scholars, though the social problems of high divorce rate and consequent disintegration of the family were not acute. We are not saying no need existed at all for the system. We are saying, even though it was lawful and realistic, the need was not strong. Social circumstances in past times did not invite its presentation. The daughter accepted her father's wishes, whatever the circumstances of the marriage, suitable or unsuitable. To refuse was a social disgrace, a dishonor that would haunt her family for years. Women's expectations of marital happiness were low. They were more willing to stay in unhappy marriages and also unwilling to be tainted by divorce. A second, third, and fourth marriage for the man was common. The man need not get acquainted with the woman, and society accepted this as normal. The scholars therefore decided not to present our system because society did not seem to need it. Now, 1,000 years later, people's understanding and situations have changed.

"Despite that, our scholars who derive their *fatwa* from Islam, which meets people's needs in every era, have given us the essentials for building the foundation of our system. Those scholars were aware of people's problems and concerns. They understood profoundly that it was the right of every person, male or female, who wanted to marry to know what the other person was like, even if only the appearance."

Dr. Omar paused to open a book. "The proof is in *Fiqh As-Sunnah*, volume 2, page 19, in the chapter on *khitbah* [the proposal]. *Hadiths* urge the suitor to look at his fiancée. Here is what came from the great Prophet (pbuh): Al-Mughirah Ibn Shu'beh narrated that **he proposed to an Ansari woman, and the Prophet (pbuh) asked, 'Have you looked at her?' He said, 'No.' The Prophet (pbuh) said, 'Look at her; this makes it more probable you will get along with each other,'** meaning it will keep harmony between you. Even more so, the book mentions allowing looking at some parts of a woman's body, such as the face, which shows whether her body suits his liking. Dawood said, 'The whole body should be looked at.' Al-Awza'ai said, **'He looks at the fleshy parts.'** The *hadiths* and opinions of scholars did not specify or emphasize which 'fleshy' parts. Rather, they were general so as to validate the concept of looking.[91]

"This is exactly what Sunni scholars state. Shi'ah scholars allowed the suitor to see his fiancée dressed in form-fitting garments to show her figure and so allow discovery of physical deformity. Today, after announcing our system, the suitor need not look at his fiancée's body based on 'the necessities allow the forbidden.' It is now based on the couple's mutual agreement.

"Our duty is to respect our minds. Life develops day after day, so we must examine whether the forbidden is still forbidden and the allowed is still allowed. We shall also stick to our belief that *Shari'ah* was revealed to serve people and help them find happiness, not restrain them, but launch them into life with a strong foundation and firm principles."

The student did not like the answer to his question. He and a small group left the lecture hall. The audience talked among themselves, and Mustafa felt it best to let them digest the walkout in this way. When they finally fell silent on their own, Dr. Omar said, "Some will object to this system. This is their business. We do not deny them the right to refute, only the right to forbid others from being convinced. On Judgment Day, how we raised of our children will be questioned. The Prophet (pbuh) said, **Every one of you is a shepherd, and every one of you is responsible for his herd.**"

At this point, a male student stood up. He appeared to be nervous and he stated forcefully, **"I understand why my fellow student got angry and walked out. It is because your leap is bigger than you realize. You say The Leap is about timing only, but you are also removing two elements that we think important and lawful: the approval of the girl's guardian and witnessing."**

Dr. Omar went on the offensive. "Before I answer," he said, "I want to know if the audience thinks getting acquainted before marriage is beneficial or not. Does anyone here believe we do not need to get thoroughly acquainted before marriage? Please raise your hand." No hands went up.

Dr. Omar continued, "I thought so. During the previous weeks, we have proved that competent men and women have the right to marry

---

[91]    Sabiq 19.

themselves off. We have proved that the Shi'ites are not obligated to have the father's approval or witnessing and that the Sunnis can accept this too. But let us take for granted that what you say is right – we need these two things for marriage to be lawful.

"Here is my example. I am the father of a daughter attending the university. She is interested in a classmate, whom she sees as a possible partner for permanent marriage. She wants to go farther in getting acquainted with this boy. She and he would like to make a temporary contract for *feeqah*. The wording, the dowry, and the timing are all there. Why should I say 'no'? My 'no' would change right into wrong, light into dark, lawful into sinful. My 'no' means God would frown on the relationship and it would therefore be unlawful. Give me a reason why I should refuse. On what basis can I refuse? If I say 'no' without a basis, then God will frown on me too.

"My agreement is the key to lawfulness. My 'yes' means God will accept the relationship. God will be happy, my daughter will be happy, and this should make me happy too. This whole system is based on my agreement, but, if I, the father, am rational and raised my daughter well, my agreement must be taken for granted. That my consent be asked is a courtesy and a formality. We can say my consent is essential, but it is not truly essential because I cannot say 'no.' For me to say 'no' is to go against *Shari'ah*.

"Once I have said 'yes,' I am automatically a witness to the relationship because I know about it. Both families know about it. There are no secrets here. The second witness could be my competent son or the boy's father. The witnessing therefore occurs informally and arises naturally out of the situation.

"We do ask for a big Leap, but it is not in fact bigger than we realize."

* * * * *

## Responsibility and Maturity

A teacher spoke for the remaining the audience when he rose to apologize to the lecturers for the students' rudeness. He also had a question. **"You quoted the *hadith* Every one of you is a shepherd, and every one of you is responsible for his herd. Based on this *hadith*, you are responsible for your family. How do you view this responsibility?"**

Seyyid Mohammed replied, "Yes, we are all responsible and will be held to account on Judgment Day. My responsibility toward my children is to build their personalities on the most noble, moral base and with the most honorable and esteemed virtues. I hand them experience from my experience and a mental outlook from my mental outlook. I put in front of their eyes the paths to safety, so they may carry righteousness and virtue in their consciences and live correctly and virtuously. My responsibility begins on the day they are born and ends when their minds have matured and they have become responsible for their actions. That is when my paternal responsibility ends as far as Allah, society, and the law are concerned. Having given them all I can, my duty is done. Now the responsibility is theirs alone. I do not interfere in their choice of career, as I do not in what they eat and drink. If they break the law and go to jail, it is their, not my, responsibility. All religions and laws accept this. The *Qur'anic* principle is: **no soul shall bear another's burden, 6:164**.

"Yes, I am responsible for their actions if I did not raise them properly before they became independent. When we talk about the girl, we talk about the one we raised and protected and to whom we gave her freedom, because she knows where her interest lies more than anyone else. Should this girl not get permission from her guardian for the contract, he should respect her choice if he raised her well – because *Shari'ah* gave her the right to make her own choice and commitment.

"A time period limits the parents' responsibility. In the *Surah Al-Isra'*, Allah says, **treat them with humility and tenderness and say: Lord, be merciful to them for they nursed [*rabbaiani*] me when I was an infant. 17:24.** The word *rabbaiani* in this verse means the parents gave me what built my personality and prepared me to face my responsibilities. The verse also means, looked at from the parents' perspective, that the parents nursed the child out of responsibility. Therefore, the request in the *Qur'an* is to nurture the child until he matures and becomes competent and responsible for his deeds."

A female student rose from the center of the audience. **"If we assume your system is correct, must not the girl be mature to enter this system?"**

"A certain amount of maturity is a requirement," said Dr. Afaf, "but our system also trains young people to become more mature. A mature person puts matters in perspective, objectively evaluates different choices, and knows where his or her interest lies. Someone who lacks these abilities often makes poor decisions.

"Our system is based on stages, whose timing considers different levels of maturity. Less mature girls must go slower and stay in the appropriate stage longer. One of our system's aims of acquaintanceship is to train girls to become vigilant and recognize good choices, and this represents a growth in maturity. Our system leads them by the hand through several stages toward the ability to ultimately make a sensible choice.

"A hasty entry into marriage by an immature girl, or boy, is not a recipe for success. Many girls quickly accept an early marriage, even if the boy lacks the qualities of a good husband. It may be due to pressure from the family, financial matters, a longing for love, or the impression – usually proved incorrect – that marriage brings more freedom. If these are the real motives for marriage and if they accompany a hasty decision, the marriage has a high probability to fail.

"In addition, some of the mental and emotional maturity for achieving the aims of marriage may be lacking. Our system realistically helps to reach this maturity if we respect the girl's freedom to accept *feeqah* and do not burden her with suspicion and prying. She may stay in *feeqah* for several years while continuing her education or career, or fulfilling any other goals in her life. Her maturity and awareness will follow its natural progression. If she moves on to *meeqah*, it will be with more emotional maturity, experience, and knowledge. She will base decisions and changes in her steps in life on an awareness attained with time and experience. This will apply when she moves toward permanent marriage.

"After society embraces our system, young people will not marry in haste. The girl will finish her schooling during feeqah, meeqah, or no relationship. Life's issues, in all its diversity and detail, will begin to show their true appearance to her eyes. When she is half way through the journey, she will be ready to begin on the other half and may move from *feeqah* to *meeqah*.

"Our system does not delay satisfaction of the girl's romantic desires during the years of study. Its natural, lawful place to be addressed is in the conditions of the contract between the young people. Whatever the details of their arrangement, the attention paid to this need will prevent the couple from straying off the path of good behavior.

The girl has come close to psychological, physical, and mental maturity. Having passed her 18th or 19th birthday, she is now 21 or 23 years old. This age is suitable for making choices and entering marriage.

"We must give our girls space to complete the process of maturity and must respect their experiences founded on lawful principles. They may then live in the present without fear or anxiety or getting lost, protected by a system that leads them toward a bright future."

\* \* \* \* \*

## Wisdom and Sex

Mustafa called on a male student who directed his question specifically to Nasser. **"Does your system build a framework for sexual satisfaction so boys and girls do not look for sex in deviant and unlawful ways?"**

"Yes," said Nasser, "sex within a lawful framework is one of the aims of our system, but not the main aim. We strive to place emotion, compatibility, and an agreement as an essential introduction in the bonding of a couple who wish to marry. We strive the most to strengthen complete sexual satisfaction in a lawful way before permanent marriage. Sex is absent in *feeqah*. We encourage the couple to prolong *feeqah* to examine each other closely – in temperament, character, mind, and education. In *meeqah*, we urge them to deepen their emotional relationship more than the sexual aspect. Sex at this stage is limited to only hugging, kissing, and touching. It is about discovery of parts of the body and sensations and is controlled by conditions to which the couple must adhere. They yet have not yet entered the stage of complete sexual activity. Our advice to the virgin who is building a relationship with a boy with the aim of permanent marriage is that the acquaintance requires *feeqah* and *meeqah* only. While disagreeing with society, we do not recommend *seeqah* because society will reject the girl for not being a virgin when she goes to her marital home. The girl begins with *feeqah*, *meeqah*, and then permanent marriage after each stage has played its part. Sexual intercourse., in its full sense, is postponed to the time of permanent marriage."

A male student asked, **"Why object to sexual intercourse when the contract is lawful? Why pay attention to society's criticism, if the relationship is lawful?"**

Nasser said, "This is where the philosophy of timing comes into the relationship, and this is linked to the mind and logic. The girl must understand the exact meaning of temporary contract. Satisfying the couple's lust may lead to pregnancy and the spinning wheel of society's criticism, right or wrong. Did this girl realistically study the boy's capability to protect her from vicious gossip by making a permanent contract with her and by considering to make her his permanent wife in front of everyone without hesitation or fear? Or will he deny it? The girl must consider the lost opportunities of marriage if the boy leaves her, especially if she has a child, plus the effect this will have on her ambitions in work and education. Another point is whether she found him competent for marriage, and responsible about what marriage concerns, such as the dowry, the house, and a reasonable income to protect against poverty. This is in addition to the morals and behavior that a girl usually wants from a husband. The girl must keep these questions in mind. Her future depends on the answers.

"Our system is divided into practical steps, based on reality and logic. The timing in the relationship and its stages serve as a safety valve for the relationship and firmly keep problems from developing. When the girl understands the aims in the timing and the stages, she will not fulfill the boy's complete sexual desires because of the possible consequences. Also, increased compatibility and meshing of their ideas contribute to the movement from one stage to another to the end of the journey. The couple does not become stuck in one stage. When we say 'stage,' the mind automatically knows it is a temporary arrangement that permits renewal or termination. The girl's comprehension of the nature of a temporary relationship will prevent her from tying herself permanently to a boy who makes her subservient to his moods or brings other liabilities to a relationship.

"As for the boys, the case for entering complete sexual activity is exaggerated relating to those ready to begin in *feeqah,* which would usually be at 18 to 21 years of age. Yes, the desire for sex increases in men as they get older and more experienced. However, in the early stages, love will triumph over sex. The previously married man is typically unwilling to experience emotional love only for one or two years before sexual activity starts. He wants sex from the first few days of the relationship, but the opposite is true of the young woman, who is more driven emotionally and romantically, than sexually.

"Sex may put its weight and pressure on boys, but emotion plays a more essential role in the relationship. This is evident because, when girls date boys, even unlawfully, they tend to preserve their virginity. Boys avoid full intercourse for many reasons, the most important being the feelings between the couple, and, second, social considerations.

"When in *feeqah*, we are talking about young ages. I ask the older people in the audience to go back to when you were young, when 'I love you' from a girl's mouth turned a boy's world glorious, and when those words played a sweet melody in the depths of his heart."

* * * * *

## The Call of Freedom

There was a pause as the audience seemed to inhale Nasser's sentiments. Then a female student's voice broke the silence. **"What is the springboard for acquaintance?"**

Dr. Omar answered, "This question takes us to the greatest humanistic issue that Allah placed in this world. It takes us to what systematizes man's movement within the framework of his responsibility, and to what creates and produces the good qualities in life in its humanistic sphere, far removed from injustice and oppression, and close to welcoming places of light.

"This question takes us to a discussion of freedom, based on the idea that the universe is governed by human relationships, through what they believe and express, and launched by their humanity and awareness without one person forcing authority on another. They reveal their manners, feelings, emotions, the spirit of good will, and the logic of justice.

"Liberty in its humanistic sense means a people give studied and detailed opinions on anything in life without being controlled, and without an authority pressuring them about their opinions. It means expressing opinions without being terrified by those seeking to attack the believers in freedom. It does not mean advocating positions that infringe on the freedom of others.

"Wars have been fought, and prisons and detention camps built in an attempt to crush freedom. However, freedom has kept flapping its wings. The body may be imprisoned, but thoughts remain free from all restraints and dark cells. Freedom will exist as long as the world exists. It is Allah's gift to humankind.

"Within the context of this humanistic, sublime, and noble concept of freedom, we say getting acquainted requires freedom of choice. In the absence of freedom, we cannot get acquainted in a healthy, rational way. In the end, we will not know how to choose a good partner. As it is our right to seek what to us are sublime ideas and righteous aims without anyone imposing their ideas and aims on us, it is also our right to choose a partner for life.

"An essential element in the young man and woman's comfort with choices and their ability to make good choices is the parents' keenness in creating an environment of freedom for their children from birth. This better enables the young man and woman to exercise their right to express ideas, have dreams, and make choices when they reach adulthood. It is the parents' duty only to direct them and to point out what is in their best interests, but the decision is for their children alone. If the choice seems poor to the parents, the children alone should take the blame.

"When they reach an age that society decides is of maturity and competency, after we have taken care of their various steps in life – by way of upbringing, teaching, directing and, advising – we must give them the freedom to choose what suits them. We may remain by their sides to offer them advice from our life experience to protect them against danger and difficulties. Then, if something goes wrong or a poor choice is made, they must take the responsibility because we have fulfilled our responsibility toward them. The son who commits a sin is alone responsible for sin, because the parents did everything Allah wanted to raise him. Of his own volition, the son strayed from the path after he became an adult. If he had strayed before reaching adulthood, the blame falls on both parties. However, his parents, who had closed their eyes to his bad behavior and poor choice of friends, must accept the greater responsibility for his downfall. They had not raised him well or given him enough of the right attention.

"Some parents must get rid of the idea that the boy has freedom to choose, plan, refuse, and accept, while the girl must accept, submit to, and carry out what others have planned for her future. This idea is wrong, because both are exactly the same when it comes to reward and punishment. All life's responsibilities are the same, except for differences in their physiology and psychology.

"When we give boys freedom, no excuse exists to withhold it from girls. We discussed this in depth at previous seminars, especially pertaining to guardianship of the girl. We provided proof to show no lawful need existed for guardianship of the girl. Rather, customs played a great role in imposing this guardianship. We came to the clear lawful conclusion that everyone is equal in Allah's eyes.

"To you, young men and women, I say, 'Be free.' I do not say rebel, but be free, armed with your vigilance, humanity, and strength of morality. Be free to know how to choose right from wrong, for you alone own your lives. You are will enter the world of marriage, and it is you alone who will be happy or sad, succeed or fail, contribute to the creation or the destruction of a family. You will determine this with this freedom, and will step over anything bad that life throws in your way. You will also know what the end of the path has hidden for you because you have used your freedom to look out for your interests in all aspects of life, and because you have logic, awareness, and the spirit of duty.

"Therefore, the springboard for acquaintance is found in freedom, and this extends to the right to be free to choose a partner. When this idea has established itself and society has adopted this freedom as it pertains to acquaintance and marriage, we will have laid a safe foundation for learning how to pick a person to get acquainted with, and consequently how to get acquainted.

Dr. Omar then continued. "We hear and read the opinions and ideas of Muslim scholars discussing a solution to a problem in marriage. The latest of these opinions is the idea of 'friend marriage' announced in a fatwa by Sheikh Abdul Majeed Al-Zindani, Head of State Council of the Yemeni Reform Party. This marriage occurs under a lawful contract and in the presence of the guardian and witnesses, but the groom remains at his parents' home and the bride remains at her parents' home. They see each other for a limited time in any place, and then return to their parents' homes after the intimate rendezvous. This marriage – Sheikh Al-Zindani believes – 'allows friendship and the exchange of sexual freedom – under a lawful contract – between young men and women, something that would make this marriage, if implemented by Muslim young men in the West, a means to prevent the evils of immoral situations, and also a means to contribute to finding lawful solutions for the crisis of spinsters and the difficulty of providing a marital home.' [92]

"First, we must salute these scholars who seek solutions for problems in society by changing the non-fixed features of *Shari'ah* without touching the fixed ones. However, why do we always search for a solution to our society's problems only after they have spread and become firmly entrenched in our reality, and after the lapse of many people into behavior that is *makrooh* [not recommended] or *haram* [forbidden] ?

"Why not answer man's needs and the possibility of problems by setting up new systems to prevent these problems. It is especially important to act swiftly, given the fast pace of today's world. We are always behind the others when we have the capacity to put the others behind us. At least let us stand side by side, which would be better.

"The respected Sheikh Al-Zindani made friend marriage Islamically allowed for our youth in the West and forbade it for our youth at home. What if a boy and girl in the East were in the same circumstances as the young people in the West? Would they be allowed friend marriage? Or would it be forbidden as long as they were in the East; so they must migrate to the West to achieve their desires?

"We do not believe in separating the needs of the East and the West. Islam is for all humankind, a religion for preventing problems before it is a system for treating problems.

"Our main social problem is not marriage. Our problem is finding the right path to an acquaintanceship with a suitable person for marriage. This path should pass through a system of lawful acquaintance, with gradual stages that facilitate making a good choice for a successful marriage. This is not what happens today.

"Today we have a serious problem and a gap in our social system by not acknowledging a person has hidden needs, feelings, and

---

[92]   *Al-Qabas*, 9 Aug. 2003: 12.

instincts in his longing for a life partner. This is the true beginning of a human being, not when he is born, as some believe. From this beginning till he finds his partner, he travels unfortunately along a path not governed by a system. Only luck governs it, or some take refuge in families and friends to find a partner for them. Some even resort to advertising for partners in newspapers or on the Internet. What kind of system is this?

"If normal man respects himself and rejects "the road of luck" for choosing a lifetime partner, the only other way he will travel is through forbidden alleyways toward what is *shobhah* [lawfully dubious] because the lawful way does not exist in our society.

"Facing this, is it possible for Divine systems and religions, which derive their greatness from the greatness of their Creator, to fail in revealing a social system that takes our youth by the hand and leads them to successful marriage?

"The system we have presented in our seminars is the one that will fill this gap and complete the circle of life. With humble pride, we declare it the correct system for the East and West and humankind, because it is the Creator's system for all people."

* * * * *

## Stability in Olden Times

The same female student was ready with another excellent question. She now told the lecturers, "**I am convinced that acquaintanceship is valid and an essential progression toward marriage. Acquaintance will show me where to put my steps. However, past marriages that did not follow the path of acquaintance seemed more stable than today's marriages. Do you agree?**"

Dr. Afaf wished to respond. "The lack of dependable information lets us assume that past marriages were happy. We have only a relatively clear history of past marriages for one or two generations, meaning back to our grandfathers and grandmothers. We may learn about the previous generation from what our parents have told us, though this is hardly scientific or accurate. But who can inform us about the tens and hundreds of previous generations? Did they have a happy life or not?

"I believe the lives of our grandfathers and grandmothers were stable, but not necessarily happy. This is because girls did not have ambition and expectations that equaled those of boys. The norm at that time forced a girl to marry, even before the age of 12 or 13. She was not allowed to go to school and be literate. If she could not read, how could her personality develop in the realms of culture, education, and society in general? On top of these were the restraints imposed on her that did not invite her to develop her general social interests for participating in educational or cultural activities.

"Where were her ambition and expectations when she had no opportunities or choices? She was raised to clean, cook, and wash clothes. With this mentality, she moved into her husband's home. She had to care for the children, including being worried about their financial needs. She often also cared for his older relatives. When her husband hit her and she ran back to her parents' home, her father returned her to the martal home. This accepted the oppression of the husband, which was allowed because he fed and sheltered her. His opinions were her opinions; she had none of her own. Her role was limited to mothering, not just in housekeeping but also in child care. She had no role in her husband's formation of hopes and ideas, but rather accepted his decisions. The absence of choices made her submissive and accepting.

"No clear vision exists to help us determine if past marriages happy, or if both partners were happy, or how they defined happiness. We deduce that many women accepted what men planned for them. The women were committed to these plans, as they had no other choice. To object would be futile."

"Today times have changed, and women have become equal to men. Beliefs and ideas that were acceptable in the past have faded away in the modern era. Women are no longer those persons on whose behalf men thought, planned the future, and determined ambitions. This change in women's status has occurred beyond our society. This is why the importance of premarital acquaintance is recognized in other nations. We differ from them in that our system of acquaintance is launched from the depths of Islam, in what it determined for humankind – in methods, vision, and ideas."

Seyyid Mohammed said with a smile, "Dr. Afaf is harsh on the old society. I am not disputing the accuracy of some of her comments, but we must not devalue the role of the woman in the past, especially in raising children as she produced great achievements. We must look at olden times objectively.

"What benefit would a woman have had 400 years ago from being a painter or a leader in a social or political position? None, because the objective circumstances that could use her energies and capabilities did not exist. It may have been men or the prevailing situations at the time that caused this. Today the opposite is true, as women acquire advanced capabilities to participate in a flourishing society and help develop it.

"I want to refer to the 'philosophy of the cave,' which is where people first lived. Back then, the wife's wish was for her husband to return safe from the great dangers of hunting for food. She had no other wishes. Today, we live in much better circumstances, where some men have comfortable offices and many luxuries. We cannot compare today's man to the caveman, who had to kill wild animals to eat and feed his family. Therefore, what a woman used to accept – only for her husband's safe return – is not enough for her today. She is dissatisfied unless he returns carrying what she, not he, has chosen.

"Does Dr. Afaf agree with my opinion?" She politely signaled to him that she did.

"Many women in the past were happy," he continued, "in the sense that they were content and accepting of their circumstances. Would they have been happier, or more content, if our system for choosing their life partner had been around and if they had been given the opportunity to apply our system? I think so."

* * * * *

## Acting a Part

A male student who was enthusiastic about the new system, but also apprehensive, addressed Dr. Omar. **"I am strongly in favor of premarital acquaintance to minimize future negative developments. However, some people, male or female, during acquaintance try to show only their good side and hide the other. They may be good actors. Their aim may not be a permanent bond, but rather time spent together for fun with no long-term**

**purpose. How can the sincere person discover if the other does not have the same aim in getting acquainted?"**

Dr. Omar replied, "The stages of our system provide a path for uncovering deception by their gradualness and by the widening of the margin of choice. We assume that those who enter these stages are aware and have good manners, that they pay attention to morals, virtue, and humanity, and that their goals in life are honourable – also, that they do not have great anxiety, mental tensions, or unstable personalities.

"If we assume a boy has the good qualities and his motive for acquaintanceship is to build a stable marriage, he will not think of acting and will present the true picture of his personality, hopes, education, status, and wealth. If he lacked the good qualities, he might fool around and act and strive to satisfy his desires or to achieve any other goal that might be useless or a waste of time. Let us say this is possible.

"But the stated intention and effort to meet another person in an attempt to create a family, and the connection of manners and righteousness, should reduce the need to act by the boy – and the girl too. If the boy follows the stages and the gradual approach of our system with precision, he will not need to act because the space to manoeuvre is wide. Later, he may lawfully enter a contract with one or two others and may choose whom he prefers. There are dozens of girls in front of him, at work, at university, and in society. It is easy to approach them, so why the need to act? Also, the courtship is public so incorrect behavior will be noticed and, if done more than once, a blot on his reputation.

"The girl is not helpless in this situation. The insincere person more and more over time reveals hints of his true nature. It is up to the girl hopefully to be able to read these signals and not renew the contract with the offender.

"Acting is more likely to occur if we delay introducing this system and we let society further close upon itself by rejecting the idea of acquaintance. Situations that breed acting occur when the acquaintance period is very short and not public, when an opportunity to meet each other has come and may never return because traditions work against making opportunities abundant, when society makes it difficult for people to seek love, or when one of the parties is

185

unaware of how to judge good character. Also, acting masters the situation if great inequality exists between the two parties in material or immaterial ways, such as differences in wealth or education. For example, if the girl has beauty and wealth and the boy does not, he may be eager to propose and he feels it better to conceal his flaws because his main aim is not her welfare, but possession of her heart, body, and money. The opposite is true in all this: a girl may be the actor and a boy the victim.

"Acting may arise when other choices are unavailable, when the proposal of marriage is based purely on selfishness, or when the noble aim – getting acquainted to achieve a happy and stable marriage – disappears.

"Our system provides an antidote to these all situations. We stand by the idea of prolonging the duration of the acquaintance period, because the longer the period in the first stages, the more discoveries there will be. Our system reveals acting even of a small degree. When a girl enters *feeqah*, she enters the primary stage of acquaintance. In *meeqah,* she will discover much about the boy, even if she has not completely discovered the whole truth about him yet. With time and the gradualness of the stages, little by little the two parties enter each other's world and are able, through their growing awareness, to discover whether the other's personality is a true or camouflaged one that changes appearance according to need. After that, the decision is in their hands."

\* \* \* \* \*

## The Principle of Paternity

A male student addressed the lecturers. **"If a young man wanted to marry but could not do so for economic reasons, he might make a temporary contract for *seeqah* because of his sexual drive only and not from paternal or familial motivation. He thereby rejects permanent marriage and one of its essential motives, reproduction. What is your opinion of that?"**

Seyyid Mohammed replied, "We have said our system is not rigid, with a one-size-fits-all formula. It is adaptable to people's different needs, but they must connect the details to the main idea in a lawful way. A person has choices that fit his or her circumstances, situation, and position.

"Let us say people might choose *seeqah* for motives and reasons that prolong its time period, and this keeps them from having a permanent marriage with family and children. These are special cases that belong to a sector of society that has its own special circumstances. These people have the right to satisfy the desires Allah gave them, provided that they do not contravene *Shari'ah*. Why it is disgraceful for a man and woman meet, under *Shari'ah*, in *seeqah* for sexual reasons, as long as this does not entail what is forbidden? When the man makes a lawful contract, he makes it not with an inanimate object, but with a human being whose desires conform with his desires. As long as sex in a temporary contract does not have to be given to him every time he wants it and only when the woman agrees to his wish, then she will be content within herself for her desires are similar to his desires.

"Allah planted this instinct deep within a person's soul. If people did not satisfy its need through the Divine system, they would collapse, completely defeated, under its pressure. In his book on our sexual life, Dr. Sabri Al-Qabani says, 'It is hard to feel happy and calm and to preserve a sober mind and a reassured state of the self, when he is in a state of constant repression or failure to satisfy the sexual call, that natural call that the Creator created inside us since eternity. We know that defying social laws usually inherits regret and punishment by the conscience and society. We must also know that defying natural laws and closing our ears to the natural sexual calls, by repressing the feelings and not answering their call, will make the person ill, stop his effort and motivation to create and produce, and punish him harshly. The drive to quench the sexual thirst is a power that cannot be subdued. Every mature understanding teenager has a sexual drive and a strong desire to satisfy it' [93]

"Sex is a desire that has a beautiful effect. Practicing it in a righteous way and with virtue is instinctive to many people, whether it is satisfied by *seeqah* or by permanent marriage. *Shari'ah* has a high regard for this instinct. When a person has sexual intercourse lawfully, he must perform *ghosl al-janaba* [total ablution]. However, if it is prayer time, he may pray and meet with his God without performing prayer *ghosl* [without the usual prayer ablution], as if Allah was letting him enter without a knock on the door and welcoming him with his mercy. Lawful sex is not dirty, but a pleasurable need that makes people happy and teaches them manners. The Prophet (pbuh) says, **If one of you came to his wife [for sex], let there be foreplay between them.**[94]

---

[93] Sabri Al-Qabani, *Hayatuna Al-Jinsiyyeh [Our Sexual Life]* (Beirut: Dar Al-'Ilm Lil Malayin, 1988) 21-22.
[94] *Wasa'il Ash-Shi'ah*, section 20, 118.

"This gives us a life system that is moral and educational. Foreplay in sex is like foreplay in life – a husband should not be rough with his wife, since the love and mercy found in sex is also be found in the general life of the couple. Sex has great benefits: it relaxes the body, reduces tension, and nurtures the brain, especially if it is practiced in the lawful way that Allah accepts.

"This is what is agreed on the subject of sex. As for reproduction, we must be realistic and sensible. Not every man or woman wishes to become a parent. This is not to deny their paternal and maternal instincts, but may relate to economic, mental, or social circumstances. They may live in this state for a long time, and it may or may not disappear. Therefore, we cannot object to them lacking this feeling or force them to accept parenthood if they do not have all the qualifications that go hand in hand with it.

"*Shari'ah* allows a married person not to have children even in permanent marriage. Sa'd Ibn Muslim said that Imam Ja'far As-Sadiq said, **It is up to the man to direct it [the semen] to where he likes,**[95] which is known in jurisprudence as *'azl* [*coitus interruptus*], or *tahdeed an-nasi'* [birth control] in the common modern terminology. In *Al-Muatta'* of Imam Malik Ibn Anas, several *hadiths* are narrated that allow this. In one of them: **It is your plantation; if you want, you may water it, and, if you want, you may leave it thirsty.**[96] And in another *hadith*, Ibn Abbas was asked about *'azl.* **He called one of his women and said: tell them, but it was as if she shied away, so he said: it is like this; as for myself I do it,** [that is, he does *'azl*].' [97]

"The principle of paternity may live in the man's unconscious mind. The woman who does not want motherhood may try to change him in that, and this may lead to separation. They would then choose more suitable partners, and that is their business.

"I want to return to the question about the economic situation preventing permanent marriage and a young man resorting to *seeqah*. If we refuse him, what would he do? He cannot set up a household and he is not capable of taking on family responsibilities, so what will he do? Do we suffocate his desire? Should we invite

---

[95] *Wasa'il Ash-Shi'ah*, section, 149.
[96] Malik Ibn Anas, *Al-Muatta'* [*The Foothold*] (Beirut: Dar Al-Gharb Al-Islami, 1984) 403.
[97] Ibn Anas 403.

him to fast? Remember the young man cannot go through with the temporary contract unless he finds a woman who has the same desires and circumstances. The young man may take this step when his aim is solely sexual gratification that does not fall into forbidden territory and when the woman has the same feeling. Even more so, she understands everything clearly: there is a dowry and a set time period, in addition to the existence of the same needs and circumstances that brought the two together. Nothing in this is shameful or wrong.

"Every human being has the right to live, especially if their lifestyle is set in a lawful framework. Society has to respect the wishes of all people and their freedom to be different. A person who wants to be single all his life and knows he will not fall into forbidden territory is free to do so, as long as he does not break the law, violate public order, and abuse *Shari'ah*. When Allah is satisfied, who are we to interfere? If we like children and are capable of raising them well, we should have them. However, we must let everyone else be free to make his or her choice regarding parenthood.

"Nevertheless, however long the period of *seeqah* with its satisfaction of sexual needs, the maternal and paternal instincts remain to be satisfied. This may be done only in permanent marriage and when suitable circumstances are provided. If they are not provided, the couple will not be able to marry and live competently with parenting and maternity, and this will be an injustice to them and the children."

The same student asked, **"If sex is free, are you not in effect permitting termination of parenthood?"**

"We are not stopping anything or breaking rules," said Seyyid Mohammed. We only make recommendations – to suit only that part of society needing *seeqah*. Your previous question focused on the idea of being incapable of setting up a home, so the man resorted to satisfying his desires through *seeqah*. Please come forward and provide a house and job for him, or let the government take responsibility and let the private associations play a role. If that happens and his fortunes improve, he will go directly into permanent marriage and have as many children as God blesses him with. He will embrace paternity, his wife will embrace maternity, and there will be absolutely no problem."

An elderly man in the audience asked, **"Is not having a child one of the principles of marriage?"**

Seyyid Mohammed replied, "If we assume this is correct, that reproduction – as some scholars say – is the essence of marriage, our system shows how a man may choose a woman who wants to have his children, and how she may choose the right, competent man to have children with. This idea is recommended, but is not obligatory. To have children, the couple must share the same vision and goals. We – in the light of the logic of the honorable questioner- state this with ease, but we cannot force someone who does not possess the traits needed for paternity or who is impotent to become a father, or someone who is barren to become a mother.

"Let us say the sexual instinct in an 18 or 19 nineteen year old boy has reached its peak. He asks his father to let him marry, and the father fulfills his wish. Is this boy driven to marry because he wants to have children or he wants to satisfy his sexual and emotional instincts? His choice is the latter. Delaying having children would allow him to build a future without burdening his wife and himself with the responsibility of raising the children, which might introduce conflict and end up in divorce. We must differentiate between sexual and emotional desires and paternal and maternal instincts

"Nowadays, some people have special circumstances and wish primarily to build their emotional bond with another person first, then move on to nurturing their paternal and maternal instincts. What happens most of the time is that their parents pressure the young couple to have children quickly. This wish is imposed on couples from society, so that their parents can see their grandchild. This pressure does not benefit the couple, if they are not mentally prepared for parenthood. We must let the couple have freedom of choice. The instinct of conceiving will one day kick in even if the married couple suppresses it at the beginning of the marriage. We advise people to consider the circumstances of those who wish to postpone having children till after they achieve certain goals, such as finishing an education, improving living conditions, finding a job that does not require constant travel, or recovering from a serious illness or injury. We also stress that other people's decisions are not our business.

"We search for the person and the lifestyle that suits us. If we secure Allah's approval and we become content while hurting no one, who has the right to confiscate our freedom?

"Look at the picture from all sides, not from only one side, so your judgment will be clear."

* * * * *

## Haste and Delay

The same student who wrongly thought the system put a stop to the parenthood addressed a question to Nasser. He asked, **"Do you really think your system will decrease the divorce rate?"**

Nasser said, "Today there is still haste in entering permanent marriage and this haste does not serve the goals of marriage. This is why there is a high divorce rate or at least many cases of a lack of stability, resulting in overreaction and tension between couples. Our system depends on delaying entering permanent marriage. The delay is a natural outcome of the gradualness of the stages used in reaching, at the end, permanent marriage.

"The main aim of this delay is to motivate young men and women to take enough time to think about their future and plan to build their lives together. The time they take in separating *feeqah* from *meeqah* contributes to nurturing their characters, and helps them to focus on making the decision without rushing and without depending on suggestions from others. It creates the mentality of responsibility, composure, and deep understanding of the role of marriage in life.

"It has been proved that many people who go straight into permanent marriage, simply to satisfy sexual and emotional desires or to achieve such psychological needs as parenthood with the absence of the main requirements for building a family, form a bond shaped by weakness. Most of the time, this leads to divorce.

"Divorce completely changes the direction of a person's life. Before marriage, a woman has many choices; after marriage, the choices decrease. If she is divorced with four or five children, is relatively old, and does not have educational qualifications or work experience, divorce may present a great problem for her. She will not be able to find opportunities to compensate her with a new family life. It is of great importance in such cases for the woman not to resort to divorce. This may have been avoided through the lawful stages of acquaintance, by her discovery of the level of sincerity, competence, and feelings of the man, and his capability of carrying out his responsibilities toward her. The divorced woman may remarry, but the opportunities of achieving that are few. Reality proves this.

"*Feeqah* and *meeqah* delay permanent marriage till a much more stable time, when true awareness of each other and understanding of marital responsibilities occur. This minimizes the possibility of divorce and also adultery.

"What we want from our system is not only to acquaint, but also to delay permanent marriage, which brings with it the responsibilities of expenses, family, and children. This must be carried out in the best way possible, without suppression of desires and with lawful emotional and sexual outlets. We may not be emotionally and financially ready to take on these responsibilities if we were to enter permanent marriage directly. This is why the periods separating *feeqah, meeqah,* and permanent marriage are insurance that provide many necessities for entering the world of marriage. The system also provides support for continuity of marriage and family stability."

One of the female guests asked, **"The two parties will get older during this delay. Might that not be in their interest?"**

Dr. Afaf answered, "To get older while we genuinely and logically study our steps before heading down a long path and stumbling into bumpy places is better than racing with the wind without discovering the dangerous places in our journey. Not discovering this will recoil on us. We will fall into an abyss and will wait for someone to rescue us and treat our wounds. Haste has unpredictable results, whereas going slowly offers the safest route for the projects or special situations that we plan for.

"Those of us who are relatively older than you, the students, are nostalgic about our youthful years – the days when we were single, the strolls on the beach, innocent games, outings among Nature, dreams, and youth's vigor and motivation. We know those days will not return. An old person cannot be a young person, those precious minutes cannot return, and gray hair – however much dye we use to get rid of it – will remain gray hair underneath and can never be beaten by attempts to hide it.

"Those who did not live their youthful years to the fullest may have future problems by regretting this, becoming unsociable, and going into isolation. Because many of us were placed at the center of marital responsibility early on, without introduction or training, its weight tired us and bent our backs. We try to escape with the excuse of divorce. If we cannot escape, we become regretful. But what good does regret do?

"*Feeqah* and *meeqah*, in addition to their importance in choosing a suitable person during acquaintance, is important in another way: the two young people live out their youth more, calmly plan more, and take all that is lawful from life and all that Allah has allowed in whatever tempts their desires. In the coming days and under the living pressures and obligations toward the family they will be burdened with, their many difficult duties may not leave moments of relaxation or offer opportunities for tranquility. If the two parties immerse themselves in the sea of responsibilities early on and have children, they will be faced, day and night, only with the demands of their obligations.

"What is the harm in getting older and not entering the world of permanent marriage right away? Why do not we think of the years as a stage for qualification and training, becoming mature at an age when we feel safe, instead of this being an anxious and stressful time? Every stage has its circumstances and principles. People should live their youthful years with what youth has given them, such as an openness to life. As they move toward middle age or elderliness, they will have taken everything in the earlier stages of their lives that satisfied their desires and refined their understanding of religious and humanistic morals.

"All we request is the principle of delay. We are not saying 10 years, but rather considering the circumstances and reasons for every case. If we delay marriage for two, three, or even five years for the circumstances and reasons mentioned, this will not affect having children. If we did delay marriage for many long years, as the questioner is suggesting, the woman may reach menopause and the man may become too old to be an appropriate father."

An audience member addressed Dr. Omar. **"You specify about 18 years of age for boys and girls to enter *feeqah* and *meeqah*. Can you guarantee those younger than 18 will not enter temporary contracts?"**

193

Dr. Omar replied, "Every rule has an exception. Some girls and boys may do this without guardian permission, but lawfully because, though they were too young, the legal aspect may be important to them. They may wish to avoid forbidden relationships. We do not encourage these relatively young boys and girls to make a temporary contract, because we fear, in the absence of parental supervision, things may occur that are not in their best interests. However, we cannot allow ourselves to forbid these relationships if they are lawfully governed.

"If we look at laws that do not allow anyone to drive a car before the age of 18, we find, even with the strict application of these laws, a small proportion of teenagers between 16 and 17 years of age who drive cars and thereby break the law. However, good parental upbringing and supervision will implant in the boy or girl the dangers of doing something at this age and that the law forbids before the age of 18. One day after reaching this age, they will drive a car and no one will be able to object. With proper guidance and education, they will understand what is right and not steal the car keys. They will know their hopes will be met, even if they must wait a year or two.

"This mental and educational directing applies to *feeqah* and *meeqah*. If we were pressure the young men and women, be harsh on them, and suggest they will never be able to enter *feeqah* and *meeqah* to satisfy their emotions, they will find dozens of other ways of doing so. They will have many plans to carry out what they want, away from the eyes of their parents and society. Destroying their hopes of a lawful relationship means trying to crush their lawful desires, which are irrepressible however much we try to thwart them. If we explain to them, through reason, the necessity of delaying entering a *feeqah* and *meeqah* relationship until a suitable age in the near future, when this relationship will be protected by Allah's blessing, the parents' agreement, and society's acceptance, then we can claim that the two parties will delay this step by understanding the postponement is temporary. They will be able to look forward to the day when they can make the decision that fulfills their wishes."

A female student stood and called out, **"Is specifying the age of 18 subject to *Shari'ah* or social law?"**

Dr. Omar replied, "This age is not determined Islamically, but by a mere social consideration. This is what society has accepted. It considers that this age marks the beginnings of *roshd*, though we sometimes see the girl starts the *roshd* stage at 16. This depends on the girl's awareness, education, and upbringing, independent of specifying an age. If we assume a girl enters a contract with a boy before this age, no sin has been committed. There are legal rulings allowing marriage contracts before puberty or sexual maturity.

"We say again: good upbringing and family care will prevent a girl from entering a contract too soon. However, if the family sees a lawful interest in allowing their daughter to date one of her relatives or friends even before turning 18, there is no Islamic problem in this. Relationships before this age are not unlawful, but they may be unwise. Obtaining parental permission is essential before 18. After this age, parental permission, agreement, or blessing is unnecessary.

"Our system is related to the moral upbringing that parents take care of – watching, guiding, and shaping a child into a decent religious being – and is related, before anything else, to the belief that God's eyes do not sleep. Anyone so brought up would consider God's satisfaction before the self's. Without such spirit and such upbringing, our system can never be implemented and will be doomed – just as permanent marriage today seems doomed when it does not follow God's rule in everything, big or small."

* * * * *

## The Relevance of *Mut'ah*

The intelligent audience now circled back to the subject of *mut'ah*. An enthusiastic male student stood and asked, "**Through all that has been discussed in these seminars, we have come to realize *feeqah*, *meeqah*, and *seeqah*, are in one category: the *mut'ah* or temporary contract or temporary marriage. Does not this concept need to be explained from an Islamic viewpoint?**"

"I thank the student for giving us an opportunity to explain this idea," said Seyyid Mohammed. "We were waiting for this chance.

"The lawfulness of *mut'ah* is disputed among Muslim scholars. Some believe it was made lawful at the time of the Messenger (pbuh) and then forbidden, with a difference over the number of times it was made lawful and later forbidden. There are also those who believe in its lawfulness at the time of the Prophet (pbuh) and the Caliph

Abu Bakr and the first part of the time of the second Caliph Omar Ibn Al-Khattab."

Seyyid Mohammed opened a book and began to read. "'The meaning of *mut'ah* marriage is that a man marries a woman for a period of time. For instance, he says, 'I marry my daughter to you for a month or a year or until the [pilgrimage] season ends or until the pilgrims return,' or the like, whether the time period is known or unknown. But this marriage is void according to Ahmad Ibn Hanbal, who said, 'The marriage of *mut'ah* is *haram* [forbidden].' On the other hand, Abu Bakr – and he is one of the grand Muslim scholars – mentioned another *hadith* that states it is *makrooh* [not recommended], but not *haram*.'

"Every issue that is *makrooh* is allowed. Anyone who wishes to make sure *mut'ah* is allowed by some Sunni scholars may refer to the text I have just read by Ibn Qodamah, who died in 620 AH [1223 AD], in the book *Al-Moghni*, volume 6, page 644. [98]

"Also, in relation to this, Dr. Sheikh Ar-Rafi'i one of the Sunni scholars says, 'Their [the Shi'ite] proof of its lawfulness is from the *Qur'an* and the *Sunnah*. As for the *Qur'an*, in the verse **istemta'tum** [for the enjoyment you have had] of them, give them their *a'jer* [dowry] as a duty, 4:24, *istemta'tum* was understood to mean allowing *mut'ah* marriage. If *istemta'tum* meant permanent marriage, Allah would have said instead, for example, 'marry them.' Scholars have also supported their belief in *mut'ah's* lawfulness from the words that immediately follow *istemta'tum* – **give them their a'jer [dowry]** – and because this *a'jer* [payment] is usually given only when there is a temporary benefit. In addition, some of the Prophet's (pbuh) companions, such as Abdullah Ibn Mas'ood, Abdullah Ibn Abbas, and Ubayy Ibn Ka'b, read the verse: **for the enjoyment you have had of them** – *ila ajalin mosamma* [for a specific time period] **– give them their a'jer [dowry] as a duty**; this was mentioned in the *tafseer* [interpretation of the meanings of the *Qur'an*] of At-Tabari and Ar-Razi.

"Also, At-Tabari narrated in his *Qur'an* commentary that Ibn Shu'beh asked Al-Hakam Ibn Otaibah about this verse, '...is it *mansookh* [voided by a later verse]?' He said that Al-Hakam said that Imam Ali

---

[98] Abu Mohammed Abdullah Ibn Qodamah, *Al-Moghni* [*The Sufficient*], vol. 6 (Beirut: Dar Ihya'a Al-Torath Al-Arabi, 1993) 644. See Document 16 at the back of this book.

Ibn Abi Talib said, **'Were it not for Omar's prohibition of *mut'ah*, no one would have committed adultery but the damned.'**

"Sheikh Ar-Rafi'i continues, 'As for the lawfulness of the *mut'ah* marriage in the Prophetic *Sunnah,* the Shi'ite Imamate believe that the *hadiths* narrated in their books by the Imams, such as Al-Bukhari, Muslim, An-Nisa'i, and Ahmad Ibn Hanbal, prove that the Messenger of Allah (pbuh) gave permission for *mut'ah,* that it was practiced in his time and in the time of time of Abu Bakr and Omar, that its lawful state is absolute, that no verse was revealed from Allah to make it *mansookh*, and that the Messenger of Allah (pbuh) did not prohibit it during his life. These *hadiths* are *mostafeedah* [numerous] and *motewaatirah* [narrated by so many scholars that the possibility of conspiracy does not exist – they must be true]. One of the *hadiths* that prove the Prophet (pbuh) gave his permission to practice it is narrated in *Sahih Al-Bukhari* [*Al-Bukhari's Authentic Hadiths*]: that Jabir Ibn Abdullah and Salamah Ibn Al-Akwa' said, 'We were in an army and the Messenger of Allah (pbuh) came to us and said, **I give you permission to practice *mut'ah,*** that is, the *mut'ah* of women. In *Sahih Muslim* [*Muslim's Authentic Hadiths*] it is narrated that these two also said, **The Messenger of Allah (pbuh) came to us and gave us permission for *mut'ah*.** Regarding the question of whether the *mut'ah* marriage was practiced in the time of the Messenger (pbuh) and in the time of Abu Bakr and in the first period of the reign of Omar, their [the Shi'ite] proof of this is narrated in *Sahih Muslim* that 'Ata said, 'Jabir Ibn Abdullah [Al-Ansari] came for *'umrah* [smaller pilgrimage]. We went to him in his house and the people asked him about things. Then they mentioned the *mut'ah* and Jabir replied, **'We practiced *mut'ah* in the time of the Messenger of Allah (pbuh), Abu Bakr, and Omar.'''**

"'Other evidence of the lawfulness of *mut'ah* marriage, according to the Shi'ite Imamate, and that it was not made void at the time of the Prophet (pbuh), is what was narrated by Imam Ahmad Ibn Hanbal in *Musnad*: that Omran bin Hussein said, **The *mut'ah* verse was revealed in the book of Allah, and we practiced it with the Messenger of Allah (pbuh), and no verse was revealed to make it void, and the Prophet did not prohibit it to his death.** This is in addition to other similar *hadiths,* from which one can understand the idea that the lawfulness of the *mut'ah* marriage – to the Shi'ite Imamate – has not been proved to have been nullified.' [99]

"Sheikh Ar-Rafi'i presents the Sunni opinion regarding the nullification of the *mut'ah* verse. Whoever wishes to know more about Sunni and Shi'ite opinions on this subject may refer to the sources from the two schools of thought, to see, in detail, their evidence and opinions."

Another male student asked, **"If your system is for all Muslims, and you claim it serves non-Muslims too, and if some scholars prohibit it and some allow it, how will everyone be able to use this system?"**

Seyyid Mohammed again responded. "From a religious view, one can obey Allah's orders free from partisanship to one scholarly opinion that objects to another scholarly opinion. A Muslim is able to use another scholar's opinion where he is satisfied with it, on the basis that the dispute between scholars stems from their differences in interpreting the text. Although some Sunnis object to *mut'ah* marriage because they invalidate the issue of timing, they do allow timing in other types of marriage. They allow marriage with hidden intention to divorce, whereas in *mut'ah* the temporary intention of the marriage is known and clear.

"As Sheikh Ar-Rafi'i says, '...the Shi'ah should not be slandered because they ruled to allow *mut'ah*. It is supported by evidence, especially after everyone agreed *mut'ah* was present at the time of the Prophet (pbuh) and after some of the grand Sunni scholars narrated that the *mut'ah* verse in the *Qur'an* was not *mansookh* [voided by a later verse]. Az-Zamakhshari mentioned in his *Qur'an* commentary *Al-Kashshaf*, narrated from Ibn Abbas, that the *mut'ah* verse is among the *muhkamat* [verses that may never be voided]. It is also untenable to say the verse **for the enjoyment you have had of them, give them their a'jer [dowry] as a duty, 4:24,** is canceled by a *hadith* because the *Qur'an* is *yeqeeni* [definite] and a *hadith* is *dhenni* [indefinite]. Moreover, those who say the *mut'ah* verse was canceled disagree on the source of this: Is it the *Qur'an* or the *Sunnah* or *Ijmaa'* [consensus among scholars]? And they disagree on the time when this claimed cancelation occurred: Was it during the battle of Awtas, Hunain, Khaiber, or Tabook, or the *Fateh Mecca* [conquest of Mecca], or the *Hujjat al-Wadaa'* [farewell pilgrimage], or any other definite time?' [100]

---

[99] Sheikh Mustafa Ar-Rafi'i, *Islamuna fit-Tawfeeq bain As-Sunnah wash-Shi'ah* [*Our Islam Reconciles Sunnah and Shi'ah*] (Beirut: Mu'assasat Al-'Alami, 1984) 147+.

"This is to say that the *Qur'anic* scripture cannot be argued about and played with or be subjected to *tahreef* [deviation or distortion]. Since a *hadith* was sometimes based on the desire or trustworthiness of the narrator, it does not carry the strength of certainty of the *Qur'an*.

"This respectable Sunni scholar's explanation clarifies the Shi'ites' conclusive evidence and proof on the subject of temporary contract. It shows the Shi'ite belief in this is justified as far as Allah's satisfaction is concerned. It is unacceptable for those who disagree with them over the ruling to accuse them of taking their jurisprudence from anywhere other than lawful sources, of which the *Qur'an* is the most important." [101]

A teacher seated in the back row spoke up. **"Dr. Omar, you said Muslims have the right to take the jurisprudence opinion that reassures them feel the most. Are there Sunni scholars who allow taking the opinions of Shi'ite scholars?"**

Dr. Omar replied, "Many Sunni scholars have no problem with permitting following of the Shi'ite Imamate school of thought. As an example, I will read the text of a historical *fatwa* published by the Sheikh of Al-Azhar in his time. He was Sheikh Mahmoud Shaltout, and his Eminence was asked:

"'Some people believe, for a Muslim's worship and transactions to be done correctly, he must follow one of the four known schools. Neither the Shi'ite Imamate nor the Shi'ite Zaidi's schools are among them. Does your Eminence agree with this opinion and its absoluteness, and so prohibit following, for example, the Shi'ite Imamate Ithna'ashari school?'

"His Eminence replied,

"'(1) Islam does not require Muslims to follow a particular school, but we say: every Muslim has the right to follow at the beginning any school that has been narrated correctly and whose rulings are written in its books. Whoever follows a school has the right to change to another – any school – and there is no *haraj* [limitation] on him in this.

---

[100] Ar-Rafi'i 153+. See Document 17 at the back of this book.
[101] Abul Hussein Muslim Ibn Al-Hajjaj Al-Nisapuri, *Sahih Muslim* [*Muslim's Authentic Hadiths*], vol. 5, An-Nawawi's commentary (Beirut: Dar Ibn Hazim, 1995), 179. See Document 18 at the back of this book.

"'(2) The Ja'fari school known as the Shi'ite Imamate Ithna'ashari school is Islamically allowed to be followed like all the Sunni schools.

"'Therefore, Muslims should know this, and get rid of prejudice against certain schools. The religion of Allah and His *Shari'ah* do not follow a school nor are they the property of one school, as all are *mujtahideen* [highest religious scholars], worthy because they are trying, to the best of their ability, to formulate new rulings acceptable to Allah. Those unworthy of formulating rulings are allowed to follow schools and to act according to the schools' rulings, if the *'ibadat* [acts of worship] or *mu'amalat* [dealings between people] are not changed.'" [102]

Dr. Omar continued, "From my knowledge of Sunni opinions on the lawfulness of *mut'ah*, I have seen *mut'ah* legislation existed at the time of the Messenger (pbuh). I have also seen its disallowance came at a later time. I saw it was permitted in the books of some Sunni scholars. I read that these scholars saw the Shi'ites had the right, based on the evidence they believed in, to allow *mut'ah*, and that their school of thought may be followed. This made me leap The Leap that we mentioned earlier. If the Sunni wants to be convinced about the lawfulness of *mut'ah* marriage, these Sunni sources are available for examination.

"However, if the Sunni insists on being unconvinced by everything we have proved and quoted, then he should transfer from one scholar to another within the Sunni schools of thought. This transfer will shorten the distance to the acceptance of the issues that are connected to the lawfulness of *mut'ah*, because the *mut'ah* contract does not need a guardian or witnesses or announcement, something that we find in the literature concerning permanent marriage. Some scholars permit a permanent marriage contract without the guardian's permission, like the Hanafis, or without witnesses, like the Malikis. So, a person may enter permanent marriage without these.

"Only one matter remains: How will Sunnis accept the timing? This is the difference between the Shi'ites and us. To solve this problem,

[102] Mahmoud Shaltout. *Fatwat Jawaz Al-Ta'abod Be Math'hab Ash-Shi'ia Al-Imamia* [*Fatwa on Allowing Following of the Shi'ite Imamate School*] (Cairo: Dar At-Taqreeb Bainal-Mathahib Al-Islamiah, Office of the Sheikh of Al-Azhar Mosque, 1958). See Document 19 at the back of this book.

we allow marriage with hidden intention to divorce, and this intention connects to timing. This marriage specifies a time in the man's mind when he is bound to his wife. When he decides this time has ended, he surprises her with a divorce. The dispute between the Shi'ites and Sunnis on the timing is restricted to revealing or concealing it. Both Shi'ites and Sunnis allow timing. The Shi'ites permit revealing and the Sunnis do not. If a Sunni is unconvinced by everything we have said, he should accept the Shi'ite school of thought and their concept of timing based on the *fatwa* of the Sheikh of Al-Azhar, Sheikh Mahmoud Shaltout (may God rest his soul). He finds it is permissible in the Shi'ite school of thought. In believing in that, a person may save himself from much complexity."

After this explanation, a male student stood and asked, **"What is the nature of *mut'ah* marriage from a jurisprudence point of view?"**

Seyyid Mohammed answered, "The true nature of *mut'ah* in the Shi'ite Imamate school of thought is a contract made up of agreement and acceptance and includes all the elements of permanent marriage and also other kinds of contracts in society, even the general elements of maturity, competence, right of choice, and satisfaction. It also has two requirements carrying the same weight as the main requirements of permanent marriage. The first is including the dowry, which, if neglected, would invalidate the contract. The second is including the time period, long or short, which, if neglected, would make the contract not be *mut'ah* and would become, according to some scholars, permanent marriage.

"There are two opinions on this issue. The argument, that it would change to a permanent one, is based on the fact that the nature of *mut'ah* and permanent marriage is the same, but that they differ in the *taqyeed* [restriction] and *itlaq* [non-restriction]. If the restriction – the timing – is not mentioned, then the contract becomes non-restricted, which means permanent. Another view believes, by omitting the timing aspect, the contract would be considered void. It is then neither *mut'ah* nor permanent, because the non-restriction that happened was unintentional and the intended *mut'ah* did not occur.

"If a *mut'ah* contract was made correctly, the husband may give his wife the whole timed period or only part of it. This means he may

201

end the marriage, even without her agreement, before the end of the duration agreed on in the contract.

"When the time period ends or he ended it before the agreed-on expiration date, the wife must wait till two menstrual periods have passed before entering into another contract with another man if she still menstruates, or for 45 days if she is at a menstrual age but is not menstruating. This is in the case when intercourse has occurred and when she has not yet reached the age of menopause. If the husband did not have sexual intercourse with her or if she has passed menopause, then there is no 'iddah – exactly like for the permanent wife.

"If her husband dies, she must wait the 'iddah of death, which is four months and 10 days – exactly like for the permanent wife.

"Mut'ah marriage is characterized by the fact that the wife gets no nafaqah [maintenance allowance], except if it was made a condition, and by the fact that there is no inheritance between the couple, except if it was made a condition. This differs from permanent marriage, where maintenance allowances and inheritance are obligatory. Even if not having them is a condition, such a condition is void. It opposes the permanent contract's principles of maintenance allowance and inheritance, and also opposes the Qur'an and the Sunnah.

"Children born through mut'ah are considered legitimate, with all the lawful rights and constraints of children born in a permanent marriage – no marriage through kinship, breastfeeding, or in-law relationship, and right of inheritance and maintenance."

Another male student wanted more details. He asked, **"What are the shared rulings between mut'ah and permanent marriage?"**

Seyyid Mohammed said, "Mut'ah marriage shares many similarities with permanent marriage. I will list the most important. They are:

- ❖ They both need a contract that includes oral acceptance and agreement. Agreement from one side only is insufficient.
- ❖ The contracts cannot be valid unless they are carried out using the words of permanent marriage or mut'ah, such as Zawwajtuka [I have married myself to you] or ankahtuka [with the right to have sex] or matta'tuka [with the right to have pleasure]

- ❖ The *mut'ah* contract, after it has been drawn up with its conditions, becomes valid, like the permanent contract.

- ❖ Making marriage conditions is permitted, provide they do not contravene the *Qur'an* or the *Sunnah* and do not make a lawful matter forbidden or a forbidden matter lawful.

- ❖ If the couple is found in *khalwah* [in a confined place alone], behind closed doors, or with curtains or the like drawn, this does not lead as a consequence to the dowry or *'iddah* becoming obligatory.

- ❖ If an unlawful point appears in the *mut'ah* contract, it will be nullified. If the couple has not had sexual intercourse, the woman does not get a dowry. If the woman had sexual intercourse without knowing about the problem in the contract, she receives the full dowry. If she slept with him and knew about the problem when the contract was made and kept it to herself, she is considered an adulteress and she does not get any part of the dowry – as in permanent marriage.

- ❖ Both have unmarriageability due to close kinship, breastfeeding, and in-law relation.

- ❖ It is forbidden to marry two sisters at the same time.

- ❖ The husband may not marry his wife's niece on either her sister's or brother's side unless she gives permission.

- ❖ It is forbidden to have sexual intercourse with the woman while she is menstruating or after childbirth.

- ❖ The *mut'ah* wife is a *firash* [bed, that is, the place where the child is born] based on *al-walad lil-firash* [the child is to be related to the father even if she had him out of wedlock] when sexual intercourse occurred. This makes it obligatory to relate the child to the husband [that is, to his or her ancestry].

- ❖ The child born in *mut'ah* has the same rights and obligations as the child born in a permanent marriage – right of financial support, inheritance, and obligations of maintenance toward parents.

- ❖ The *'iddah* is obligatory for the woman after the completion of the *mut'ah* duration, similar to the *'iddah* after divorce in a permanent marriage, when the woman has had sexual intercourse.

- ❖ There is no *'iddah* if the woman has not had sexual intercourse.

- ❖ The *'iddah* in death of the husband lasts four months and 10 days."

The same student suggested, **"It would be helpful if we might look at the rulings pertaining to *mut'ah*."**

Seyyid Mohammed replied, "*Mut'ah* marriage has many rulings. Here are the most important:

- ❖ The necessity of stating the proposed dowry.
- ❖ The necessity of stating the proposed time period.
- ❖ There is no maintenance allowance, unless it is a condition. In the permanent marriage, the allowance is obligatory and cannot be canceled as a condition because it is a marriage principle laid down in *Shari'ah*. But, if the maintenance allowance owed by him was for a certain number of months, then she may give it up or reduce the amount.
- ❖ *Mut'ah* has no divorce. The woman and man separate when the contract ends.
- ❖ She cannot return to him [unless it is with a new contract] during her *'iddah*, as opposed to the divorced woman in a permanent marriage.
- ❖ If her husband dies before the end of the period and she has not had sexual intercourse with him, the total dowry is rightfully hers. By contrast, in the permanent one, if her husband dies and she has not had sexual intercourse with him, the prevalent ruling is that she gets half the dowry.
- ❖ The *mut'ah* partner has the right to receive her total dowry when the period ends, even if she has not had sexual intercourse with her partner.
- ❖ There is no *muhallil* [the second husband whom she marries after the third divorce from her first husband so that she may remarry her first husband] in *mut'ah* after the third divorce. This practice is confined to permanent marriage, provided she has had intercourse with the first husband.
- ❖ The man is allowed to renew his contract with the woman a second, third, fourth time, and more, with a new contract every time. A *muhallil* is not needed."[103]

A different male student now asked for even more detail. **"As we know, the couple in permanent marriage, separates by divorce and the husband and wife inherit from each other, but,**

---

[103] Mohammed Ibn Ismael Al-Bukhari, et al. *Al-Mut'ah wa Mashroo'ietuha fil Islam* [*Mut'ah and Its Lawfulness in Islam*] (Beirut: Dar Az-Zahra', 1991) 129+.

in *mut'ah,* there is no divorce and, unless made a condition, no inheritance between husband and wife. How can *mut'ah* therefore be lawful?"

Seyyid Mohammed said, "I would like to correct this information for the honorable student. There are cases where the permanently married couple may *tebeen* [separate] without divorce. Here are several:

- ❖ The wife is a *mula'inah* [curser].
- ❖ The wife is a slave.
- ❖ The husband is insane.
- ❖ The Muslim husband or wife rejects Islam.
- ❖ The husband or wife, when a child, had been breastfed by the other's mother and they have, in effect, become siblings.
- ❖ The wife, when a child, had been breastfed by his former or older wife and she has, in effect, become his child.

"This is in Shi'ite jurisprudence. For the Sunnis, there are similar cases where the marriage may be severed without divorce, such as:

- ❖ The husband or wife rejects Islam.
- ❖ The husband and wife are discovered to be breastfed siblings.[104]

"Most rules have exceptions. So, there are also cases of permanent marriage where there is no inheritance. A few examples from Sunni rulings are:

- ❖ A sick man marries a wife and dies before he has slept with her.
- ❖ The wife is non-Muslim.
- ❖ The wife is a slave.
- ❖ The wife kills her husband.
- ❖ The husband kills his wife.

"This is the ruling of the Sunni scholars on inheritance. It is detailed in the book *Al-Mirath Al-Muqaren,* starting on page 81, by Badran Abul

---

[104] Sabiq 212 and Al-Jaziri 375.

'Aynain Badran, *Shari'ah* teacher in the College of Law at Alexandria University.[105]

"We agree the woman has no inheritance rights in temporary marriage when she has not set this as a condition because *feeqah* and *meeqah* are based on the aim of acquaintance, in the hope of permanent marriage. It occurs when the couple finds they are good for each other. This system does not aim to establish a full sexual relationship. So, what right does the woman have to inherit without having given the man complete sexual pleasure and without having had his children? She does not have rights over him as the wife in a permanent marriage would. If a lawful contract was made between them for a month or a year to explore compatibility, without obligations imposed on the two parties except for what was stated in the contract, including a dowry (the woman's only right in this contract), how can the woman claim an inheritance if the man dies? An accident may happen a month, a week, or even a day into their contract. It is Allah's through mercy if such an event does not happen.

"In the same way, what right does the man have inherit from the woman if he did not present her with anything or assume the obligations of marriage and she did not perform any duty for him? *Feeqah* and *meeqah* are only stages of acquaintance, not a state of permanent marriage continuing for decades, during which the couple made sacrifices and assumed many obligations toward their family home and children.

"This also applies to the absence of a maintenance allowance. When the contract term is short, why should the man pay if the woman falls ill and needs a hospital, is injured in an accident, has university fees, or needs new clothes? We must be rational. Allah was merciful when he created many systems for us to move through life. We take from these systems whatever makes sense and does waste our many opportunities.

"When the man is unsure if the woman is right for him as a wife, or if he is right for her as a husband, why should we force him to pay an allowance when he is just starting to know her? Some of us ask

---

[105] Badran Abul 'Aynain Badran, *Al-Mirath Al-Muqaren* [*Comparative Heritage*] (Cairo: Dar Al-Ma'aref, 1971) 81+.

for things when it is not in our right to do so, and it is not in the best interests of the other person to grant them.

"Through contracts, Allah set up two systems. Some of us want only one system, as if to impose what we want on Allah, He who is most knowing of what is best for us. We say, if you want an inheritance and an allowance, go for permanent marriage. If your aim is to study of the possibility of reaching a permanent relationship with another person, then, for the duration of the contract, you are free to give an allowance, or not, and to accept a condition of inheritance, or not. It is your choice."

* * * * *

## Considering the Forbidden

No one argued with the Seyyid's logic on inheritance and allowances. A male student now moved the discussion in a new direction. He asked, **"Some scholars say temporary marriage does not *yohassin* [protect from falling into forbidden sexual acts] the man as much as permanent marriage does. Do you agree?"**

The Seyyid continued to handle the questions. "We need to clarify the understanding of *Ihsaan* [protection from falling into forbidden sexual acts]. When it is used in the scholarly definition, it means acts that would lead to punishment by *Shari'ah* of the husband or wife who have committed adultery. Scholars also explained that the person deserving punishment is the one with a partner who can provide sexual intercourse whenever he wished. The man who entered a lawful temporary contract with a woman has no right to sexual intercourse. The permanent wife is required to live with the husband and provide him with sexual fulfillment, except during menstruation and after childbirth. The woman under a temporary contract is not required to do so. The man has no right to invite her to bed and, if he did, she is not obliged to agree. It is correct that the temporary contract does not *yohassin* the man. The permanent contract does *yohassin* him because he has the 'bed right.' This is one of the positive aspects of our system, not a negative one to be held against it."

One of the female students stood and asked, **"In a televised symposium, participants mentioned that most *hadiths* state**

**the right to perform sex is for the man only. Do you agree with this opinion?"**

"The question outside our subject," said Seyyid Mohammed, "but there is no harm in answering it briefly. Most Sunni and Shi'ite scholars believed the woman's right to have sex should be once every four months, but some Sunni scholars specified it should be once a month. Today, there seems to be an increase in sexual desires due to television programs, art magazines, and so on. Life nowadays drives you to excitement. We therefore lean toward the opinion that the woman's right to have sex should be once a month. Also, the Shi'ite members of this team leaped and took this opinion."

A teacher directed her question to Nasser. **"We understand from your speech on *mut'ah* that a man should choose a chaste woman, but what if he chooses a prostitute? We hear about men abroad or even in their country who enter into *mut'ah* contracts with prostitutes and pay no attention to the lawful requirements of *mut'ah* marriage. Does this keep *mut'ah* forbidden as a *Qur'anic* law?"**

"During the team's meetings, we discussed this because it is part of the concerns surrounding our system. Our obligation is to confront all the bad effects that may occur to best prepare for applying of this system.

"If we suppose that some use *mut'ah* marriage incorrectly, then there is a contradiction between theory and practice. Sometimes, the theory is in an exalted position and the application, by contrast, is more mundane. Allah's laws may be applied incorrectly, or taken advantage of in a way that is removed from the spirituality of *Shari'ah*. This wrongful application and exploitation do not invalidate the law's significance. As this issue relates to *Shari'ah*, it also applies to trade, and the difference between dealing honestly and cheating or lying. This is no reason to forbid trade – because there are individuals or organizations who violate trade laws and ethics. This goes for permanent marriage too. We meet individuals who take advantage of this marriage for their personal benefit, who unleash their pathologies and hurt others, but we do not dare to say permanent marriage is an incorrect institution.

"The responsibility of scholars is called on here to show the negatives and to work in revealing the truth of these rulings so people will not stumble into bad ways – specifically so those who go abroad will not make temporary contracts with prostitutes in the name of Islam because this will yield problems as far as *Shari'ah* is concerned.

"I see the need to dwell on this problem primarily to present our view on how to treat the problem. First, we must define the difference between a prostitute and an adulteress. Not every adulteress is a prostitute, because the prostitute sells herself at any time and rarely rejects a customer. An adulteress is a woman who sins with a man not her husband. She may have fallen into sin in a moment of weakness as a consequence of a love relationship. She did not trade her body for money. We do not have the right to describe every married or unmarried woman who has had a sexual relationship outside marriage as a prostitute, because a prostitute presents her body on the street, rarely refuses someone who pays her, and is with a new man every hour or so. We should not use the term 'prostitute' unjustifiably for any woman who has had a forbidden sexual relationship that may have been the first and last one in her life.

"To those Muslims who come up with excuses for their wrong actions by hiding them beneath a 'lawful' blanket, we answer from a moral and religious perspective. From a moral perspective, they are having relations with a woman who sells her body as a profession. She stands half-naked on the street, or waits for the phone to ring to grant the wishes of whoever calls. This relationship is unlawful. From a *Shari'ah* standpoint, we must understand the lawful issue: No man must make a contract with a woman while she is in her *'iddah*; so what reassurance does he have that she is not? How does a man know a woman of that kind has not slept with another man an hour earlier or a day earlier, or will not sleep with another man an hour or a day later? Can he be sure she will observe an *'iddah* when the *'iddah* after temporary marriage requires two menstrual periods?"

The teacher replied with a question. **"What if these men say the woman is to be believed regarding what she claims about her sexual activity?"**

"Yes," said Nasser, "there are those who say the woman is responsible for her own body. It is not a man's responsibility to check what she did in the past and what she will do later. It is up to her if she is in her *'iddah* and she did not wait. She must take the lawful responsibility of that. However, this kind of reasoning deceives the inner-self. No man with the right mind that Allah has given him would think like this. The previous would apply only to an honest woman. As for a prostitute, she is too far removed from *Shari'ah* and its constraints to make such excuses plausible.

"Let us not deceive ourselves. Those who hold this opinion, when they eat out, choose a suitable restaurant with suitable prices in a suitable area. Many of them ask about the type of food and if the meat is *halal* [slaughtered according to *Shari'ah*]. When they buy a car, they check it thoroughly so they will not have problems with it later. This is how we see them in their professions: examining, asking questions, and setting conditions before signing any contracts. They are cautious and must have everything be completely clear. But, when they want to find pleasure with a woman from the streets, they will settle the price with her in five minutes or less and a person can befriend her very quickly – and they say she is responsible for her own body. What kind of logic is that?

"If a prostitute comes one day to a man she has slept with and claims to be pregnant with his child, what would his position be? If he wanted the child and was sure of her honesty, he would believe her. However, as a principle, he does not want to be connected to her in any permanent way as she is a prostitute. He will therefore reject her, because he made a wrongful contract with a woman of the streets. When she claims pregnancy, he will refuse her claims because she has had sexual intercourse with an unlimited number of other men.

"How can he accept a child whose mother is prostitute? By the way, I must apologize to the audience for having used this term. Is he ready to give the child his name and financial support, while its mother moves from one city to another, from one man to another?

"We must be truthful with ourselves when we accept *Shari'ah*, not be haphazardly driven by sexual desires without considering Allah's rulings on this subject."

A female student asked, **"Are there not *fatwas* allowing marriage to a woman known to be committing *zina* [unlawful sex]?"**

"This is correct," said Nasser, "but the scholars emphasized the necessity of avoiding sin and directing her to the right path, to try to rescue her from the pit of corruption and moral decay and to take her to a clean place. Allah will greatly reward whoever can help this woman. The issue is not limited to permanent contracts, if the man's intention was to marry her. He could offer a *mut'ah* contract, but not for one or two hours, because this short time does not allow her to get out of her bad situation and psychological and moral dilemma. It needs a long time, and the man must sacrifice much comfort, time, and money. One of the reasons that drove this woman to prostitution was financial need or mental anxiety, so how much time and money are needed to supervise and rescue her? Does he have enough resources, powers of persuasion, perseverance, and the intellectual and religious capacity? After asking these questions, he will be able to choose. If he offers help, the woman must also work hard to get out of her old situation so the man may be sure her intention is real.

"Young men should not read the *fatwas* based on **do not approach your prayers, 4:43**.[106] Whether they wish to be tied to a woman permanently or temporarily, they should note the verse **Women are your fields, 2:223**. They must concentrate on choosing the right 'land.' Is it good for cultivation? Will its fruit be sweet or bitter? These questions should be constantly in mind before we own and touch this land.

"Here, we see the importance of our system. If society establishes the lawful measures in the man and woman's relationship and works to apply *feeqah*, *meeqah*, and even *seeqah* in this relationship – that is, if it accepts the idea of temporary marriage – I am sure we will not find so many men associating with prostitutes to satisfy their sexual thirst momentarily when such activity has so many legal and moral complications. The problem is that the lawful element that comes from the allowed category was often neglected, or, worse, society forbad this lawful element. The result was that urgent sexual desires drove many young people were driven to do forbidden things. This wrong outlook on temporary contracts as 'lawful adultery' has caused these contracts to lose their role in preventing young people from entering unlawful relationships. Society bears the responsibility

---

[106] This is part of a *Qur'an*ic verse: **Believers, do not approach your prayers when drunk, but wait till you can grasp the meaning of your words, 4:43**; this is often used as an example of how people manipulate the verses, *hadiths*, or *fatwas* because they say the *Qur'an* itself prohibits prayer when they quote **do not approach your prayers** and neglect to mention the rest of the verse!

to Allah over its position, as it fostered the spread of adultery and other deviant sexual behavior.

"I sum up by saying: the wrong application of temporary contracts by some people cancels neither their lawfulness nor their ethical, social, and humane importance. Having an relationship under a 'lawful' covering with a woman known to be living a life of sin is illogical and forbidden, especially if the man has no real intention and capability of rescuing her from her corrupt environment.

"Even if a man can deceive himself, he cannot deceive Allah."

**\* \* \* \* \***

## Second Marriage

A female student had a concern about multiple marriages, which she viewed in a negative light. She asked, **"To what extent will *feeqah* and *meeqah* reduce the number of second marriages, which, although allowed and Divinely legislated, is a major cause for the increase of social problems? I ask Dr. Omar."**

Dr. Omar replied, "The results of applying any system in the beginning will be different from the later results. The social mentality needs time to experience the full implications of a new system's meaning, especially understanding and appreciating its importance and its capability to solve problems. We are not expecting quick results. Even if results do come quickly, they are accompanied by negatives from misunderstanding and incorrectly applying the system, or by incompleteness because the system's spread in society has not yet is limited and has yet been reached everyone. Early positive results will not be the same 50 years later.

"Any individual feature in the system also requires the application of the rest of the features because the individual features make up the complete system. They complement and interact with each another. This also goes for the social system. With the codification of lawful relationships like marriage, morals and correct upbringing must govern and must have a strong presence in these relationships. Otherwise, the laws may not contribute to the stability of marital life because it has lost an essential element in these relationships: morals. When we present *feeqah* and *meeqah*, we must be aware of many essential issues – lawful, ethical, and humanistic – for the application to carry a high percentage of positive results. That occurs when society is convinced of the rightness of the idea and carries it forward dutifully. This we leave to time. The idea is a seed that needs time to germinate.

"We believe in the coming years the application of *feeqah* and *meeqah* will reduce, God willing, not just the number of divorces and adulteries, but also the number of multiple marriages. We will not see the positive effects quickly when implementing the system, but they will occur in the future. When young people delay marrying till they reach 25 or 26 or even a little older, with their emotional and sexual outlets controlled by a lawful temporary contract, they will have enough time not to rush into entering permanent marriage and end up – as a consequence – with divorce or a second marriage, which is a choice only for men. The young men and women will find the right person for building a shared marital life through the application of our system and its gradual nature The problems will not be so many that they will badly affect the reassurance and stability in this marital life. The man will not be obliged to look for more wives, and the wife will live safely out of range of the weapon of divorce."

Here, a teachers joined in. **"Divorce, though lawful in *Shari'ah*, is strongly not recommended by *Shari'ah* and society, whereas *Shari'ah* has encouraged second marriage when needed and also when not needed. Therefore, how can you deny a man the right to marry a second time?"**

Seyyid Mohammed responded, "No one can forbid second marriage as long as Allah, the legislator, allows it, and not even forbid third and fourth marriages, whether caused by ordinary or pressing circumstances. However, we, the team, believe whoever makes a second marriage usually does so as a result of special circumstances and sometimes under pressure. Although some people do not think it essential and important, those who marry several wives often do feel it is necessary. It is a act that stems from the heart of the need.

"We have no right to denounce it. We can never object or come up with new ruling on any ruling that is confirmed in the *Qur'an*. This is indisputable. However, when the questioner suggested that our system would reduce the rate of second marriage, then we say there is an ongoing problem that customs and traditions have made eternal between men and women – that a woman will not accept sharing her husband with another woman. This team is made up mainly of men, but we have an honorable Sister among us, Dr. Afaf. We have discussed this topic more than once and we still differ. Dr. Afaf thinks a man does not have to marry a second wife – of course, not as an objection to the legal ruling – unless it is for unusual circumstances. She thinks, if he wants sex, he has a wife and, if he assumes he can be just with his two wives, he is mistaken. Therefore, according to Dr. Afaf, there must exist some compelling circumstance that allows the man to marry a second time. The men on the team do not share the same opinion with me.

"We hope to reach a stage where the circumstances that encourage a second marriage will disappear or be greatly reduced. This may be a wish and may not have practical application. It is similar to what some countries do when announcing a 'year without accidents,' while knowing some accidents will still occur. Aiming for zero accidents will bring them closer to that goal. The rate of accidents will be reduced as a result of the warnings that alert people to be careful. Eventually, people will try better to avoid danger, be cautious, and care more about their lives and the lives of others.

"We have no right to reject *Shari'ah*. Instead, we must use it to achieve exalted goals that bring us good in this life and in the hereafter."

* * * * *

## A Few Side Issues

Some students wanted to explore side issues. One male student stood and inquired, **"Putting aside the aim of *feeqah* and *meeqah* to reach permanent marriage, some people think there are women who make *mut'ah* marriage a profession. They transform *mut'ah* into a money-making pursuit. What is your opinion?"**

Seyyid Mohammed said, "It is not only some lay people who think this way, but also some scholars and intellectuals. These scholars forbid temporary marriages altogether, even though they know all the books of the Ja'fari school of thought, especially the jurisprudence ones, rule it is necessary for women to have a lawful *'iddah* after she leaves *mut'ah*. Despite this, they accuse those who say *mut'ah* is allowed of having daughters who move from one man's lap to another. This is not just a slight on *mut'ah* marriage, but also an obvious lie with no connection to the truth. Any lawful sexual relationship in permanent or temporary marriage must be come after the woman's *'iddah* – three menstrual cycles after permanent marriage and two after *mut'ah*.

"If a woman was temporarily married to a man, let us say, only for one hour and they had sexual intercourse, she will not be able to be with another man until after two menstrual cycles have passed. If we were also to assume two menstrual cycles average between 45 and 60 days depending on when the cycle started, then after that she is able to directly enter another relationship. But, from a psychological and practical perspective, she can prolong the period for six months so that she can find a person whom she feels comfortable with. This woman can make a contract with only two or three men a year, so how large will her dowry be in a temporary marriage to be sufficient enough to become a big fortune?

"If we were to assume that some women do not have true feelings and normal emotions, they might accept a temporary marriage from any man regardless of his character. After such a woman makes a contract with the first person for an hour, and then it ends after an hour, she is able to make a new contract after 45 days. If this irrational process occurred, she would be able to make five or six contracts a year.

"If we were to extremely exaggerate the dowry and assume the woman would request a dowry of $1,000 for the duration of one hour, how many men would give a woman $1,000 for an hour? If she were able to make five temporary contracts a year then the money she would receive from these contracts would be $5,000. With this annual income, we deduce that she might probably save $1,500. Where is the great profit she is making out of these temporary contracts?

"I hope we can be rational about everything that questions our system. A woman is incapable of taking advantage of *mut'ah* if she applies it lawfully. The *'iddah* that Allah commanded, during which the woman must abstain from marriage, is not solely to clean her uterus and to ensure she is not pregnant. There is also psychology: for the woman to love a man and to live with him, she needs time. How much spare time does she have to love a man during a short contract time before leaving him and yet also receive a great sum of money?"

One of the teachers in the audience asked, **"The *iddah* in permanent marriage is three menstrual cycles and in temporary marriage is two. Why is that?"**

The Seyyid again answered, "Divorce becomes inevitable after many problems and difficulties. There is a great possibility that the marriage has produced children. Allah, by his mercy in his *Shari'ah*, has given the divorcing couple a period of three menstrual cycles, especially in the *raj'ee* divorce, where the couple may return to each other without a new contract if they return during the *iddah*. This gives them up to three months to rethink their actions, solve their problems, look after their children, and hopefully regain stability at home. As for why it is three menstrual cycles, some believe it is not for the purification of the uterus because one menstrual period is enough to do that, and a second makes doubly sure of it. It is really about being a long enough time for the couple to think calmly and study the possibility of returning to their family home.

"When we come to the *iddah* after the temporary marriage and its specification of two menstrual periods, we must consider the separation does not stem from divorce as a result of problems. It is the end of the contract time between the man and woman, which was fully agreed on and accepted by both parties. The *iddah* is two menstrual periods after the temporary marriage – also by Allah's mercy – so that the woman is not compelled to stay longer than necessary without a new contract, whether permanent or temporary, with a man who suits her."

\* \* \* \* \*

## Back to Emotion

A female student took over to bring back the topic of love from earlier in the seminar. **"Some researchers believe love makes the two parties compatible. With love, they move to permanent marriage in harmony. If this is true, why do you need *feeqah* and *meeqah*? Let their friendship be innocent, and love may determine the choice."**

Dr. Afaf answered, "If we were look at the marriage registers, we would find many divorced couples who were once in love. We cannot go into the philosophy of love and talk about the forms and schools that have discussed and studied it extensively. This is an area requiring long research. What is agreed on is that superficial love exists. It results from the pressure of selfishness and stems from the quick bedazzling glance of the man or woman's appearance, money, family background, or social status. This is what two people probably experience, stemming from various types of selfishness that aim for marriage as one of its means, not an aim in itself. Therefore, we can give this love a label: it is the quick love that happens quickly and goes quickly as a result of changing circumstances that laid this love on the surface but not deep inside. Beauty will wither away, and money may run out or one of the couple does not benefit from this money as was expected and so the goals are not achieved. We are not against this love, for people are free to do what they want. But we deduce that this love is not a firm basis for marriage.

"We believe in love that achieves compatibility and agreement and creates a wide space for happiness to dwell in. For this to come true, a lawful acquaintance is needed to reveal the truth about each person. This is what *feeqah* and *meeqah* ensure, as they are influenced by a gradualness that is capable of showing this truth to both of them. Their compatibility and agreement intensifies the degree of their love. They move toward marital life while carrying reassurance and happiness that result from a love connected to a lawful contract, which also prevents the two from erring into what Allah has forbidden. The longer the time of acquaintance, the greater will be one person's knowledge of the other. Fewer disputes will arise in their marital life, not solely because of love, but because of their understanding and consideration of each other – and this agreement on matters may be regarded as a kind of love. Agreement will lead to stability, just as love will lead to happiness.

"As for why *feeqah* and *meeqah* are needed, if there is an innocent friendship between two young people, I ask: what is the system of innocent friendship and what are its limits and restraints? We do not think anyone has laid down a system for friendship between a young man and woman except for some general ethics and advice without the foundation that would give friendship the characteristics of a system. Our system's refusal to adopt this kind of friendship avoids imitating the West, where friendships are not governed by any order. I remind you of the ISO philosophy that, for any system to be formulated and to take on the characteristic of a system and become a system in all the senses of the word, it must have good characteristics, controls, limits, and aims and ambitions that are

217

crystal clear. Without the presence of these characteristics, this would not be a system. The way of getting to know one another in the West is based on a friendship that does not follow a specific system or constraints. Friendship's definition and expectations differ from country to country, and from society to society, from era to era, and from individual to individual. What was unacceptable in friendship and acquaintance 50 years ago has become acceptable now. This proves that friendship in the West does not follow an order, because a good order sets firm boundaries suitable for every era. It places non-fixed constraints within the system without affecting the fixed ones. What we witness today are movable boundaries often driven by greed or selfishness. This is why Islam differs from the Western way, as it provides all the answers for life and the fixed and non-fixed constraints for all eras and places. When we see friendship as the essence of getting acquainted between a young man and woman, we ought to know what the structure of friendship is based on, and where the fixed and non-fixed constraints lie.

"The West has no firm characteristics for friendship and so no system. Therefore, the solution for getting acquainted in a lawful and healthy way is to be found in Islam. The lack of commitment to a system is an acceptance of chaos. The balanced person does not accept chaos in relationships, for himself, his sister, and whoever is around him."

A male student stood and asked: **"Do you not feel this love that you called superficial or interest-bound can transform, through *feeqah* and *meeqah*, into a deeper love during the long period of acquaintance?"**

Dr. Afaf said, "Thank you for reading my mind. This is what I wished to comment on. Our system may benefit even love that is based on selfishness. The period of acquaintance may drive the man and woman who love each other for superficial reasons to change their outlook on each other. This time period assists them in discovering the moral and personal attributes they were unaware of before, because greed for money, beauty, family background, or social status had blinded their ability to appreciate the more important traits in a human being. At the moment of awareness of the other person's goodness, this passing love transforms into a deep one.

"The opposite may also occur. The deceived person may discover the selfishness of the other person who is attracted to his or her beauty or money, and prefer to escape from living with that person the under the same roof. Also, the deceiver may discover bad traits and conclude that personal ambition is not worth the punishment of being made anxious for a lifetime. Beauty and money do not compensate for a marital hell with the only refuge being divorce.

"*Feeqah* and *meeqah* help to discover the positives and also the negatives. When things become clear, we are able to balance the two on a scale and see which are the heavier. If the positives weigh more, we move forward to the next stage. If the negatives weigh more, we do not renew the contract and we leave the relationship with the least possible loss and with no regrets.

"We are for love, but we believe *feeqah* and *meeqah* signal the pathway to a vigilant love. The experience of acquaintance will either strengthen this love or clarify what we were deluded by – that the other person's love was nothing but a mirage."

Another male student was thinking of the final stage of the new system. He directed his question to Nasser. "**Your system encourages lawful acquaintance between young men and women to find understanding and compatibility, so they may later enter into permanent marriage with full clarity. In your opinion, where are the married couples in this system?**"

Nasser responded, "Any close relationship between a man and woman – if there is honesty – creates feelings of affection or love. A person in this case must make sure his dreams are based on correct principles and firm ground, before being swayed by feelings and emotions. He must know that entering love is not the same as leaving it. Entering love is much easier. In building a relationship, the door may be open. If he wants to leave, he may find the door shut. We stress the need for clarity and gradualness in the relationship. If one of them wants to leave, he or she can do so calmly, without animosity developing between them.

"One of the results of *feeqah* and *meeqah* is to make certain of love in the relationship by discovering the true feelings, or to leave the relationship but with understanding and without disputes.

"It is correct that our system is for younger people and those who wish to marry permanently, but married people may benefit from it as well. We include even those already married and whose lives are dominated by special circumstances and situations that they have concealed and are concerned about. There are men who are married and want to marry a second wife for a specific reason: his wife may be barren or the marriage may be unsuccessful and he does not want to separate from his small children. There are those who want to enter *seeqah* as they are financially incapable of supporting a new family and a new house. There are those who are divorced and want to remarry. We advise all of them to enter *feeqah* and *meeqah* first.

"Our system is a general one and its benefits are not limited to a certain kind of people. It is for the whole society because it is in essence a Divine ruling that Allah laid down to serve everyone."

* * * * *

## The Unmarriageables

The same professor who had taken part directed had comments and a question for Seyyid Mohammed. **"The consequences of permanent marriage are also present in the temporary marriage as far as the *maharim* [unmarriageable relatives] are concerned. When a boy and girl make a contract, her mother becomes forbidden to him and she becomes forbidden to his father. Your system encourages those aiming to choose a partner to get to know many people. As a consequence, unmarriageable relatives will increase. What if a boy and girl enter into a contract and one day later he enters into another contract with her mother? They marry permanently and have children. Do you not think this will result in mixed up ancestry?"**

The Seyyid replied, "The probability of that occurring is rare. Usually the boy enters into a contract with a girl close to his age. Her mother would be older and this makes unlikely the possibility of this boy marrying the mother as she is too old and is unsuitable to be his permanent wife. However, given the improbability of the assumption, if Islamic relationships of acquaintance were occurring secretly without the family's knowledge, then this issue might become valid. A boy and girl may enter into a lawful contract in any of the stages and, if we assume this boy does not have experience in marital affairs and in what is allowed and forbidden, then after the contract ends, he may make a contract with her mother if she was widowed or divorced. He would be sinning and committing a legal error. If she conceived, then the ancestry would indeed get mixed up.

"This statement is correct under two circumstances: when contracts are made in secret and when those who enter contracts are ignorant about *Shari'ah* rulings on marriage. The fear of mixing up ancestry may be wiped out easily if society accepts *feeqah* and *meeqah*, where contracts are in front of people's eyes, far from fear and secrecy. Society's acceptance of this Islamic system saves us from many problems, especially when we know that Islam is the religion of light, not darkness. It is the religion of daytime, not the nighttime of disguise, isolation, and fear. When a young man and woman go out together within a lawful contract, and with their parents' permission and with society's respect for their relationship, then there will be no mixed up ancestry. The young man would not even think of asking for her mother's hand when relationships are in the open, even if he did not have a background in jurisprudence. However, if their outings occurred under the wings of darkness, and their parents had no knowledge of it and secrecy is the master of the situation, then we would expect lawful problems to surface.

"The problem may not only be ancestry. It may arise from breastfeeding in secret, when the nurse conceals she is breastfeeding a child who may grow up to marry his sister. Thus, if we accept the matter and are convinced of its lawfulness, then all the relationships of acquaintance will not be secretive and eventually the fears and dangers will disappear."

The professor then said, **"Will not having many lawful relationships increase the number of unmarriageable relatives?"**

"What is wrong with that?" asked Seyyid Mohammed rhetorically. "This situation would be a half full cup, not a half empty one. An advantage of having more than one wife is that it creates closer social relationships. It is good for a boy to have the same number of mothers-in-law as the number of his lawful temporary contracts. The boy will have older women to visit them to ask for advice and to offer his assistance when needed. It is also good for a girl to have as many fathers-in-law as her number of lawful temporary contracts. These older men will be able to help her when needed. She, in turn, will love them like a daughter loves her father, and they will love her as their own daughter, even if permanent marriage does not take place.

"We must always look for positive, for the half full cup. Having many unmarriageable relatives is a healthy for society because it strengthens bonds and relationships. It gives more weight and seriousness to *feeqah* and *meeqah*, by bringing relationships out to the open, especially if we respect *Shari'ah* and let people live freely, without complications, and do not surrender to customs that were laid down by a mentality that won people's conviction rather than Allah's approval.

"The West cannot but envy the East in its close social ties and the bonds that connect the youth to their in-laws and vice versa. Our system values these relationships because they achieve family support. Having many in-laws makes the young people assume and commit to more precise responsibilities."

* * * * *

## Agreement and Disagreement

A male student stood to present a point that would have inevitably been mentioned later. **"You say there must be agreement on the essentials between the young man and woman before getting married. Do you think all young men and women have the level of understanding of marital life to agree on these essentials before marriage? Second, do you not think marriage is as much an agreement on shared compromises as it is on rights and duties?"**

Seyyid Mohammed answered, "There are obvious issues that do not need a contract for agreement, such as running the household and nursing. They happen with a joint understanding. It is the woman who nurses, and usually cleans, cooks, and is in charge of the household chores. The man's duty is to support the family financially as much as he can.

"Nevertheless, the household jobs that the woman has assumed alone are no excuse for the man to forget that he should give her a hand at home. His manliness will not be tarnished by helping his wife clean, cook, and watch the children from time to time. In this way, his wife will not feel she does only lowly chores and nothing else is her specialty.

"We will not talk about the many individual things that sow love and devotion between a married couple, except to say that joint work and shared household responsibilities are essential for creating love. Our seminars are not about this.

"When the couple differs on major issues, they must return to what they agreed on in their marriage contract to get out of the problem without one team scoring points over the other team. These points can hurt like wounds and cause discomfort to dignity."

Another male student asked, **"What are the major issues?"**

Mustafa saw that Dr. Omar wanted to answer, so he transferred the question to him.

Dr. Omar began, "They are the issues where the solution should be ready when there is a conflict. They are restricted to divorce and its effect on the dowry, alimony, and care of the children. For the couple not to get tangled up in disputes, and to avoid the spite that increases when one triumphs and the other is defeated, there must be a agreement based on simplicity and practicality. For example, when the woman lays down a condition of a high dowry before marriage and the man accepts, his acceptance should be supported by a competent mind that agreed to the condition after studying his capability to implement it. The man should study the possibility of divorce first, then agree to the dowry with conditions for the way to pay the dowry. If he can pay it, he should not delay in giving her this right. If he is unable to pay it in one installment, she should be considerate of his circumstances in the method of payment for him to be able to fulfill his promise.

"We now come to the children after divorce. There should be agreements linked to the children's future – the responsibility of raising them, the amount of the allowance for their support, the school they will attend, the father's visits if they are in their mother's custody or vice versa, and the environment that will be provided for them after divorce. The existence and nature of these agreements and their details will have a big impact on the children's lives. They will be spared being overwhelmed by the anxiety that comes from hearing the parental quarrels that usually occur in divorce. The greatest losers in these fights are the children. For them to keep their identities in the future, there must be agreements before marriage – in case of divorce later – for them to live in a safe and correct environment along Allah's rightful path of light. Otherwise, the impact of divorce on one or more of the children might be catastrophic. They might take the wrong paths that lead to the eventual destruction of their lives. The importance of this cannot be overemphasized.

"Our enthusiasm for agreements springs from the fact that the husband will have all the winning cards if the woman does not have the capability of acquiring similar winning cards. These will help her under certain circumstances, such as if he throws her and her children out of the house, and her parents are unable to take on her or the children's responsibilities. Such issues should be agreed on before marriage. Is the house for the husband or the wife? Is the husband supposed to find accommodation for the wife right after the divorce, or does she share the house with him because the house may be owned by both? The house in this case would be split up according to the lawful way, or the dowry may suffice.

"These are the issues that no one cares about, not even a little, until it is too late. Yet, they should be at the top of our priorities. Has society, the parents, the school, or the people who give advice been able to make our youth understand that circumstances and situations change and divorce may occur, so that, when married couples encounter problems, they face the new circumstances with responsibility, humanity, and good ethics?"

Dr. Afaf wished to comment on Dr. Omar's remarks. She said, "To carry on from where Dr. Omar left off, I will go back to and answer the rest of the previous question about the amount of understanding young men and women have of these matters.

"I think that young men and women do not have different level of awareness on these matters. The adoration and love that one has for the other can blind them from the beginning. Also, most of them lack the necessary experience in marriage and its problems to set down the arrangements and conditions at the start of the journey. Here, the roles of the parents, society, and law courts are significant in clarifying marital affairs and all the problems that may arise. At a time when the two sides enter the stage of lawful acquaintance, experienced people should be by their sides to explain what is concealed from them and what they should know. These elders may know more about the problems of life or may themselves have experienced or witnessed divorce, and deeply understood the wrong initial steps and wrong results. They can advise the young couple while they are still in *feeqah* and *meeqah* – when they are planning their future in the early stages of happiness and acquaintance – to help them lay down the agreements that would offer realistic and practical solutions should they have problems or disputes.

"The responsibility of this is a collective responsibility that obliges us to care for our children, who are still vulnerable and have not experienced life deeply. We must guide them to the right path for alleviating their problems, and even offer solutions to the problems they may face in the future. In this way, they will have immunity that removes them from battle with the least loss.

"Our duty obliges us to bear responsibility in all this – the mother with her daughter, the father with his son, the religious scholar with his society, and the judge with himself during the writing of the marriage contract, when he should ask the couple about any omitted agreements in case disputes occur.

"We, along with the young men and women themselves, know that for every three or four marriages, one divorce takes place. So, why should not my daughter or son, or you or me, be among one of the divorced?

"We leave our homes every day and are certain that an accident will take place somewhere. Who can guarantee that one of us will not be the victim?

"We have life insurance, so why cannot we create 'marriage insurance'? We can, but it can be accomplished only through premarital agreements."

Nasser saw an opportunity to contribute. "Laying down conditions is not a major factor in preventing disputes between married people, but it can certainly diminish the problems that often occur after their separation. In addition to what Dr. Omar and Dr. Afaf have said, there are three fundamental points on the issue of agreements and conditions.

"First, if agreement on conditions occurs before marriage, then executing them will often be fair and logical for both parties – if they observe them. Once, they were two loving people, but, after divorce, they are likely to be overtaken by enmity. The outcome often depends on who can hurt the other more or destroy the other's life more, or take more. In the end, there is no winner and two losers.

Laying down conditions comes from the fear of one becoming unjust to the other after divorce, something that is highly likely.

"Second, the reasons for divorce should not be trivial or silly. Agreements serve as a barrier to divorce, as each party would know in advance what he or she would endure after divorce.

"Third, if divorce occurs, and assuming that conditions and agreements exist and the two parties are humane, moral, and observant of their religious duties, then they shall be able to solve their problems face to face, without the kind of complications or problems that require lawyers and courts to solve.

* * * * *

## Fate and Multiplicity

One male student stood and said, **"Some people say marriage is *qismaw wa naseeb* [an outcome of fate]. Where does choosing the other party come into it?**

Nasser seemed ready to answer any question. He said quickly, "Personally, I do not believe in fate in marriage. Marriage is a matter of facts, planning, and circumstances that make us go ahead or not. Our choice will be right or wrong, and we achieve this by our own will. People before marriage do not care about *qismaw wa naseeb*. After marriage they say it, whether the marriage is succeeding or failing. Before marriage, no one acts like this is a consideration, since, with the margin of choice – whether narrow or wide – the boy and the girl can choose, and no one talks about fate. Even those who believe in it do not sit at home waiting for fate to arrive. They look, reject, and finally approve someone that one, albeit without searching deeply. If we accept the principle of *qismaw wa naseeb,* then we accept being compelled and not free. This also implies we are not responsible for our choices and actions. Believing this is the opposite of reality.

"The will of Allah in blessing a person in his marriage is absolutely undeniable. This is part of Allah's knowledge that one may or may not get. The matter of fate will then be the positive opportunity that we call luck, which is pure choice if he or she succeeds in utilizing the opportunity given by fate in a positive direction. If a person is rich, his wealth is not separated from the means he used to change his circumstances from poverty to wealth. If he had not used the means, some of which are effort and hard work, he would have stayed poor and not found his way to wealth. Therefore, choosing and specifying the target are what led him to achieve his wish. It is the same in marriage.

"Even with a belief in fate, humans practice freedom of choice because they try to make changes. A man can make a change if he discovers a woman is unsuitable for marriage. A woman can, if she discovers unsuitability soon after marriage, postpone producing children. By this action, she may guarantee her freedom and get out of the marriage by divorce with the least loss. It is incorrect to view *qismaw wa naseeb* as a state we cannot get out of. Allah says, **Verily, never will Allah change the condition of a people until they change it themselves [with their own souls], 13:11** This means: change yourself so that you change your situation."

A male student now asked Dr. Afaf, **"Your colleague talked earlier about differentiating between true love and suspicious love. The girl was cautioned that a boy's love might be unhealthy and clouded by suspicion. He shows love and protective jealousy, but he is really suspicious within. How may the girl discover that?"**

Dr. Afaf replied, "We do not mean all young men are suspicious, but this mentality does affect some people of both sexes. Here, we are more concerned with male suspicion because of the greater power males have in our society. A man's suspicion may harm a woman more than her suspicion may harm him. As an example, let us assume the boy is the jealous one and the girl needs to differentiate between true love and suspicious love. In this case, she is the only one who can judge. It is enough for us to warn her and she can, with her awareness and capabilities, know whether or not the boy's strong interest in her comes from healthy love. One sign of a suspicious mind is that the boy is often checking up on her. A second is that he accuses her wrongfully of not being truthful. A third is that he speaks of distrusting many other people. If this forms a pattern, the boy is 'bad news.' If he has made one small mistake, his basic nature may not be suspicious.

"Allah has given women powers that enable them to discover that, due to the interconnections between the right and left parts of the brain in women more than in men, and they have the ability to use the two parts of the brain more than men. Therefore, 'they are generally better than men at knowing the emotional differences in voices, moves, and facial expressions.' [107]

"We, as a team, do not claim to have all the knowledge in such matters and their intricate details. You have the knowledge. You alone have the ability to differentiate between true love and suspicious love as it concerns you personally. The matter is in your hands. Our care for you and your future life makes us try to open the correct road in front of you to prevent you from stumbling into difficult terrain.

"Our warning in this matter is for a purpose. If suspicion enters in *feeqah,* how will it affect the relationship in *meeqah* and beyond? The girl may hold dear her freedom and set out to benefit from life. She may proceed from goals she has given herself, whether it is education, career, or friendships. The boy, however, may show suspicion of her actions and want to limit her freedom. What would her future situation be, after this boy becomes her life partner? If the girl wishes to give up her rights and believes she can live with a suspicious person who wants her under constant observation, this is up to her and no one will object to her stance. However, if she fears that she may not be able to tolerate his suspicion or get along with this mentality, we advise her from the start to make her position clear so that she does not come to regret it. Maybe she can tolerate suspicion in *feeqah* and *meeqah*, but how would the situation be after giving birth to four children?

"If there is a problem, it is up to you to deal with it."

One guest stood and said, **"You talked about gradualness in the relationship between the young man and woman in *feeqah* and *meeqah*. You also say multiple approaches are allowed, one following another. How do you explain this multiplicity?"**

Dr. Omar, "Our system stands for gradualness and multiplicity. In gradualness, the boy or girl discovers positive and negative points in the other, but there may be difficulty in making a choice because if there is no comparison. We say everything is relative. How good or how bad are these positive or negative points compared with those of another person? Also, the discovery is not complete and

---

[107] Anne Moir and David Jessel, *Brain Sex: the Real Difference between Men and Women* [*Jins Ad-Deemagh*], Trans. Badr Al-Munayyis (New York: Carol Publishing,1991) 73.

has some gaps. Here, hesitation in accepting or rejecting occurs. All the positives present in a person cannot be known completely, especially when the relationship is between one boy and one girl and so the knowledge is limited to a narrow margin. Therefore, we see the need for multiplicity with gradualness: the boy gets to know more than one girl and she gets to know more than one boy. This is accompanied by study, analysis, and comparison of several possible future partners. The choice is then made with more clarity and in the context of reality.

"In gradualness, one party may find likable merits, but they may be minor not major ones. Some positive merits may not be clear even though they are fundamental in marriage, while desire and love prevent a correct vision. He or she may make a bad choice. This is due normally to the lack of experience of that boys and girls have of each other. Lack of experience may fool the two parties. They may assume that the merits in the other party are found in the entire gender or that only this other party has this wonderful merit. As for multiplicity, we discover positive points and psychological, moral, and aesthetic merits that we do not find in those who we had thought were suitable.

"Based on this, we prefer freedom of multiplicity, but we also believe entering all stages gradually is even more important than having multiple relationships. If we cannot have both, we would choose gradualness over multiplicity.

"We do not mean multiplicity in sexual relationships, but multiplicity in getting acquainted with others within the framework of religion and morals. There should be no new relationship before leaving the first one. This must be understood so that no one thinks the girl in particular is allowed to know, within the religious framework, more than one boy at the same time.

"It is not us who decide the number of people whom the boy or girl may get to know. This is subject to each person's circumstances. You should decide on the number of people you get to know. Generally, we support the idea that a boy or girl should get acquainted with two or three others during their search and discovery process so as to choose the most suitable person for the future wife or husband. Because boys are bolder in trying to know young girls, within the religious framework, the girl will know through his actions if he has a relationship with another girl. If she wants to accept this, she is free to do so.

"It is lawful, though it may be impractical, for a boy to have several *feeqah* and *meeqah* agreements at the same time. However, if he has an exclusive contract with a particular girl and he is violating this condition, then he has broken the contract. When the girl discovers he is cheating and lying, she may ask him for early termination of the contract.

"We warn every girl not to fall into the net of the first boy she is introduced to, believing rightly or wrongly that he is suitable and that no one matches his morals, character, and knowledge. Many girls fall into this incorrect belief because, at the start of their dating life, they assume their knowledge of the boy is enough and there is no need to meet others. But, as life goes on, with its complexities and changing hopes and ambitions, we may regret having had only one acquaintance when we maybe could have found a more suitable person, one who would have assisted more with our life's endeavors and offered us more security.

"There are needs and essentials we discover after marriage, but what stops us from knowing these needs before getting married – especially if society believes we have the freedom to know people, through gradualness and multiplicity, and therefore we advise you to grasp multiplicity, provided that it falls within the Islamically allowable arena of intermixing that occurs before *feeqah* or during *feeqah* or *meeqah*. You will then discover merits that you failed to notice when acquaintance is limited to one person only.

"Encouraging multiplicity in acquaintance does not mean abandoning the first person for the second or the third person that we became acquainted with, even if we did not find in them the merits we were seeking. We can go back to the first one, if he or she is still available, because he or she may be seen as more suitable after we have had experience with others.

"Moving from one relationship to another does not necessarily mean severing the first or second relationship, which was for the aim of marriage. The boy and girl may continue to be a sibling to each other, even if they were unsuitable as lifelong partners in marriage. Humanistic links and bonds that gather people together based on love, respect, and appreciation should be preserved. We hope our relationships remain untainted by selfishness and desires originating from selfish thinking, which makes people constantly want profit and benefits from other persons, even if this contradicts all other values.

"This is what the Islamic *Shari'ah* has emphasized – in permanent marriage, and when separation and divorce occur. The *Qur'an* has laid down an exalted moral approach that may be summarized by **...or separate with kindness, 2:229**. This is after a relationship between the couple may have lasted many years with its shared experiences, challenges, and children. Double kindness may therefore apply when ending a relationship where the two parties have specified when it will be over and where children, problems, or disputes are not involved.

"It is highly moral to leave a relationship, in which we have specified when it ends, as brothers. I wish we could reach the level of transparency and truthfulness in our relationships in which each one of us gives up his or her selfishness and does not say to the other, 'you are an unsuitable spouse for me,' but rather, 'I am an unsuitable spouse for you.' This represents higher morals, more humility, and more consideration for the other person's feelings.

"Morals are essential to the extent that they are the basis of society's straightforwardness, and their absence destroys society and leads people to live sin a jungle. Morals are the noblest elements in the universe. This is why the Messenger of Allah (pbuh) said, **I was sent only to complete the best of morals.**"

A male student remarked: **"Gradualness and multiplicity allow a girl to go through many experiences with the aim of marriage before she settles on one person. However, boys reject marrying a girl who has had experiences with other boys."**

Nasser replied, "We are an Eastern society. Much that we reject or accept is not governed by fixed religious parameters, but by customs and traditions that the Eastern mentality created due to circumstances and formed over the years and through many generations till it came down to us and became embedded in our minds as fixed concepts and facts that we cannot pass over or reject.

"We need time for it to become clear to the generations that these traditions do not represent anything on a religious level. We have much hope because aware and knowledgeable people in past generations rejected many traditions that no longer fit their way of life. When we present our ideas, we are betting that the present generation of aware and intellectual youth will, through their religion and knowledge, begin to improve the current reality.

"If we want to follow the mentality represented by the student's remark, we would say the divorced woman, even if she has not given birth to children, is not sought after by men, so what about the divorcée who has four children? Does any blemish – on an Islamic level – stick to the woman because of her divorce? Of course not! Does Islam accept that we reject marriage to a widowed woman when the Messenger of Allah (pbuh), the Imams, and the Prophet's companions have married widows and divorcées? There was nothing wrong with that at all, for the Messenger of Allah (pbuh) is above blemish or shortcoming.

"Divorce or widowhood does not stain women. Nonetheless, some people in our society look down on them. Whoever wants to marry a divorcée or a widow faces huge resistance and rejection, especially from a young man's family. Is this accepted by religion, reason, or logic? Do we accept it? Allah says one thing and some of us say another. How distant is what we say from what Allah says!

"The girl who has had Islamically allowed experiences, and known a past romance with someone other than you, will give you a stronger and richer romance than the girl who has not. Whoever experiences love knows love, just as whoever experiences generosity knows the nature of generosity. Eastern women have a firm nature and generally believe that love should not be given except to their husbands. They may be naïve or may be perceived to be naïve in how to offer love and sex to a man. Therefore, Eastern men sometimes marry Western women who have had sexual experience – even though they have religious reservations about how she got that experience. Some Eastern men are attracted to foreign women because they believe these women understand passion and can better satisfy a man's desires.

"There are illnesses ravaging our society. They are the reason for its backwardness and isolation, and for the killing of the spirit of ambition and innovation within it. If we do not treat these illnesses with potent remedies, they will continue to be a killer and we shall continue to see correct things upside down.

"What is the objection to a girl searching on her own for her life partner, while holding on to her religion, upbringing, and gracious morals? Let our women see Khadija and take her example. She searched for the most honorable person on earth to be her husband and found the Messenger of Allah (pbuh).

"Let us move away from social hypocrisy. Why does the boy accept this for himself and reject it for his sister? It is typical selfishness that we men find wide areas for ourselves to choose and search for whom we think might become our life partner, but we refuse this right for the same life partner!

"All people are the same in Allah's appraisal. Men and women's responsibilities are the same toward Allah. Some of us say this is a male society, but this is a rejected theory. Society is one with all its people, men and women, even if roles are different and every member, man or woman, fulfills a role conforming to their creation.

"Social hypocrisy is an illness. No magic recipe can wipe it out of our lives. The only solution that can rip the illness out of our souls and minds is to make *Shari'ah* the arbiter in our life: accept what Allah accepts and reject what Allah rejects.

"Our hope is in our young men and women, and in future generations. We hope their minds start to get inspiration from Islam as a system for living. We have to plant the good seed in the earth so it shall rise one day toward the sky, and ask for its help. Look at the Muslim woman in past times and look at her today. Today she approaches life in all its breadth to get, alongside men, the most important scientific, cultural, and social positions."

* * * * *

## Exploring the Negatives

A university teacher who had listened intently to the discussion raised a question of general importance. **"When we look into the details of your system, we recognize a strong insistence and extreme desire to change some features that have become firmly embedded in the mentality regarding the man-woman relationship. This insistence and desire are based on clear Islamic foundations. However, new thinking cannot change,**

**certainly not quickly, the ideas, customs, and traditions that have become firmly embedded in the mind. How are we going to deal with this problem?"**

Nasser answered, "The problem is not the thoughts and concepts that society has become used to or not used to. We believe in original thinking. However much society tries to lock it up, one day its dawn will come and it will spread. No one will be able to stop it. At the heart of the matter is changing people, who, by nature and by accustomization to social or conceptual norms, are controlled by habit. They fear breaking free of it and breaking the social and educational systems that have become part of their personalities and beings. All that is new and different from what has become firmly established in their minds will be rejected immediately, especially if they have not analyzed or discussed a new concept or system. If they are accustomed to walking on a certain road and we show them a new road, even if it is an easier one, they will hesitate and fear traveling on that road. Ignorance and fear of new things make people reject them. Imam Ali Ibn Abi Talib said, **Man is an enemy of what he is ignorant of.**

"This applies to *feeqah, meeqah*. As a whole, they are not new at all because they come from *Shari'ah*. What is new is the approach in defining the allowable relationship between the man and woman and pointing out the woman's rights.

"When we face this great number of questions about our system, we understand the natural position of the questioners. It comes from a fear of the results and how to control them. Because they do not know the positive and negative points that would result from implementing this system, and the horizon – wide or narrow – that governs this implementation, fear of the unknown molds the rejection of this system.

"This is natural because rejecting change comes from not being sure of one's ability to control the results and direct them along the road they should take. We often think of change as having unknown results and distance ourselves from accepting it out of caution. We imagine falling into dilemmas we do not want to fall into, and falsely think we would have no power to get out of them.

"We do not suggest accepting any new thing without analyzing it closely or accepting it without expecting clear results. We invite everyone to study our steps, strategies, and probable outcomes. We encourage an open and aware mentality that does not accept an idea in a foggy way, not knowing whether it is in their interest or will benefit everyone. Entering into a new arena without planning is illogical, and Allah may not accept it. If someone objects, saying society does not accept the idea of the system for fear of wrong implementation by some people, we say: we have established that the system is good and that it provides a big opportunity for young men and women to know what they are doing when they enter into permanent marriage.

"There are deviant men who, with their wrong actions and desire to fool young women, may tarnish the system and delay society's acceptance of it. We ask: does the presence of some bad people in our society make us reject good ideas? Do wrong implementations of a system mean we have to cancel it? This is unreasonable. I do not think any of you accept it. What we should do is to cancel the role of the bad people in society, and keep the good idea and strive to firmly establish it. If we accept the illogic, we must cancel permanent marriage because certain individuals, with their wrong actions, do not rise up to the sanctity of permanent marriage. Does anyone follow this thinking? I do not think anyone in this hall would. Listen to what God says: **...and you were on the brink of the pit of Fire and He saved you from it, 3:103** He saved them with what? He rescued them with the Messenger of Allah and the Message of Islam. They were going astray and deviant and He sent the Message to show them how to stay on the path of correctness and truth. Allah did not wait for them to become good people before sending Islam to them. If He had done that, they would not have stayed on the brink of Fire. They would have fallen in!

"Our system's release to society has been long delayed. The delay of its realization has opened the door for many people to pursue adultery and other sins. Therefore, society must fight these negatives by accepting our idea and living its benefits and positiveness.

"Because our system is new in its approach and method, we try to study in advance of implementation all the negatives that may result. A probability remains that some negatives may still occur."

A member of the audience asked, **"Then, you admit your system has negatives?"**

Nasser answered, "There are no negatives in the basics of the system. Some people may not apply all the features of this system and may not realize its Islamic dimensions, foundations, or starting points so bad implementation may occur. This is not the system's fault, but the fault of those who implement the system in the wrong way. They alone should bear the responsibility toward Allah and society. We can reduce these negatives when implementing the system if scholars, society, and the officials fulfill their role in clarifying its foundations and methods and in specifying its goals, and also in firmly establishing its culture and concepts in minds and souls. With this, we guarantee minimizing the probability of errors and negatives.

"Whether we like it or not, some negative things will happen for various reasons, some deriving from the system's absence of clarity for some people. This is their responsibility, not the system's. Some other people lacking morality and Islamic constraints may be unjust in implementing it or may abuse certain situations that were not expected by the other party. This is where society plays a role in preventing such negatives from happening – by clarifying the Islamic visions of the system, by applying the constraints and fixed features that ensure the relationship between the man and woman is based on clarity, and by warning that fooling one another or engaging in any such behavior may destroy the relationship, may make it a hostage to selfishness or to the control of one party, or may destroy a person's reputation.

"Our detailed study of this system allowed us to talk in detail about the negatives and to define solutions that we presented on this stage. We hope on behalf of all scholars, researchers, and parents that, when this system is implemented and negatives occur, they will put every effort in presenting their ideas and opinions to address these negatives, especially as they will involve the non-fixed aspects, such as the contract, as well as what is allowed and forbidden. The negatives will be about ethics and will not affect the fixed aspects of *feeqah* and *meeqah*.

"The fear of change is natural and to be expected. We respect the fear of the fearful people. At the same time, we say: change is essential. In these seminars we have tried, with you, to arrive at common visions that make logical and acceptable the change in the way to enter into marriage."

A male student asked, **"Why present this particular system? Why not search for another system?"**

Nasser said, "Search. You are free to search for a better system if you can find one, but your search should be based on Islamic precepts taken from the *Qur'an* and the *Sunnah*, not from a secular logic or any logic that contradicts Islam or is unacceptable for the Islamic reality. Search, and this is what we want, and our emphasis on our system does not deprive you of your right to search. We have searched much in various social systems, materialistic and secular, but could find nothing better than the system of Islam. This is not simply a partisan stance, though we are honored to be Muslims. This is reality."

* * * * *

## Benefiting Non-Muslims

A male student who had silently attended all the seminars now stood for the first time and announced, **"I am Christian and respect what you have presented in your social system taken from *Shari'ah*. I have listened carefully to all your explanations. What most held my attention was your statement in the first seminar that your system will benefit non-Muslims. I have been waiting patiently to hear about this benefit, but have so far heard nothing of what you have promised. I hope now to hear about this benefit."**

Mustafa asked Nasser to continue speaking. Nasser said, "I apologize on behalf of the team for delaying mentioning of this. Even if the honorable student had not spoken, it was not absent from our minds. We were merely waiting for the opportunity to talk about it.

"The features of our system come from Islam, and from moral, educational, and humanistic concepts that do not contradict Islam. Muslims, because of their religious beliefs, will benefit most from our system. This does not stop anyone who follows other religions from benefiting from it too. Our system concentrates on concepts that interest and concern everyone. These concepts are morals, acquaintance, gradualness, constraints, and limits in the relationships between people. Of utmost importance is specifying time periods for the stages of these relationships. These concepts are all universal and not restricted to any religion.

"Muslims and Christians may benefit and so may anyone else who follows another religion and who wants to implement these concepts, if he or she adheres to them and lives by them. The Christian, when he wants to marry, is free to be guided by the features of his own religion, but very little in our system contradicts his religion. He may concur with the Muslim on the matter of gradualness in romantic and social relationships and in identifying his choices. Gradualness is logical in any relationship, and continuing it or severing it is subject to the common or different convictions of the two parties. The same applies to conditions: the Christian puts conditions on his relationship with the other person that conform to his religious beliefs, just as the Muslim makes conditions that do not contradict his religion's fixed ideas. It is likewise for constraints and morals – they are general principles for which Christians consult Christianity and Muslims consult Islam. Living up to promises, not hurting the dignity of the other party, and liking for the other what you like for yourself are principles accepted by all religions. If people followed these principles, they would relieve much stress and avoid much disturbance that usually occur between couples and later within families.

"As in *Shari'ah*, the contract, right to sexual pleasure, inheritance, financial maintenance, and other marital duties are also defined in Christianity. We conclude that followers of Christianity should specify a system of gradualness in their relationships before committing to marriage, and should find wording as in *feeqah* and *meeqah*. This would be better for them than the current system of knowing each other, which is chaotic and not based on fixed religious concepts. We find especially in the West, where, during the last 40 to 60 years, the restraints have been lost and features of relationships have become unclear. This is what completely separates Western customs from our society's current practices or from our future system presented at these seminars. If we wanted to discuss this, we would find a clear difference in how women are viewed.

"The relationship in the West is not governed by laws or frameworks or limits. On many occasions, it has no readily definable features. We can use clothing as an example. Muslims think the *hijab* for women is an Islamic system that defines exactly what it allows women to uncover. We are not discussing this subject here, but just let me say the aim of this is to preserve the value of woman – and it is a system (like ISO) for society for now and the future, a system that defines for men too limitations regarding dress. Our vision contradicts completely the Westerner's impression that the *hijab* limits the freedom of women and reduces their value. If we follow this thinking, we might ask: if the *hijab* reduces the value of women, what is the system in the West? What are the characteristics of dress for Western women and how does it preserve their value and dignity?

"This question has no answer because of the confusion resulting from lack of a system. The proof of this is that women in the West wear what they like when they like. In Miami, USA, for example, women have freedom to walk in the streets wearing swimsuits, even to enter restaurants wearing only bikinis. The same woman, if dressed that way outdoors in New York City, will be violating the law and will be prevented from doing so. Another woman during an evening occasion may wear a dress that exposes her breasts and back. All those present view that dress as normal and see no harm in wearing it. The next day, if the same woman wears the same dress to her workplace, the same people who were present the night before will without doubt object to the dress. Some of them will even suggest that the woman does not respect herself or her place of work and her co-workers. It is puzzling that a woman is decent at night but not during the day! How they dress and behave depends on the time, on the location, and, if there is a party, on the rules set by the host. Where therefore is the system in the West? Such flexibility is not a system.

"When we believe in a system, we believe it can be suitable for all times and locations. *Shari'ah* is a Divine law that did not come down for a specific time, for night and not day, or a specific location, for one town and not another. It is suitable for our women past, present, and future, and this is what the West lacks.

"At the same time that the West calls for firmly establishing the ISO system in institutions, factories, and governmental and private companies, it does not call for establishing a system in social and acquaintance relationships. Why is there this contradiction?

"Our system builds its social relationships on a type of ISO. The person knows how to enter into relationships and when and how to leave them, and what are the consequences, laws, guidelines, responsibilities, duties, and rights. And like the ISO, some features are changeable and some not. Through these features, the person knows how to place his steps on the road."

A female stood. **"I too am Christian,"** she said. **"Other than promoting more conformity in attire, which I am not sure I agree with, it is still unclear to me how we non-Muslims can really benefit from your system. Can you be more specific regarding dating between men and women?"**

Dr. Afaf indicated she wanted to respond. "Certainly. We sense unease and anxiety in the early stages of acquaintance among non-Musiims because of this lack of a system. When a boy asks a girl or a girl asks a boy for company at a social occasion – be it a party, a ballgame, a museum, a movie, lunch, or dinner – the asking party's motive is unclear. Is it *feeqah, meeqah,* or *seeqah*? No one knows, maybe even including the asking party. You do not completely understand what to wear, how to prepare for the occasion, or what to expect. Sometimes you make a mistake – say the wrong thing or act the wrong way – and are embarrassed.

"With our system, the boundaries are clear. Therefore, there should be no confusion and consequently little or no anxiety at the starting of a relationship. Further, we advocate always starting with *feeqah* to allow people to get acquainted gradually before moving to a more serious relationship. Many non-Muslims, especially in the West, start their dating relationships with *seeqah*. They get sexually and emotionally involved too soon and cannot see the other person clearly. Many marry because the sex is good while being blinded to their incompatibility in other crucial ways. The high divorce rate in the West is partly based on this."

The same student said, **"It also sounds like Westerners have leaped far ahead of us. Is this true?"**

Nasser leaned toward the microphone and answered, "Not at all. Rushing ahead to a higher stage of acquaintance is not what The Leap means. The Leap is about morality and about the Muslim's need to recognize the difference between *Shari'ah* and traditions or customs. Once this difference is recognized, a lawful system can be developed for allowing people to get acquainted before marriage. Presenting such a lawful system to you is what we have done.

"Now let me amplify on Dr. Afaf's last statement. First, let us not overlook The Leap of morality, which every well-intentioned person may benefit from no matter where they live or what religion they practice. I attended university in the West and remain in touch with the friends I made during that time. The stories they have told me of their dating experiences, and these days of their children's dating experiences, are sometimes hair-raising. Many people in the West have lost their courtesy and respect for each other and simply do not know how to behave on a date, whether the date is proving successful or not. A person in the West may even start the evening on a date with one person, sneak away, and come home with someone else! Ending relationships in the West, whether after short-term dating or long-term marriage, more often than not occurs without kindness. Also, dating begins too early in the West, both with and without parental knowledge, and the result is often pregnancy among single girls who are only from 13 to 16 years old. Some of them travel the road of abortion, some give birth and keep the baby, and some offer the child for adoption. In many respects, there is chaos in the West and within this chaos, someone often gets hurt.

"You cannot tell me that non-Muslims, whether in the West or the East, would not benefit from a system that, first, promotes behavior based on a morality that teaches people how to respect each other and put long-term decency above short-term pleasure and that, second, promotes using gradualness, responsibility, and awareness as tools for making the most important decision of your life: choosing a marriage partner.

"In the past, Westerners had stages of acquaintance leading to permanent marriage that they called dating, going steady, and engagement and these correlated loosely to *feeqah, meeqah,* and *seeqah*, respectively. These stages were usually sealed with a gift or exchange of gifts, like a brooch, bracelet, and engagement ring. This formality broke down in the late 1960's and has never returned. While there are features to admire in the West, like the legal rights of women and their ability to gain experience through multiple relationships without tarnishing their reputations, on the whole, the chaos in their dating lives does not allow many to find their most suitable lifetime partner. Sometimes, after several serious relationships or divorces, they learn and are lucky enough to meet the right person. We say it is better to make the right choice earlier in life. It spares everyone much grief, especially children who were produced during a relationship.

"Let me add that we do not seek to tamper with the good features in the West. Rather, we can learn from each other and try to apply one another's good features when they do not violate our beliefs."

One of the teachers wanted to know, **"Which specific feature of your system can non-Muslims benefit from the most?"**

Nasser continued, "There are really three that are most applicable: (1) gradualness, whose relevance Dr. Afaf just explained for reducing divorce in the West; (2) the timing; and (3) the dowry. The timing is important because it is an indication of how much interest the parties have in each other. The longer the time of the contract(s), the more it shows serious interest in each other, and the shorter the time, the more it shows doubts about their compatibility. It is also important in fostering separation with kindness. It is clear from the start – the temporary contract has an end date and one of the parties may not want renewal. Things cannot drift. A decision is required at a particular time that both parties are aware of. This allows the party not wanting to renew to simply state that and may avoid the invention of petty reasons that people use to justify a breakup or the discourtesy of 'disappearing' by, for instance, not returning phone calls. Many relationships in the West end with fights and much pain. The timing can teach people to separate with kindness and civility. As for the concept of the dowry, I believe in giving a small gift at the start of a new stage of a relationship or at the renewal of a relationship. It helps to formalize the contract and a return to some formality is what the West needs. Social chaos and anarchy are unhealthy and do not promote human happiness. Chaos can allow poor behavior to thrive and can lead to a breakdown in the respect that humans should have for each other."

A different female student now asked, **"Your system includes the terms *feeqah*, *meeqah*, and *seeqah*. What are the alternative terms for non-Arabic speakers and non-Muslims who accept the system?"**

Nasser again answered, "It is appropriate for any society that finds our system useful and wishes to implement its approach to use the same terms. The words are easy for all eyes and tongues in the world. Germans, French, Americans, and others can, just as Arabs can, read and say *feeqah*, *meeqah*, and *seeqah*. While we emphasize this, we also say that the use of other more complicated expressions, such as *sadaqah Shari'ah* [Islamically allowed friendship] or *ta'arof Shar'i* [Islamically allowed acquaintance], is for Muslims only.

"Other people do not have the same beliefs as Muslims. If this system is implemented in non-Muslim societies, even if after decades from now, we would prefer that they use our terminology. These words represent gradual stages that suit and fulfill the needs of all societies. They bring us nearer to the globalization, in its social and humanistic dimension, that everyone talks about nowadays.

"We will not be surprised if our ideas will initially appeal more and be adopted sooner by Muslims in the West than here in Lebanon."

* * * * *

## Precise Words

A female student had a question related to the marriage contract's detail and precision. She asked, **"What is the terminology of the contract, or, rather, what is its wording?"**

Seyyid Mohammed answered, saying: "The marriage contract, whether permanent or term, is subject to specific words to be said by the two parties. The mere uttering of the words of the contract makes the relationship lawful

"For the permanent contract, the woman says to the man: '*Zawwajtuka nafsee 'alaa mahrin wa miqdaaruhu* _____, *li aqrabil ajalayn.*" ['I have married myself to you at a dowry of _____ (to be paid to me) at whichever of the two times comes first.'] [108] The man says: '*Qebilt.*' ['I accept.']

"For the temporary contract of *feeqah*, the woman says: '*Zawwajtuka nafsee bishert al-feeqah 'alaa mahrin ma'loom wa miqdaaruhu __ _____ wa li muddet ma'looma miqdaaruha _____.*' ['I have married myself to you, on the condition of *feeqah,* at a known dowry of _____ for a known time of _____.'] The man says: '*Qebilt.*' ['I accept.']

"For the temporary contract of *meeqah*, the woman says: '*Zawwajtuka nafsee bishert al-meeqah 'alaa mahrin ma'loom wa miqdaaruhu*

_____ *wa li muddet ma'looma miqdaaruha* _____.'
['I have married myself to you, on the condition of *meeqah,* at a known dowry of _____ for a known time of _____.']
The man says: *'Qebilt.'* ['I accept.']

"For the temporary contract of *seeqah,* the woman says: *'Zawwajtuka nafsee 'alaa mahrin ma'loom wa miqdaaruhu* _____ *wa li muddet ma'looma miqdaaruha* _____.'* ['I have married myself to you at a known dowry of _____ for a known time of _____.'] The man says: *'Qebilt.'* ['I accept.']

"We advise that the temporary contract specify the period in days or weeks, not months, so no problems arise from the difference between *hijri* [lunar calendar] months and *meeladi* [solar calendar] months. For example, the agreement will be for 90 days or 13 weeks if the couple wishes the period of the contract to last three months."

One male student was surprised by the ease with which the contract is done. **"According to your previous explanations, the contract holds great responsibilities. Do these few words make the temporary contract Islamically legal and accepted by Allah?"**

"Yes," answered the Seyyid. "These two words also make the permanent marriage Islamically legal and accepted by Allah. Just as entering permanent marriage, with its big responsibilities, duties, and rights, occurs easily with these words, entering temporary marriage is easy too, but its responsibilities are also big."

The voice of a male student rang out sharply, **"Do you accept the responsibility of all this toward Allah when you make it allowed for young men and women to make marriage contracts so simply?"**

This time Dr. Omar answered, "I ask the brother with that question: after the judge [register official] in the court carries out the contract between the couple, will he be responsible if the man later does an injustice to his wife? Will the judge be responsible if the woman is unfaithful to her husband? Will the judge be responsible for their failure to raise their children properly or their failure to meet their familial duties in general? Will the couple's parents, after carrying

---

[108] The "two times" mean divorce or death.

244

out the contract, be responsible for problems that arise in the marital relationship? I reply with one word: No!

"The same goes for the temporary contracts proposed within our system. The couple who does or does not abide by the terms of the contract or meet their obligations regarding their promises and covenants, and regarding what Allah has made allowed and what He has prohibited, should themselves bear the responsibility – and absolutely no one else.

"For having clarified that these temporary contracts are Islamically allowed because we are not presenting anything that is not clear and explicit in *Shari'ah*, we say, yes, we are responsible for that – yes, I and my four colleagues bear full responsibility toward Allah."

* * * * *

# CHAPTER SIX
## The End of the Last Seminar

* * * * *

### Nasser's Review

A male student stood during Dr. Omar's last answer. He looked like he had a comment or wanted to ask a question. Mustafa politely apologized to him and added, "The time is almost up and the university examinations are approaching. We must begin the ending of this, our last seminar. First, we will have a summation. Then, I have written questions from the audience that were handed to me during today's discussion. They relate to the details of temporary marriage and must be answered. Finally, each lecturer has a few words about the system we have presented. I apologize and announce the end of discussion."

Mustafa now wished Nasser to give a brief account of the philosophy of the system and how to enter into it. In response to Mustafa's request, Nasser said: "We have elaborated on our system during the last two lengthy seminars. Despite that, we have not given the subject the attention it deserves. Our system is taken from the Islamic schools of thought, meaning from Islam itself and nothing other than Islam. We presented it to you in response to a fundamental need in our life. We had found the way through which people were entering into the world of marriage lacked a system to help them build a happy, healthy family.

"This system, with its main feature of gradualness, makes a realistic assumption that a young man and woman want to know each other before getting married. It is natural that they disclose their wish of acquaintance to each other – something that normally occurs when they meet. This meeting should not be one of *khalwah* [unmarried man and woman being alone] and should be without forbidden things. This first stage of getting acquainted does not oblige them to be two parties to a contract as long as their meeting is governed by the elements of decency and morality.

"When they find out for themselves that they want to know each other more comprehensively, this will certainly call for private meetings. They will feel the need to do so away from the eyes of the people, and they might get alone in a *khalwah*. Their agreement on being alone together means the two desire to reveal some of their feelings. These desires must be expressed within an Islamically acceptable atmosphere – and the Islamically acceptable, as we emphasize and insist on, is the system that governs such tendencies and deeds. There must be a contract that provides these meetings, or this *khalwah*, with *Shari'ah* lawfulness. The contract will then be a kind of framework for the relationship when emotion starts to surface.

"This is stage of the contract known as *feeqah*. This first *feeqah* contract in the getting-acquainted stage should be for a short time. The young couple may at the beginning make this contract for a week, for instance, and then renew the contract for the same *feeqah* stage for a longer time, according to their circumstances and to how they are getting along. They may also decide to stop furthering this experience at this stage permanently or perhaps considering resuming the acquaintance if other opportunities arise in the future.

"The same is true for the *meeqah* stage. The couple should not insist that it lasts for two years immediately. Make it for a shorter period, as was done in *feeqah*, then renew the contract within this stage several times. This is because getting along well in *feeqah* is no guarantee that the couple will get along well in *meeqah*.

"This advice is directed in particular toward girls, who may wrongly think a contract for a longer time will give them more emotional security in their relationship and will give them more value as persons. This is false because, even if the girl gave herself to the boy for a long period, what will guarantee that his proper treatment of her and his exchange of feelings will last for a long time? Girls may also think it not worth committing their emotions to a short period, but this is an error. The relationship is not connected to emotions alone, for the contract comes with responsibilities. Emotions have no given time span. They start and end at a certain time not connected to contracts, but responsibilities are subject to the timing of the contract. In this contract, the girl commits herself to certain responsibilities – and so does the boy – more than to the emotional engagement. In light of this, our system is governed by gradualness in all the aspects of the relationship between two people: in time, emotions, commitments, and promises.

"So, the couple meets, they are alone together, their emotions are moved, they want to have an Islamically allowable relationship, and they are convinced of the need for gradualness and for multiple short relationships in every stage so as to best study and choose. Under such circumstances, a contract becomes a must.

"For the contract, the girl says: '*Zawwajtuka nafsee bishert al-feeqah 'alaa mahrin ma'loom wa miqdaaruhu_____ wa li muddet ma'looma miqdaaruha _____.*' ['I have married myself to you, on the condition of *feeqah,* at a known dowry of _____ for a known time period of _____.'] The boy says: '*Qebilt.*' ['I accept.'] The dowry and the time period are what they have agreed on, with their knowledge of the limits of *feeqah.*

"After their relationship develops more and becomes deeper, they may enter into the second contract stage called '*meeqah.*' If the time period of the contract for *feeqah* has ended, they renew the contract, agreeing on the dowry and time period, but under the conditions of *meeqah*, the limits and dimensions of which you know. As for *seeqah*, we recommend it to divorcées and widows.

"There are fundamental details, one of which is that, because the girl is usually naturally shy, she may appoint the boy as proxy to carry out the contract on her behalf. After agreeing on the dowry, the time period, and the type of relationship (*feeqah* or *meeqah*) and after making an appointment for the ceremony, she gives him the right to be her proxy and he says: '*Zawwajtu muwakkilatee li nafsee 'alaa mahrin ma'loom miqdaaruhu _____ wa li muddet ma'looma miqdaaruha _____ bishert al-feeqah or al-meeqah.*' ['I have married my proxy to me, on the condition of *feeqah* or *meeqah*, at a

known dowry of _____ for a known time period of _____
____.'] Then he adds: '*Qebilt.*' ['I accept.')

"If the proxy changes the agreed-on conditions during the uttering of the words of the contract, the contract becomes void – unless the girl wants to accept the changes, and then the contract is valid.

"Because we strive for transparency and clarity in the contract, the girl should insist on conditions suitable for her during her appointments with the boy. She should not give the boy the freedom to choose the time period, dowry, or nature of the relationship, meaning *feeqah* or *meeqah*. The concern is that the boy might be unfair and impose conditions that best suit only himself.

"At the same time, the boy must understand that he should not try to take advantage in any way. Whatever he may gain temporarily, he would lose in the long run. When fairness is practiced, in the long run, both parties benefit."

* * * * *

## Final Questions and Answers

While Nasser had been talking, Mustafa handed the papers with the audience's questions to Seyyid Mohammed. The Seyyid read the questions to himself and organized them by importance. When Nasser had finished speaking, the Seyyid read each aloud and answered them one by one.

"Question 1. **Is it allowed, while in *feeqah*, to go into *meeqah* before *feeqah* has ended?**

"There is no dispute that this contract in *feeqah* is an Islamically legal contract based on a comprehensive system Everything in this stage – and everything concerned with the relationship between the two – is subject to the condition that the boy treats the girl within the limits and constraints that Islam allows between him and a sister regarding speaking, looking, and touching. If we imagine a boy who does not abide by this condition and starts trying to seduce the girl, to fool her, or in any other way to move on to *meeqah* prematurely by making inappropriate suggestions or flirting sexually with her without her consent, the contract continues to be valid but the boy is committing a sin. The girl should be vigilant regarding her relationship with him.

He may not be trustworthy. It will be up to her, when the period of the contract ends, to decide whether to continue with the relationship or sever it. However, if she accepts what he is doing, she would have allowed him not to abide by the conditions.

"Moving from one stage to another must be explicitly asked for and it must be by both of them. It may not be implicit. If they both agree, then, yes, they may move to *meeqah* and no need to end the remaining time of the original *feeqah* contract.

"Question 2. **There is no divorce in temporary marriage. The couple separates when the contract's time period ends. What if they both want to end the relationship before the term of the contract ends? What should they do?**

"Just as divorce in the permanent marriage is the man's right, he also has the right in a temporary marriage, before the end of the time period, to give to the girl the rest of the time. He says: *'Wehebtokee al-moddah al-motebekkiyah.'* [I give to you the time period that is left.] The girl becomes – by these words – free. The girl has no right to take for herself the time left, unless she has put that as a condition when making the contract.

"Question 3. **What if the couple forgets or disagrees on the time period of the contract and the dates that they agreed to begin it and to end it?**

"In this case, and so that they do not fall into prohibited acts, the man gives to the woman the time period that remains. They then make a new contract if they both wish it.

"Question 4. **The *'iddah* after temporary marriage requires two menstruations to pass if full intercourse has occurred. If the man ends the contract during her menstruation, would this count as the first menstruation?**

"Of course not. This present menstruation is occurring during the agreed-on time period. The woman must wait for two more menstruations, after the current one, to come out of her *'iddah*.

"Question 5. **If the man dies before the time period ends, must the woman observe an *'iddah*, whether or not she has had full intercourse?**

"Yes. Just as after permanent marriage, there is an *'iddah* of death after temporary marriage. The woman's *'iddah*, when the man dies, is four months and 10 days."

Mustafa gestured that time was short. From among the remaining questions, the Seyyid chose one last one.

"Question 6. **In temporary marriage [*seeqah*], does the girl have the right to ask for any amount of dowry, given that the time periods for temporary marriage are usually short?**

"This is up to both of them. Islam does not interfere in specifying the value, but it recommends that the dowry be small and reasonable. If there was full intercourse and because the man is not obliged tc pay a maintenance allowance, the woman may ask for a dowry that equals what she needs during two menstruation periods, which is normally two months. This is because she has no right to enter into a contract with a man before the end of her *'iddah*, which is two menstrual cycles or 45 days for young women who do not menstruate."

With this answer, the Seyyid finished answering the written questions addressed to the lecturers.

* * * * *

## What Is the System?

Mustafa now asked the lecturers to explain what the system meant to them. He called on the Seyyid to go first.

Seyyid Mohammed began, "Our adherence to this system comes from a deep conviction that Islam has solutions for all our social situations. Islam's vision and concepts make it suitable for every time and place. The unchangeable teachings will always stay as the original principles that outline the approach, while the particular changeable rulings come from the unchangeable teachings themselves. This flexibility is the greatness of Islam as it flows with every age and every reality.

"During the years when we were writing the principles of this system, we were – with all objectivity – searching among all religious and secular ideas for a system to help people enter the world of marriage and to create a solidly-built family. We wanted a system based on transparency and gradualness, placing in front of the man and the woman the smallest details and clearest path psychologically, socially, and even economically. We could find nothing except our system derived from Islam. It is now in your hands.

"It is a system for the girls, whom we hope to see become capable and aware women and to whom we hope to see marriage become a pioneering and humanistic reality. They must ride smoothly into the world of marriage, committed to the founding of our system, which provides for them a gate of light to enter this world with firm strides and a clear vision. Our ideal is that not even one of them becomes a divorcée who must suffer – as happens so much nowadays – a disintegrating relationship with her husband and an unstable family environment that caused her to live with worry, regret, sorrow, and fear throughout her life.

"It is a system for the boys, the bright hope in our world, who, if they follow this system, will find their entrance into marriage not depending on a stroke of luck or a jump into the unknown whose harvest may be nothing but hopelessness, divorce, and the search for a new wife. Absent will be the pressures of divorce – the children for whom he must shoulder great responsibilities, the divorced wife from whose lawyers he awaits a monthly court order obliging him to pay alimony, and the many other obligations resulting from divorce, all adding up to a heavy burden.

"May Allah be the guide to success for all of them."

Dr. Omar took over. "I address everyone, but especially the Sunnis, of whom I feel proud to be one. We strove, in our presentation of this system, not to clash with the approach of the Sunnis, but to view Islam as a whole. My Leap was in accepting the 'time period.' For many years, I had thought about and searched for a system suitable for building a happy, healthy family. I found no alternative but to accept the temporary marriage contract with *feeqah* and *meeqah*. Having a time period for the contract does not clash with the spirit of Islam. Though our Sunni scholars have reservations about it, claiming that these reservations are in the interests of the children and family structure, this hesitation should become immaterial because our feeqah and meeqah have no sex. Without sex, there are no children born and no excuse to oppose our system.

"We have built into *feeqah* and *meeqah* a mechanism between the boy and girl that allows them to get acquainted without launching into family or children until this acquaintance process has created a lasting relationship, if the two continue toward permanent marriage, where their intent will be to produce children and form a family.

"Our goal conforms to the goal of our Sunni scholars, and does not oppose it. They strongly desire to protect children and want them to live within the security of a family, and this is our aim too. We believe building a coherent family after entering a permanent marriage will not be possible except through getting acquainted within temporary marriage contracts that pave the way to arrive at that goal.

"Because I believe in the freedom of opinion that is based on reason and logic, I do not see why those who reject our system would jump to condemn those who accept it. This Leap is not big in that it stays within the boundaries of the real, unchangeable teachings of our belief. It is a simple and reasonable Leap. It is a real and fundamental Leap of religion and morals, which takes us into the wide and open areas of all that is truthful, just, beautiful, and good in life. If we reject this, what is the alternative?

"Our system is a system of the allowed and the forbidden, plus careful planning for the future of our children.

"It is a system of balance, which does not deny desires nor free them without restraints, but organizes and soothes them and shows how to deal with them gradually with preciseness and care

"It is a system of responsibility, which specifies rights and duties, so no one inflicts injustice on another, since all things relating to marriage will be clear and without confusion.

"It is a system of introducing people to each other based on the *Qur'anic* verse: **Men, we have created you from a male and a female, and made you into nations and tribes, that you might get to know one another, 49:13.**

"It is a system of introducing people to each other based on freedom of choice, but with precision in the choosing, where morals and humanistic feelings govern the relationship between people.

"It is a system of clear agreements that minimize problems and create solutions for all problems. The people entering into it know what they are doing. The people leaving it know what is involved and how to separate when they want to and do so as painlessly as possible.

"It is a system that lays the first brick of society – the family that is coherent and stable.

"It is a system of insurance in marriage, in what it represents in terms of a father, a mother, children, and a family home – where ambitions harmonize, thoughts meet, and goals are set.

"It is a system based on a Leap that knows exactly where to place its feet on the road and that calls for courage, awareness, and rejection of all inherited norms that do not conform to religion or logic.

"It is a system of an approach that brings us from darkness into light.

"When we call on our young men and women to adopt this system, it is because we strongly desire that they achieve stability in their family lives. Many scientific, social, economic, and development objectives lie before them in life. Without this stability, they will never be able to carry out their roles in these important fields. The system we propose, and hope that society implements, is a big step for the future."

It was now Dr. Afaf's turn. She said, "Women today are often the weaker link in the marriage relationship. This system is designed to make women as strong as men, in a balancing process between the two. Equality and justice govern this relationship, while acknowledging there are psychological and physiological differences in men and women.

"Just as the man has full freedom of choice, in our system the woman has the freedom to accept or reject. The man lays down the conditions that suit him, and the woman also lays down the conditions that suit her.

"Customs and traditions that contradict Islam have no place in this system, nor does it require the woman to abide by customs while the man may ignore them.

"Just as doors are opened to the man to build a new future after divorce, the woman will also have the same right. Just as he has rights in the home, she will – under her conditions – have similar rights. This will apply to the children and finances, since she will ensure the children will not be used against her nor will she be kicked out the house and forced to beg for kindness from others to offer her shelter and charity.

"This system protects all this, and gives the woman the ability to protect herself from such calamities.

"Through our system, we give the woman a pioneering role that fulfills her wishes and hopes, and her very existence. All this is within the framework of Islam, which is itself characterized by justice and the correct solutions to all complexities that occur between a couple.

"I have great confidence in all our young women and men. They are able – with their awareness, culture, and morality – to translate practically the features of this system It will show them the way to a bright and secure and happy future. Thank you."

Nasser took over last and said, "This system is the fruit of an effort of long years spent in research and careful investigation. The goal of our work has always been the satisfaction of Allah before anything else. It is toward this goal that we have proceeded, having pondered and reflected on the disturbed situation of family life today. We were hurt by the floundering we all observed in the approach to marriage, and by the lack of the clear vision of a solid system that would make marriage coherent and strong. In answer to this, we formulated an approach for a healthy relationship between a young man and woman while they got to know each other and made their choice, taken in gradual stages and with carefully programed details.

"Our system emerged as one founded on knowledge, not assumptions, and based on **Are those who have knowledge the equal of those who have none? 39:9**.

"It is a system of equality and responsibility, which specifies their rights and duties to all involved.

"It is a system of transparency and clarity that spurns tricks and cunning ways. It builds a relationship between two human beings, in which the approach to the relationship is blessed with the brightness of sunlight and sheltered from the darkness of night.

"It is a system of gradualness, in which firm steps are taken to move from one situation to the other and from one reality to another. Allah says: **Who is more rightly guided, he who goes groveling on his face or he who walks upright on a straight path? 67:22**.

"It is a system of simplicity, not difficulty. The Prophet (pbuh) said, **I was sent with the easy *haneefiah*.**

"It is a system of fairness that lives up to its promises, and corresponds in implementation to the verses **speak for justice, even if it affects your own kinsmen; be true to the covenant of God, 6:152,** and **Believers, fulfill your obligations, 5:1.**

"It is a system that addresses issues both allowed and prohibited, as Dr. Omar has pointed out. It is a system where each partner does not put one step forward or backward unless it meets with Allah's satisfaction, as the *hadith* says. In the relationship with the other person, we enter into this system within the allowable, and then either stay or leave it within the allowable.

"It is a system of justice and respect for the other person's rights.

"It is a system in which we know ourselves and the other person, and differentiate between longing and doubt, right and wrong, reason and emotion, logic and ignorance.

"Finally, we should consider that we are between two eras. The era of the past had a system that worked for its people. Because of all the changes in society, we do not see it as a good system for the future. So we are between that old system and an era of fast changes that requires a new system whose goal aims at strengthening the disintegrating family structure. In implementing this new system, we will face, as with any new idea or reform, problems and difficulties. It is important that this implementation be done with great caution, awareness, and respect. Here in Lebanon, where openness and freedom are wide, we can accept new ideas. This is not true for all Muslim societies, where the social norms and prevalent traditions have caused young men and women to lose the capability and experience to get to know each other before marriage. When we ask them to embrace the idea of our system, they should develop the idea inside themselves and take care when entering into it to tread cautiously and not stir up complexities that might slow down implementation of the system.

"Because it is our strong wish that our young men and women achieve Islamic responsibility, we hope – so we may guide them –

that they will keep in contact with us. We have set up an Internet site for this purpose. Through further future contact, we can open the way toward practical solutions in implementing the system, clarification of issues they may have missed here, and clear methods that are non-deviant and straightforward.

"These are the features of the system. The experiment is worth pursuing. Let us be up to the challenge. Thanks to all, and my prayers to you for guidance and success."

Nasser's speech marked the end of the seminars. Most members of the audience stood to cheer and applaud all the lecturers for several minutes.

When the cheering and clapping ended, the final word was left to Mustafa. He said, "We are grateful for your enthusiastic response. We have now arrived at the end of these valuable seminars. On behalf of the honorable lecturers and myself, I thank you for your attendance, participation, and continued interest. I thank the university's Dean and Trustee, who provided all the necessities that gave these seminars the chance to succeed. I thank you all – teachers, students, and guests, the university's administrative staff, and the audiovisual technicians who recorded our sessions. We look forward someday to having more seminars to explore our subject in more depth.

"Meanwhile, we may all stay in touch through our website www. alousra.com and through our e-mail address dar_al_ousra@hotmail. com.

"Peace and mercy be with you. Farewell till we meet again."

* * * * *

# Checklist for Permanent Marriage Contract

* * * * *

Ideas are presented here for conditions to be considered when creating a permanent marriage contract. Some of these may be taken for literal use or they may serve as "food for thought" for a couple to debate and agree on before entering into permanent marriage. The ideal marriage contract should offer protection for both parties, especially the wife, and should consider the possibility of divorce. Some conditions listed here may also be applied to temporary contracts.

- ❖ Dowry – size, terms of payment, conditions for return
- ❖ Wedding – number of guests, invitations, food, clothes, who pays for what
- ❖ Treatment of each other – respect, courtesy, good manners, honesty, openness
- ❖ False information – previous or second marriage; grounds for voiding marriage
- ❖ Family interference – how to handle
- ❖ Decision-making – mutual agreement
- ❖ Solution to big problems – professional marriage counseling or someone respected by both families
- ❖ Privacy – not gossip about each other outside of home
- ❖ Marital home – live with relatives or independent home
- ❖ Type of home – house or apartment; size; style; furnishings

* ❖ Entertainment in home
* ❖ Joint decision on inviting temporary or permanent guests
* ❖ Maintenance allowance – what percentage of salary
* ❖ Cars – number; type
* ❖ Servants – number; type
* ❖ Housework – assistance from husband when needed
* ❖ Right to education – how much
* ❖ Right to career – before and after childbirth
* ❖ Children – number, when, their education, sharing of guardianship
* ❖ Second marriage – permitted or not
* ❖ Assignment out of country – how to handle
* ❖ Partner becomes physically or mentally incapacitated
* ❖ Partner commits crime
* ❖ Separation with kindness
* ❖ Right to divorce for the wife
* ❖ Divorce considerations:
    division of property – furniture, house, car, pets, gifts
    alimony – amount; terms
    child support – amount; terms
    custody – sole or joint; right to leave country with children
    visitation rights – husband, wife, and other family members
* ❖ Inheritance
* ❖ Renegotiation of marriage contract conditions if circumstances change

* * * * *

# Glossary

## Pronunciation Guide

### Vowels

| | |
|---|---|
| a | cat or father |
| ai / ay | aisle |
| au / aw | out |
| ee | feel |
| i | big |
| oo | moon |
| u | put |
| ' | (catch in voice, like diphthong) |

### Consonants

| | |
|---|---|
| b | bone |
| d | dog |
| dh | them |
| f | far |
| gh | (like gargling) |
| h | home |
| j | job |
| k | keep |
| kh | loch  (Scottish) |

261

| | |
|---|---|
| l | love |
| m | man |
| n | night |
| q | (like soft q + h) |
| r | ram (rolled slightly) |
| s | sand |
| sh | short |
| t | ten |
| th | thank |
| w | want |
| y | yard |
| z | zebra |

* * * * *

# Definition of Arabic Terms

Note: Terms are arranged according to the English alphabetical order. Symbols not used in English do not affect the order of the terms.

**Abu** – father of; part of some men's names; see also Ibn

**AH** – *Anno Hegirae* (in the year of the *Hegira*, Mohammed's (pbuh) flight from Mecca to Medina in 622 AD; it began the Islamic calendar); see also *hijri*, *meeladi*, and *Rabi' Al-Awwal*

> to convert roughly the lunar Islamic calendar into the Western solar calendar:
> $$32 \div 33 \times AH \text{ year} + 622 = AD \text{ year}$$
> to convert roughly the Western calendar into the Islamic calendar:
> $$33 \div 32 \times AD \text{ year} - 622 = AH \text{ year}$$

*a'jer* – payment for a job usually given after the work is done; part of the *Qur'anic* verse 4:24; sometimes translated as "dowry"; see also *ila ajalin mosamma, Qur'an,* and *sadaq*

**Al-Azhar** – The Flourishing; mosque and university built in Cairo around 360 AH [971 AD]; the prestigious Al-Azhar Sheikh is the mosque's leader and is respected by Muslims worldwide; all *fatwas* for Egypt are issued from Al-Azhar; see also *fatwa*, mosque, and Sheikh

**Al-Fatiha** – the opening chapter of the *Qur'an*; consists of seven short verses of prayer; was traditionally read aloud together by future brides and grooms to seal their pledge of marriage; see also *Qur'an*

**Allah** – the name of God in the Islamic religion; see also Islam

**'ameeqah** – deeper; basis for creating the word *meeqah*; see also *meeqah*

**Ansar** – Muslims of Medina; see also Medina

**'aqilah** – responsible; girl responsible enough to make decisions; see also *rashidah*

**arkan** – pillars; applied to the elements of marriage; see also *ijab, nikah, qubool,* and *sadaq*

**Ayesha** – one of the wives of the Prophet Mohammed (pbuh); see also Mohammed

**'azl** – *coitus interruptus*; incompletion of full sexual intercourse

**baligh** – mature (male); see also *buloogh*

**balighah** – mature (female); see also *buloogh*

**buloogh** – Islamic legal age of maturity; opinion varies among scholars whether it is puberty or 15, 17, or 18 years of age; see also *baligh* and *balighah*

**Caliph** – past male leader of a Muslim state; see also Imams and Sheikh

**da'wah** – missionary work; call for Islam

**Dhahiri** – school of thought that accepts the literal meaning of the text

**dhenni** – indefinite; said of the *hadiths*; contrasted with *yeqeeni*; see also *hadith*

**dinar** – a currency of historical times and still in use in some countries today

**dofoof** – tambourines; a metaphor for announcing a marriage

**Fateh Mecca** – the Muslim conquest of Mecca in 8 AH (630 AD); see also Mecca

**fatwa** – Islamic legal ruling; *fatawa* plural; see also Al-Azhar, *ijtihad, mufti,* and *mujtahid*

**feeqah** – the second stage of acquaintance in the system of The Leap; between introduction and *meeqah*; the boy and girl arrive at a temporary contract and get acquainted by treating each other as siblings; the contract may or may not be renewed; the contract may be renewed for *feeqah* again or for *meeqah*; see also The Leap, *meeqah,* and *rafeeqah*

**fiqh** – *Shari'ah* jurisprudence; understanding; see also *fatwa, fuqaha, hadith, Shari'ah,* and *Sunnah*

**firash** – bed; the place where the child is born; based on *al-walad lil-firash,* meaning the child is to be related to the father even if born out of wedlock

**fitneh** – a disturbance

**friend marriage** – new form of lawful marriage, similar to *milcheh,* proposed by Sheikh Al-Zindani of Yemen for people not ready to set up a marital home; the groom lives with his parents and the bride lives with her parents; the couple is allowed to meet for intimate encounters; see also *milcheh*

**fuqaha'** – *Shari'ah* jurists; see also *fiqh* and *Shari'ah*

**ghosl** – partial ablution

**ghosl al-janaba** – total ablution after sex

**Gulf countries** – the six countries along the southwestern Arabian Gulf coast (Bahrain, Kuwait, Oman, Qatar, Saudi Arabia, and the U.A.E).; see also U.A.E.

**hadith** – narration by a prophet of Islam; see also *dhenni, mostafeedah, motewaatirah, mukhtalafun 'alayh,* Prophet's (pbuh) companions, and *sahih*

**Hafsa** – one of the wives of the Prophet Mohammed (pbuh); see also Mohammed

**hajr** – under guardianship due to incompetence; see also *safih, safihah,* and *wilayah*

**halal** – actions that are religiously lawful; allowed by *Shari'ah*; contrasted with *haram*; see also *makrooh, mustahabb,* and *Shari'ah*

**Hanafi** – Sunni school of thought; see also Sunni

**Hanbali** – Sunni school of thought; see also Sunni

**haneefiah** – message

**haraj** – circumstances or activity leading to critical embarrassment or difficulty

**haram** – actions that are religiously unlawful; forbidden by *Shari'ah*; contrasted with *halal* and *Shar'i*; see also *Ihsaan, makrooh, mustahabb, Shari'ah,* and *zina*

**Hashemite** – royal family member claiming direct descent from the Prophet (pbuh); see also Mohammed

**hijab** – headscarf worn by a woman to cover her hair and neck

**hijri** – lunar calendar; contrasted with *meeladi*; see also AH and *Rabi' Al-Awwal*

**Hujjat al-Wadaa'** – the last pilgrimage to Mecca made by the Prophet (pbuh); see also Mecca and Mohammed

**'ibadat** – acts of worship; contrasted with *mu'amalat*; see also mosque

**Ibn** – son of; part of some men's names; see also Abu

**'iddah** – time period that a divorced woman, if she had sex in her marriage, waits before entering into the next temporary or permanent marriage; the *'iddah* after divorce from temporary marriage is two menstrual cycles (45 to 60 days) or 45 days for young women who do not menstruate; the *'iddah* after divorce from permanent marriage is 3 menstrual cycles (75 to 90 days); divorced women after menopause have no *'iddah*; all widows observe an *'iddah* of four months and 10 days

**Ihsaan** – protection from falling into forbidden sexual acts; see also *yohassin* and *zina*

*ijab* — the first part of the proposal in the marriage contract; the words uttered by the woman or her proxy that state the basis for the agreement of the marriage; answered by *qubool*, the man's acceptance of the terms of the agreement; one of the requirements of the temporary or permanent marriage contract; see also *arkan, nikah,* and *qubool*

*Ijmaa'* — opinion that all or almost all scholars agree on; see also *jomhoor*

*ijtihad* — intellectual process for reaching a *fatwa*; see also *fatwa* and *mujtahid*

*ila ajalin mosamma* — a specific time period; part of the *Qur'anic* verse 4:24; see also *a'jer* and *Qur'an*

**Imamate** — Shi'ite school of thought that believes in all 12 Imams; see also Imams and Shi'ite

**Imams** — male religious and secular leaders exercising authority in an Islamic state; see also Caliph, Imamate, and Sheikh

*'ishhad* — witnessing of a contract, including marriage; two witnesses are needed

**Islam** — religion that is based on the teachings of the Prophet Mohammed and the worship of Allah as God; the word Islam has a double meaning: peace and submission to one God; see also Allah

*'ismah* — the right to divorce

*istemta'na'* — (sexual) enjoyment; see also *nestemti'* and *testemti'oo*

*itlaq* — non-restriction; concept used in the marriage contract; contrasted with *taqyeed*

**Ja'fari** — Shi'ite school of thought; see also Shi'ite

*jahili* — ignorant; mentality of the *Jahiliah* (pre-Islamic era)

*jomhoor* — majority; refers to majority of scholars; see also *Ijmaa'*

*kafa'ah* — mental competence; see also *rashid* and *rashidah*

**Khadija** – first wife of the Prophet; a wealthy businesswoman who proposed marriage to Mohammed (pbuh); see also Mohammed

*khalwah* – situation when a man and woman are alone together; they are not closely related or married to each other

*khitbah* – proposal of marriage; see also *ijab*

*khul'* – type of divorce; the wife gives up her dowry so the husband will grant the divorce; once divorced, they cannot reunite without a new marriage contract even during her *'iddah*; contrasted with *raj'ee*; see also *'iddah*

**The Leap** – a system for lawful acquaintance before marriage between a man and woman; the aim is to find the best possible partner for permanent marriage; based on morality, good intentions, freedom of choice, multiple relationships, and the principle that thorough and gradual acquaintance is required for marriage to succeed; there are five stages: introduction, *feeqah*, *meeqah*, *seeqah*, and permanent marriage; the middle three are bound by lawful temporary contracts; see also *feeqah*, *meeqah*, and *seeqah*

*maharim* – unmarriageable relatives

*makrooh* – actions that are not recommended, or are recommended to abstain from; not as acceptable as *halal* or *mustahabb* or as unacceptable as *haram*; contrasted with *mustahabb*

**Maliki** – Sunni school of thought; see also Sunni

*mansookh* – verses that may be voided; contrasted with *muhkamat*; see also *Qur'an*

*ma'thoon* – a licensed cleric; he can perform marriages and grant divorces

**Mecca** – the holiest city of Islam; birthplace of Mohammed (pbuh); also called Mecca Al-Mukarramah (Holy Mecca); see also AH, *Fateh Mecca, Hujjat al-Wadaa'*, Mohammed, and *'umrah*

**Medina** – the second holiest city in Islam; city that Mohammed (pbuh) fled to after announcing Islam and where he is buried; this flight marked the start of the Islamic calendar; see also AH and Ansar

*meeladi* – solar calendar; contrasted with *hijri*; see also AH

*meeqah* – the third stage of acquaintance in the system of The Leap; between *feeqah* and *seeqah* for non-virgins and between *feeqah* and permanent marriage for virgins; the boy and girl arrive at a temporary contract and get acquainted with greater intimacy than in *feeqah* but not with sexual acts that require an *'iddah*; the contract may or may not be renewed; the contract may be renewed for *meeqah* again or for the next stage; see also *'ameeqah, feeqah,* The Leap, and *seeqah*

**Messenger of Allah (pbuh)** – the Prophet Mohammed (pbuh); see also Mohammed

*milcheh* – preliminary marriage that resembles an engagement; the couple is lawfully married, but they need more time to get acquainted; they agree not to have sex for, say, six months or a year; see also friend marriage

*misyar* – type of marriage; the husband and wife do not live together; he visits her at intervals and is not financially responsible for her upkeep when he is away unless the marriage contract requires an allowance; sometimes the marriage is kept secret

**Mohammed (pbuh)** – Prophet of Islam; also called the Messenger, the Messenger of Allah, and the Prophet; see also Ayesha, Hafsa, Hashemite, *Hujjat al-Wadaa'*, Khadija, Mecca, Medina, pbuh, Prophet's (pbuh) companions, Safiah, and Zainab

**Moses (pbuh)** – Prophet who married Shu'aib's (pbuh) daughter; see also Shu'aib

**mosque** – Islamic house of worship; see also Al-Azhar, *'ibadat,* and Islam

*mostafeedah* – numerous; a *hadith* that is true because it is narrated many times; see also *hadith*

*motewaatirah* – a *hadith* that must be true because it is narrated by so many people that the possibility of conspiracy does not exist; see also *hadith*

*mu'amalat* – dealings between people; contrasted with *'ibadat*

*mufti* - scholar capable of issuing religious rulings; see also *fatwa* and *mujtahid*

**muhallil** – intermediate husband; a man married by a thrice-divorced woman; her intention is to divorce him to allow her marriage to her first husband for a fourth time

**muhkamat** – verses that may never be voided; contrasted with *mansookh*; see also *Qur'an*

**mujtahid** – highest religious scholar capable of interpreting *Shari'ah* and formulating rulings; *mujtahideen* plural; see also *fatwa, ijtihad, mufti,* and *Shari'ah*

**mukhtalafun 'alayh** – no agreement among scholars on accepting a *hadith*; see also *hadith*

**mula'inah** – wife who curses

**Muslims** – followers of the Islamic religion; see also Islam

**mustahabb** – recommended, but not obligatory; not as acceptable as *halal* but more acceptable than *makrooh*; contrasted with *makrooh*; see also *wajib*

**mut'ah** – a temporary marriage by mutual agreement between a man and a woman; full sexual intercourse is allowed

**nafaqah** – maintenance allowance paid by the husband to the wife; not obligatory in temporary marriage unless included in the contract

**nakahtoum** – to marry; part of the *Qur'anic* verse 33:49; see also *nikah*

**nestemti'** – (sexual) enjoyment; see also *istemta'na* and *testemti'oo*

**nikah** – the marriage contract; used metaphorically for sexual intercourse; see also *arkan, ijab, nakatoum, qubool, sadaq,* and *tan-kah* and the different types of contracts (*feeqah,* friend marriage, *meeqah, milcheh, misyar, mut'ah, seeqah, 'urfi,* and *zawaj bi-niat al-talaq*)

**oukeya** – measurement of weight; 1 *oukeya* = about 200 grams (1/5 of a kilogram)

**pbuh** – peace be upon him; written or said after mentioning the Prophet Mohammed (pbuh); *salle Allahu 'alaihi wa salaam* in Arabic; see also Mohammed

**Prophet's (pbuh) companions** – the male contemporaries of Mohammed who knew him and converted to Islam; responsible for the transmission of the *hadiths*; see also Mohammed and *hadith*

**qintar'** – treasure or massive amount of money or goods

**qismaw wa naseeb** – belief in fate

**qiyas** – comparison; a method of determining *Shari'ah* lawfulness by comparing situations that have recommended versus obligatory features

**qubool** – the second part of the proposal in the marriage contract; the word uttered by the man or his proxy that states his acceptance of the *ijab*, the terms of the agreement; the man says, "*Qebilt.*" ["I accept."]; see also *arkan, ijab,* and *nikah*

**Qur'an** – the Holy Book of Islam containing the word of Allah; see also *a'jer, Al-Fatiha, ila ajalin mosamma, Surah Al-Isra', mansookh, muhkamat, tafseer,* and *yeqeeni*

**Rabi' Al-Awwal** – third of the 12 lunar months of the Islamic calendar; see also AH and *hijri*

**rafeeqah** – companion; basis for the word *feeqah*

**raj'ee** – type of divorce; the wife can return to her husband during her *'iddah* without a new marriage contract; contrasted with *khul'*; see also *'iddah*

**rashid** – rational and competent (male); contrasted with *safih*; see also *kafa'ah* and *roshd*

**rashidah** – rational and competent (female); contrasted with *safihah*; see also *'aqilah, kafa'ah,* and *roshd*

**reeba** – with wrongful intent

**roshd** – having a responsible character; see also *rashid* and *rashidah*

**sadaq** – the marriage dowry; one of the requirements of the temporary or permanent marriage contract; may also be called *'iwathun 'anil bith*; see also *a'jer, ila ajalin mosamma,* and *nikah*

**sadaqah Shari'ah** – friendship allowed by *Shari'ah*; see also *Shari'ah* and *ta'arof Shar'i*

**Safiah** – one of the wives of the Prophet Mohammed (pbuh); see also Mohammed

**safih** – irrational (male); contrasted with *rashid;* see also *hajr* and *wilayah*

**safihah** – irrational (female); contrasted with *rashidah*; see also *hajr* and *wilayah*

**sahih** – authentic; describes sayings that are definitely *hadiths*; see also *hadith*

**seeqah** – the fourth stage of acquaintance in the system of The Leap; between *meeqah* and permanent marriage; the man and woman arrive at a temporary contract and get acquainted with greater intimacy than *meeqah* with full sexual intercourse that requires an *'iddah* after the contract time is up; recommended for non-virgins only; the contract may or may not be renewed; the contract may be renewed for *seeqah* again or for permanent marriage; see also *'iddah*, The Leap, and *meeqah*

**Seyyid** – honorific title given to the male descendants of the Prophet Mohammed (pbuh); see also Mohammed

**Shafi'i** – Sunni school of thought; see also Sunni

**Shar'i** – religiously lawful in Islam; contrasted with *haram*; see also *halal, Shari'ah,* and *ta'arof Shar'i*

**Shari'ah** – Islamic law; see also *halal, haram, mujtahid, sadaqah Shari'ah, Shar'i, shobah,* and *tahreef*

**Sheikh** – title of a Muslim male of high stature; see also Al-Azhar, Caliph, and Imams

**Shi'ia** – member of the Shi'ite sect; see also Ja'fari, Imamate, and Shi'ite

**Shi'ite** – the second largest sect of Islam; see also Ja'fari, Imamate, and Shi'ia

**shobhah** – lawfully doubtful; see also *Shari'ah*

**Shu'aib (pbuh)** – Prophet whose daughter married the Prophet Moses (pbuh) after he helped her draw water from a well; see also Moses

**Sunnah** – the life, deeds, practices, and sayings of Mohammed (pbuh) recorded as examples of perfect conduct; everything announced by Mohammed is considered *Sunnah*, meaning true; also refers to a collection of rulings by scholars based on the words of the Prophet Mohammed (pbuh); see also *hadith* and Mohammed

**Sunni** – the largest sect of Islam; its main schools of thought are the Hanafi, Hanbali, Maliki, and Shafi'i

**Surah Al-Isra'** – the 17th chapter of the *Qur'an*; see also *Qur'an*

**ta'arof Shar'i** – acquaintance allowed by *Shari'ah;* see also *sadaqah Shari'ah* and *Shar'i*

**tafseer** – interpretation of the meanings of the *Qur'an*; see also *Qur'an*

**tahdeed an-nasi'** – birth control

**tahreef** – deviation from or distortion of *Shari'ah*

**tan-kah** – to have intercourse; part of the *Qur'anic* verse 2:230; see also *nikah*

**taqyeed** – restriction; concept used in the marriage contract; contrasted with *itlaq*

**tebeen** – separation of husband and wife

**testemti'oo** – (sexual) enjoyment; see also *istemta'na* and *nestemti'*

**thayyib** – non-virgin woman

**U.A.E.** – United Arab Emirates; a confederation of seven independent states on the southern coast of the Arabian Gulf (Abu Dhabi, Ajman, Dubai, Fujairah, Ras Al-Khaimah, Sharjah, and Umm Al-Qaiwain); see also Gulf countries

**'umrah** – performing certain rituals while visiting the *kaaba* (House of God in Mecca) at any time of year except during the *hajj* (a specific time when the major annual pilgrimage is made to Mecca); see also Mecca

**'urfi** – a type of unregistered marriage; recognized in Islam but not in the secular courts; occurs mostly in Egypt

**wajib** – obligatory; see also *mustahabb*

**waliyy** – guardian; usually the father of the family; see also *wilayah*

**"Wehebtokee al-moddah al-motebekkiyah."** – "I give you the time period that is left."; words used by the boy to release the girl from the full term of the temporary contract

**wilayah** – guardianship; see also *hajr, safih, safihah,* and *waliyy*

**yeqeeni** – definite; said of the *Qur'an*; contrasted with *dhenni*; see also *Qur'an*

**yohassin** – protect from falling into forbidden sexual acts; see also *Ihsaan* and *zina*

**Zainab** – one of the wives of the Prophet Mohammed (pbuh); see also Mohammed

**zawaj bi-niat al-talaq** – marriage with hidden intention to divorce; the wife does not know the husband's premeditated intention to divorce her until he does it

**zina** – sex with another person that is religiously unlawful; see also *haram* and *Ihsaan*

* * * * *

# Qur'anic Verses

* * * * *

These verses are excerpts from the Holy Book of Islam. They all appear in the text of this book, sometimes more than once. The arrangement reflects their order in the Qur'an, not the order of their appearance in the text.

**...but when they have purified themselves, you may approach them [in any manner, time, or place] ordained for you by Allah, 2:222.**  (pages 46-47)

**Women are your fields. 2:223.**  (pages 157 and 211)

**Divorced women must wait [keeping themselves from men] three menstrual courses, 2:228.**  (page 164)

**...or separate with kindness, 2:229.**  (pages 158 and 231)

**...until she has _tan-kah_ [wedded] another man, 2:230.**  (page 120)

**If a man has renounced his wife and she has reached the end of her _'iddah_, do not prevent her from remarrying her husband, 2:232.**  (page 71)

**...you shall not be blamed for what they may do for themselves lawfully, 2:240.**  (page 69)

...call in two male witnesses from among you, but if two men cannot be found, then one man and two women who you judge fit to act as witnesses, so that if either of them commit an error the other will remind her, 2:282. (page 63)

Oh, believers! When you contract a debt for a fixed period, put it in writing; let a scribe write it down for you with fairness; no scribe should refuse to write as God has taught him; therefore let him write; and let the debtor dictate, fearing God his Lord and not diminishing the sum he owes; if the debtor be an ignorant or feeble-minded person, or one who cannot dictate, let his guardian dictate for him in fairness; call in two male witnesses from among you, but if two men cannot be found, then one man and two women who you judge fit to act as witnesses, so that if either of them commit an error the other will remind her; witnesses must not refuse to give evidence if called on to do so; so do not fail to put your debts in writing, be they small or big, together with the date of payment; this is more just in the sight of God; it ensures accuracy in testifying and is the best way to remove all doubt; but if the transaction in hand be a bargain concluded on the spot, it is no offence for you if you do not commit it to writing; see that witnesses are present when you barter with one another, and let no harm be done to either scribe or witness; if you harm them you will commit a transgression; have fear of God; God teaches you, and God has knowledge of all things. 2:282. (pages 63-64 and 65)

And if any one of you entrusts another with a pledge, let the trustee restore the pledge to its owner, 2:283. (page 64)

...and you were on the brink of the pit of Fire and He saved you from it, 3:103. (page 235)

...marry women of your choice, two, or three, or four, 4:3. (page 62)

And give the women [on marriage] their dowry as a free gift, 4:4. (pages 58 and 59)

...even if you have given the latter a whole treasure for a dowry, take not the least bit of it back; do you take it by slander and a manifest wrong? 4:20. (pages 59-60)

...if you decide to take one wife in place of another, even if you have given the latter a whole treasure for a dowry, take not the least bit of it back; do you take it by slander and a manifest wrong? And how could you take it when you have gone in unto each other, and they have taken from you a solemn covenant? **4:20-21.**  (page 57)

...for the enjoyment you have had of them, give them their *a'jer* [dowry] as a duty,  **4:24.**  (pages 196, 198, and 297)

Believers, do not approach your prayers when drunk, but wait till you can grasp the meaning of your words,  **4:43.**  (page 211)

Believers, fulfill your obligations,  **5:1.**  (pages 69, 139, and 257)

Believers, do not forbid the good things God has made lawful to you; [but] do not exceed the limits: God does not love those who exceed the limits.  **5:87.**  (page 298)

...speak for justice, even if it affects your own kinsmen; be true to the covenant of God,  **6:152.**  (page 257)

This path of Mine is straight; follow it and do not follow other paths, for they lead you away from My way,  **6:153.**  (page 82)

...no soul shall bear another's burden,  **6:164.**  (page 174)

Verily never will Allah change the condition of a people until they change it themselves [with their own souls],  **13:11.**  (page 227)

Those who keep faith with God do not break their pledge,  **13:20.** (page 139)

The day when every soul will come pleading for itself; when every soul will be repaid for its deeds; none shall be wronged,  **16:111.** (page 138)

...treat them with humility and tenderness and say: Lord, be merciful to them for they nursed me when I was an infant.  **17:24.** (page 174)

Keep your promises; you are accountable for all you promise,  **17:34.** (page 139)

Had the Truth followed their desires, the heavens, the earth, and all who dwell in them would have surely been corrupted, 23:71. (page 89)

Marry those among you who are single, or the virtuous ones among your slaves, male or female, 24:32. (page 62)

Father, take this man into your service; men who are strong and honest are the best you can hire, 28:26. (page 168)

I want to give you one of my two daughters in marriage if you stay eight years in my service; but, if you wish, you may stay 10; I shall not deal harshly with you; God willing, you shall find me an upright man, 28:27. (page 168)

And who is in greater error than the man who is led by his desire without guidance from God? God does not guide the evildoers, 28:50. (page 88)

Among His signs is this: that He created for you wives among yourselves, that you may find repose in them, and He has put between you affection and mercy. Verily, in that are signs for a people who reflect. 30:21. (page 72)

...each party is happy with what they have. 30:32. (page 86)

It is not for true believers – men or women – to make their choice in their affairs if God and His Messenger (pbuh) decree otherwise, 33:36. (page 81)

If you *nakahtoum* [marry] believing women and divorce them before the marriage is consummated, you are not required to observe an *'iddah*, 33:49. (pages 120 and 163-164)

...and any believing woman who gives herself to you [the Prophet (pbuh)], and whom the Prophet (pbuh) wishes to take in marriage, this only for you [the Prophet (pbuh)] and not for the believers. 33:50. (page 169)

Are those who have knowledge the equal of those who have none? 39:9. (page 256)

And now We have set you on the right path; follow it, and do not yield to the desires of ignorant men; for they can in no way protect you from the wrath of God; the wrongdoers are patrons to each other; but the righteous have God Himself for their patron, 45:18-19.  (page 88)

Men, we have created you from a male and a female, and made you into nations and tribes, that you might get to know one another, 49:13.  (page 254)

Who is more rightly guided, he who goes groveling on his face or he who walks upright on a straight path? 67:22.  (page 257)

\* \* \* \* \*

# *Hadiths*

\* \* \* \* \*

These *hadiths* are excerpts from narrations of the prophets of Islam. All these excerpts appear in the text, sometimes more than once. The arrangement reflects their order in the text.

**No man and a woman get together without Satan becoming the third.** – Prophet Mohammed (pbuh)   (pages 13 and 81)

**You have taken them by the trust of Allah, and had them become sexually allowable to you by the word of Allah.** – Prophet Mohammed (pbuh)   (page 57)

**The woman is a seller and the man a buyer and the selling cannot be done without a price.** – Prophet Mohammed (pbuh) (pages 58-59)

**Seek even if it is an iron ring.** – Prophet Mohammed (pbuh)   (page 59)

**No prayer is accepted from the mosque's neighbor except that which is performed in the mosque.** – Prophet Mohammed (pbuh) (pages 61 and 65)

**No marriage is without witnesses.** – Prophet Mohammed (pbuh) (page 61)

**I was sent with the easy *haneefiah*** – Prophet Mohammed (pbuh) (pages 64 and 257)

**Prostitutes marry without witness** – Prophet Mohammed (pbuh) (page 65)

**No marriage is valid without a *waliyy* [guardian] and two reliable witnesses.** narrated by Omar Ibn Al-Khattab   (page 65)

**A girl went to the Prophet (pbuh) and said: 'My father married me to his nephew, but I do not like it. He answered, 'Let what your father did become valid [that is, accept it].' She said, 'I have no desire for what he did.' He answered, 'Go and marry whom you want.' She said, 'I have no desire to go against what my father did. I wanted women to know that fathers have no say in their daughters' matters.'** narrated by Ibn Abbas   (pages 68 and 107)

**No marriage is valid without a guardian.** narrated by Abu Musa Al-Ash'ari   (page 70)

**If any woman marries without consent of her guardian, the marriage is void.** Ayesha, the wife of the Prophet (pbuh), quotes the Prophet (pbuh)   (page 70)

**No guardian consent is to be sought for the widowed or divorced woman** – Prophet Mohammed (pbuh)   (page 70)

**The old unmarried woman has more right over herself than her guardian does** – Prophet Mohammed (pbuh)   (page 70)

**The widowed or divorced woman has her right, but the virgin's father gets asked for acceptance.** – Prophet Mohammed (pbuh) (page 70)

**If it is someone whose piety and manners meet your satisfaction, then accept his marriage proposal. If you do not, a *fitneh* [disturbance] and great corruption will take place.** – Prophet Mohammed (pbuh)   (page 74)

**Ignorant leaders who, if asked, give rulings without knowledge; they have gone astray and led people astray.** – Prophet Mohammed (pbuh)   (page 88)

**A man who got engaged to a barren woman said, 'Oh Messenger of Allah (pbuh), I am engaged to a woman of status and beauty,**

but she cannot bear children.' The Messenger of Allah (pbuh) did not advise him marry her. 'Marry the wife who is loving and childbearing since I want to have you be more than other nations on Judgment Day. – Prophet Mohammed (pbuh)  (page 99)

Like for your brother what you like for yourself and hate for him what you hate for yourself. – Prophet Mohammed (pbuh)  (pages 112 and 163)

If a man, whose religious observance and morals satisfy you, comes [proposing to your daughter], give him [your daughter] in marriage. – Prophet Mohammed (pbuh)  (page 157)

A woman from Ansar [Muslims of Medina] came to the Prophet (pbuh) and entered the house of Hafsa  [a wife of the Prophet (pbuh)]. The woman was well-dressed and her hair was combed. She said, 'Oh, Messenger of Allah (pbuh), a woman does not ask a man to marry her. I have had no husband for a long time, and I have no son. Do you need a wife? For I am here, I am offering myself to you if you accept me.' Mohammed said good words to her and prayed for her, then said, 'Oh, you Ansari woman! May Allah reward you, you the Ansar, for your men have supported me, and I have desired your women – or your women have desired me. You may go now, may Allah have mercy on you; Allah will reward you with Paradise because you wanted me and for your presentation of love of me and joy for me; my answer will come to you, God willing.' – Prophet Mohammed (pbuh)  (pages 168-169)

Al-Mughirah Ibn Shu'beh narrated that he proposed to an Ansari woman, and the Prophet (pbuh) asked, 'Have you looked at her?' He said,' No.' The Prophet (pbuh) said, 'Look at her; this makes it more probable you will get along with each other,' (page 171)

Every one of you is a shepherd, and every one of you is responsible for his herd. – Prophet Mohammed (pbuh)  (pages 172 and 173)

If one of you came to his wife [for sex], let there be foreplay between them. – Prophet Mohammed (pbuh)  (page 188)

**It is your plantation; if you want, you may water it, and, if you want, you may leave it thirsty.** – Prophet Mohammed (pbuh) (page 188)

Ibn Abbas was asked about *'azl*. **He called one of his women and said: Tell them, but it was as if she shied away, so he said: It is like this; as for myself I do it** [that is, he does *'azl*]. (page 188)

**We were in an army and the Messenger of Allah (pbuh) came to us and said, 'I give you permission to practice *mut'ah*, that is, the *mut'ah* of women.** narrated by Al-Bukhari that Jabir Ibn Abdullah and Salamah Ibn Al-Akwa' said (page 197)

**The Messenger of Allah (pbuh) came to us and gave us permission for *mut'ah*.** narrated in *Sahih Muslim* that Yezid, by which he meant Ibn Zuray', said that Rawh, by which he meant Ibn Al-Qasim, said that 'Amr Ibn Dinar narrated from Al-Hasan Ibn Mohammed from Salamah Ibn Al-Akwa' and Jabir Ibn Abdullah (pages 197 and 299)

**The *mut'ah* verse was revealed in the book of Allah, and we practiced it with the Messenger of Allah (pbuh), and no verse was revealed to make it void, and the Prophet did not prohibit it to his death.** narrated by Imam Ahmad Ibn Hanbal in *Musnad* that Omran bin Hussein said (pages 197-198)

Jabir Ibn Abdullah [Al-Ansari] came for *'umrah*. We went to him in his house and the people asked him about things. Then they mentioned the *mut'ah* and Jabir replied, **'We practiced *mut'ah* in the time of the Messenger of Allah (pbuh), Abu Bakr, and Omar.'** narrated in *Sahih Muslim* that 'Ata said (page 197; see also page 299)

**The representative of the Messenger of Allah (pbuh) came out to us and said: 'When the Messenger of Allah (pbuh) gave you permission to carry out *testemti'oo* [sexual enjoyment], he meant the *mut'ah* of women.'** Mohammed Ibn Beshshar said that Mohammed Ibn Ja'far said that Ibn Shu'beh said that 'Amr Ibn Dinar said that he heard Al-Hasan Ibn Mohammed narrating that Jabir Ibn Abdullah and Salamah Ibn Al-Akwa' said (page 299)

**I was sent only to complete the best of morals.** – Prophet Mohammed (pbuh) (page 231)

**Man is an enemy of what he is ignorant of.** Imam Ali Ibn Abi Talib said   (page 234)

Jabir Ibn Abdullah came for *'umrah* and we came to him in his house; and the people asked him about things, then they mentioned *mut'ah*, so he said: **'Yes, we carried out *istemta'na* [sexual enjoyment] at the time of the Messenger of Allah (pbuh), Abu Bakr, and Omar.'** Al-Hasan Al-Halawani said that Abdul Rezzaq said that Ibn Jurayj said that 'Ata said   (page 299; see also page 197)

**We used to carry out *nestemti'* [sexual enjoyment] for a handful of dates or flour, at the time of the Messenger of Allah (pbuh).** Mohammed Ibn Rafi'i said that Abdul Rezzaq said that Ibn Jurayj said that Abu Zubair said: 'I heard Jabir Ibn Abdullah saying   (page 299)

* * * * *

# Selective Documents: Excerpts

\* \* \* \* \*

**Document 1** Sabiq, *Fiqh As-Sunnah*, vol. 2, 30.
Marriage with Hidden Intention to Divorce

"Scholars agree that, if a man marries a woman without revealing his intention to divorce her after a particular time, such as after he finishes work or study in the country where he temporarily lives, the marriage is still valid."

المصدر : كتاب فقه السُّنَّة ج ٢، ص ٣٠   مستند رقم ١

العَقْدُ على المَرأةِ وفي بِنيةِ الزَّوج طَلاقُها : أتَّفَقَ الفُقَهاءُ على أنَّ مَن تزوَّجَ امرأةً دون أن
يشترطَ التوقيتَ وفي نِيَّتِهِ أن يُطَلِّقَها بعدَ زَمَنٍ، أو بعدَ انقضاءِ حاجَتِهِ في البلدِ الذي هو مقيمٌ به،
فالزَّواجُ صحيحٌ .

**Document 2** Al-Dubai'i, *Idah Hukmu Az-Zawaj Bi-niat Al-Talak*, 40.
Marriage with Hidden Intention to Divorce

"One of the most renowned scholars of our time was his eminence Sheikh Abdul Aziz Ibn Baz, the general *Mufti* [scholar capable of issuing *fatwas*] of the Kingdom of Saudi Arabia. He issued a *fatwa* allowing marriage with the hidden intention to divorce. One person sent a question to ensure the *fatwa* was given. The Sheikh answered, 'Yes, a *fatwa* from the permanent committee, and I am its president, allows marriage with hidden intention to divorce, if it is between a man and God, if he marries in expatriate lands and intends to divorce when he his study or work is finished. The *jomhoor* [majority] of scholars have no problem with it. The intention is between him and Allah and is not a condition.'

"According to *Majmoo' Fatawa wa Maqalat Mutanawwi'ah*, volume 4, page 30, 'The difference between this and *mut'ah* is that in *mut'ah* has a known requirement of a time period, such as a month or a year or two years. When the time is over, the contract ends. This is the invalid *mut'ah* marriage. But, if he marries her on the *Sunnah* of Allah and His Messenger (pbuh) and his intention is not known and not a condition except between him and God, but in his heart knows that, when he leaves that country he will divorce her, this does him no harm. It protects him from adultery and infidelity. Also, his intention may change.' This the opinion of the *jomhoor* of scholars narrated by Abu Mohammed Abdullah Ibn Qodamah (may God rest his soul), the author of *Al-Moghni*."

المصدر : إيضاح حكم الزواج بنية الطلاق، ص٤٠ مستند رقم ١٢

## رأي سماحة مفتي عام المملكة في

## الزواج بنية الطلاق

من أبرز علماء الاجتهاد في هذا العصر الحجة الثبت سماحة الشيخ عبد العزيز بن باز الذي أفتى بجواز النكاح مع اضمار نية الطلاق ، فوجّه اليه احد المستفتين ليتأكد من صحة الفتوى فأجابه وفقه الله

بقوله : ( ج ):(نعم لقد صدر فتوى من اللجنة الدائمة وأنا رئيسها بجواز النكاح بنية الطلاق اذا كان ذلك بين العبد وبين ربه ، اذا تزوج في بلاد غربة ونيته انه متى انتهى من دراسته أو من كونه موظفاً وما أشبه ذلك ان يطلّق فلا بأس بهذا عند جمهور العلماء ، وهذه النية تكون بينه وبين الله سبحانه ، وليست شرطاً .

والفرق بينه وبين المتعة : ان نكاح المتعة يكون فيه شرط مدة معلومة كشهر أو شهرين أو سنة أو سنتين ونحو ذلك ، فاذا انقضت المدة المذكورة انفسخ ، هذا هو نكاح المتعة الباطل ، أما كونه تزوجها على سنة الله ورسوله ولكن في قلبه انه متى انتهى من البلد سوف يطلقها ، فهذا لا يضره وهذه النية قد تتغير

288

وليست معلومة وليست شرطاً بل هي بينه وبين الله

فلا يضره ذلك ، وهذا من أسباب عفته عن الزنى

والفواحش ، وهذا قول جمهور أهل العلم حكاه عنهم

صاحب المغني موفق الدين إبن قدامة رحمه الله

اهـ ( ١ ) ( ١ ) .

_____

( ١ ) مجموع فتاوى ومقـالات متنوعة ج ٤

ص ٣٠

**Document 3** Az-Zahabi, *Ash-Shari'ah Al-Islamiah*, 69.
Witnessing

"Imam Malik, in a well-known opinion, said witnessing is not a reason for validating the marriage contract because the *Qur'an* does not make it a marriage requirement. The relevant scripts of the *Sunnah* are not explicit in requiring witnessing. The general announcement suffices for the contract to be valid, based on the saying of the Prophet (pbuh): Announce the marriage even if with *dofoof* [tambourines]. The Malikis said, "Since the forbidden part of this act does not occur unless the man and woman have secret intercourse, the allowable does not occur but in its opposite. For that the mere announcement suffices." Witnessing is only recommended when doing the contract, and is obligatory before the marriage, that is, intercourse. If the contract was witnessed, the obligatory and the recommended were achieved. If witnessing occurred after the contract but before intercourse, the obligatory was achieved and the recommended missed.

"The Ja'faris and the Dhahiris said witnessing is absolutely not a requirement for validating the marriage contract because the *Qur'an* did not explicitly point to it when discussing marriage. It pointed to what is less important than marriage – the contract for trade and for loans. They said the *hadiths* regarding witnessing are a recommendation, in case the marriage needs to be confirmed in front of a judge if denial takes place."

289

المصدر : كتاب الشريعة الإسلامية، ص٦٩

وذهب الإمام مالك ـ في المشهور عنه ـ إلى أن الشهادة ليست شرطا في
صحة إنشاء العقد ، لأن القرآن لم يشترط الشهادة في انعقاد الزواج ، ونصوص
السنة الصحيحة ليست صريحة في وجوب الشهادة بخصوصها ـ ويكفي لصحة
إنشاء العقد مطلق الإعلان لقوله عليه الصلاة والسلام ( أعلنوا النكاح
ولو بالدفوف ) . قال المالكية ، ( لما كان حرام هذا الفعل وهو اتصال الرجل
بالمرأة ، لا يكون إلا سراً ، فالحلال لا يكون إلا بضده ، ويكفي في ذلك
مجرد الإعلان) أما الشهادة فهي مندوبة فقط عند العقد ، وواجبه قبل
الدخول ، فإن وجدت الشهادة حال إنشاء العقد ، فقد حصل الواجب
والمندوب ، وإن وجدت بعد تمام العقد وقبل الدخول ، حصل الواجب
وفات المندوب .

وذهب الجعفرية والظاهرية ، إلى أنه لا تشترط الشهادة لصحة عقد
الزواج مطلقاً ، لأن القرآن لم يبه عليها عند الكلام عن النكاح مطلقاً ؛
مع أنه نبه عليها فيما هو أقل خطراً من الزوج ، وهو عقد البيع ، وعقد
المداينة . قالوا والأحاديث الواردة في الشهادة محمولة على الندب ، أو على
الإشهاد لإثباته عند القاضي ، لو وقع التجاحد .

**Document 4** Fawzi, *Ahkamul Usrah fil Jahiliah wal-Islam*, 54.
Witnessing

"Al-Bukhari, Muslim, and Malik state several of the Prophet's (pbuh)
companions and their sons were married without witnesses, but
simply with a wedding party. They mentioned Abdullah Ibn Omar,
Al-Hasan Ibn Ali, Abdullah Ibn Az-Zubair, and Salim Ibn Omar. They
also said, without witnesses, the Prophet (pbuh) married Safiah and
gave a dinner with dates and leafstalk, and married Zainab and held
a party in which a small calf was served. Narrated by all five except
An-Nisa'i."

روى البخاري ومسلم ومالك عن عدد من الصحابة وأولاد الصحابة أنهـم تزوجـوا
بدون شهود ، مكتفين بحفلة عرس أو وليمة ، وقـد ذكروا منهم : عبدالله بن عمـر ،
والحسن بن علي ، وعبدالله بن الزبير ، وسالـم بن عمر . وقالـوا عن النبي (ﷺ ) أنه
تزوج من ( صفية ) بدون شهود وأَوْلَمَ بتمر وسويق . وتـزوج من ( زينب ) بدون شهـود
وأولم بشاة (٢٦)

(٢٦) رواه الخمسة إلا النسائي .

## Document 5   *As-Safir*, 12 Feb. 1999, 7.
*Misya*r and *'Urfi* Marriage

"Egyptian newspapers reported that Imam Al-Azhar Sheikh Mohammed Seyyid Tantaoui announced misyar marriage is lawful as it has all the elements of marriage, but secret marriage is 'adulterous and forbidden.'"

"*Al-Wafd* [*The Delegation*] reported that Sheikh Tantaoui, during a symposium at the 31st Cairo Book Exhibition, accepted misyar marriage. He said, 'This marriage is not found in Egypt. I heard it is found in other countries, and it is Islamically legal. What is new is that a woman does not ask a man for anything except the dowry.' He added '*Misyar* is found in the Gulf, especially in Saudi Arabia. Its name comes from the husband's practice of usually visiting his wife in her home during the day, and also he is not committed to meet her financial responsibilities.'"

"The Imam of Al-Azhar also added, according to *Al-Wafd* and *Al-Gomhuria* [*The Republic*], 'All scholars agree secret marriage is invalid' and is 'adulterous and forbidden.' He said marriage practiced in Egypt as *'urfi* marriage 'has all the elements, but lacks documentation. I personally do not witness it, nor like it, nor sit when it is done, because it results in the loss of the woman's rights and breaks the law of the state. Also, it is *makrooh* [not recommended].' The Sheikh called for 'passing a law with specific punishments for whoever does that, to protect women.'"

"Egyptian newspapers confirm 'urfi marriage is widespread in Egypt among artists and university students. Egyptian courts do not recognize it, but the law does not punish those who commit it."

المصدر : جريدة «السفير» اللبنانية، ١٢ شباط (فبراير) ١٩٩٩م. مستند رقم ٥

## إمام الأزهر: زواج المسيار شرعي

أعلن إمام الأزهر الشيخ محمد سيد طنطاوي ان زواج المسيار زواج «شرعي» تتوفر فيه اركان الزواج اما الزواج غير المشهر فقال انه «زنا وحرام»، وذلك في تصريحات نقلتها أمس الصحف المصرية.

ونقلت صحيفة «الوفد» عن الشيخ طنطاوي قوله خلال الندوة التي احياها في إطار معرض القاهرة الـ٣١ للكتاب، هذا الاسبوع ان «زواج المسيار شرعي».

وقال: «هذا الزواج غير موجود في مصر، وإنما سمعت به في بعض الدول، وهو زواج شرعي والجديد فيه ان المرأة لا تكلف الزوج شيئا إلا المهر».

وزواج المسيار موجود في الخليج، لا سيما في السعودية. وهو اخذ اسمه من كون الزوج يقوم عادة بزيارة زوجته في منزلها نهارا، كما انه ليس ملزما بمديد شيا بند بمل مسؤولياتها المادية.

واضاف إمام الأزهر في تصريحات نقلتها «الوفد» و«الجمهورية» ان «العلماء اجمعوا على بطلان الزواج السري» الذي وصفه بأنه «باطل ويعد زنا وحراما».

وقال ان الزواج السري المعروف باسم الزواج العرفي في مصر، «تتوافر فيه جميع الاركان لكن ينقصه التوثيق وأنا شخصيا لا اشهده ولا احبه ولا اجلس في مجلسه لانه يترتب عليه ضياع حقوق المرأة ومخالف للنظام الذي وضعته الدولة، كما انه مكروه».

ودعا الشيخ طنطاوي الى «إصدار قانون يعاقب من يسلك هذا المسلك بعقوبات معينة حماية للمرأة».

وتؤكد الصحف المصرية انتشار الزواج العرفي في مصر بين الفنانين وطلبة الجامعات، وهو زواج لا تعترف به المحاكم المصرية، لكن القضاء لا يعاقب عليه.

(أ ف ب)

**Document 6** Al-Jaziri, *Al-Fiqh Ala Al-Mathahib Al-Arba'ah*, vol. 4, 28. Witnessing

"The three [Hanbalis, Hanafis, and Shafi'is] agreed two witnesses must be at the marriage contract for the marriage to be valid. The Maliki school, however, said two witnesses are essential on the wedding night when the couple consummate their marriage, while their presence at the contract is only recommended."

المصدر : كتاب الفقه على المذاهب الأربعة ج٤، ص٢٨.

(٧) اتفق الثلاثة على ضرورة وجود الشهود عند العقد فإذا لم يشهد شاهدان عند الإيجاب والقبول بطل . وخالف المالكية فقالوا إن وجود الشاهدين ضروري ولكن لا يلزم أن يحضرا العقد بل يحضران الدخول أما حضورهما عند العقد فهو مندوب فقط .

**Document 7** Al-Jaziri, *Al-Fiqh Ala Al-Mathahib Al-Arba'ah*, vol. 4, 46. Guardianship

"The Hanafis rejected this *hadith* because Az-Zohri, when asked about it, said he did not know it."

المصدر : كتاب الفقه على المذاهب الأربعة ج٤، ص٤٦.

وقد أجاب الحنفية عن الحديث الأول بأنه مطعون فيه ،وذلك لأن الزهري نفسه قد سئل عنه فلم يعرفه

**Document 8** Al-Jaziri, *Al-Fiqh Ala Al-Mathahib Al-Arba'ah*, vol. 4, 33. Guardianship

"If the first marriage was a bad choice and if the one who made the bad choice again married her off, this time to a suitable man with a usual dowry, the contract is valid. She has no choice, even if he married her off while drunk."

المصدر : كتاب الفقه على المذاهب الأربعة ج٤، ص٣٣.

إذ بزواج الأولى عرف بسوء الاختيار، فإذا زوجها المعروف بسوء الاختيار من كفء وبمهر المثل فإنه يصح ولا خيار لها كما إذا زوجها وهو سكران كذلك،

**Document 9** Al-Jaziri, *Al-Fiqh Ala Al-Mathahib Al-Arba'ah*, vol. 4, 46. Guardianship

"The Shafi'is and Malikis agreed guardian consent is fundamental to marriage, and marriage is invalid without it. The Hanbalis and Hanafis agreed it is a requirement and limited what is fundamental to the proposal and its acceptance. The Hanafis added it as a requirement to validate the marriage of an underage boy or girl, and insane man or woman even if they are adults. They ruled no one has authority over the marriage of the girl who is *balighah* [mature] and *'aqilah* [responsible], whether a virgin, widow, or divorcée. She has the right to enter into a contract with whomsoever she chooses on the condition of suitability. Only then may the guardian object and sever the contract."

المصدر : كتاب الفقه على المذاهب الأربعة ج٤ ، ص٤٦.  ‏مستند رقم ٩‏

قد عرفت مما ذكرناه أن الشافعية، والمالكية اصطلحوا على عد الـولي ركناً من أركان النكـاح لا يتحقق عقد النكـاح بدونـه، واصطلح الحنـابلة والحنفية على عـده شرطـاً لا ركنـاً، وقصروا الركن على الإيجـاب والقبول، إلا أن الحنفيـة قالـوا: إن شـرط لصحة زواج الصغيـر والصغيرة، والمجنون والمجنونة ولو كباراً، أمـا البـالغـة العاقلة سـواء كانت بكـراً أو ثيباً فليس لأحد عليها ولاية النكاح، بل لها أن تباشر عقد زواجها ممن تحب بشرط أن يكون كفـأ ، وإلا كان للولي حق الاعتراض وفسخ العقد .

## Document 10 Sabiq, *Fiqh As-Sunnah*, vol. 2, 38.
Witnessing

"Malik and the scholars of his school ruled witnessing marriage is not obligatory. It is not one of its requirements or fundamentals. An announcement and public knowledge are enough. Their argument was that Allah mentioned witnessing of commercial contracts and that such witnessing was proved to not be required. Marriage, for which Allah did not mention witnessing, is more worthy than commerce. The aim is to announce and so protect the ancestry. Witnessing of the contract is acceptable to avoid disputes later between the couple. If the contract is made without witnesses, but witnesses are called before marriage, that is, intercourse, the contract will not be severed. If marriage occurs without witnesses, the couple should be separated."

المصدر : فقه السّنة، ج٢، ص٣٨.  ‏مستند رقم ١٠‏

مذهب مالك وأصحابه أن الشهادة على النكاح ليست بفرض . ويكفي من ذلك شهرته والإعلان به واحتجوا لمذهبهم بأن البيوع التي ذكرها الله تعالى فيها الإشهاد عند العقد . وقد قامت الدلالة بأن ذلك ليس من فرائض البيوع . والنكاح الذي لم يذكر الله تعالى فيه الإشهاد أحرى بأن لا يكون الإشهاد فيه من شروطه وفرائضه وإنما الغرض الإعلان والظهور لحفظ الأنساب . والإشهاد يصلح بعد العقد للتداعي والاختلاف فيما ينعقد بين المتناكحين، فإن عُقِد العقد ولم يحضره شهود ثم أشهد عليه قبل الدخول لم يفسخ العقد، وإن دخلا ولم يشهدا فرق بينهما .

**Document 11** Al-Jaziri, *Al-Fiqh Ala Al-Mathahib Al-Arba'ah*, vol. 4, 21.
Witnessing

"Provided the couple believes it was acceptable for the marriage contract to be made, it is valid even though witnessed by drunkards – if they acknowledge that their witnessing will validate the contract, even if they may not remember the contract after sobering up."

المصدر : كتاب الفقه على المذاهب الأربعة ج :٤، ص٢١.

وينعقـد بحضرة السكارى إذا كانا يعرفان أن هذا ينعقد به النكاح، ولو لم يدركوه بعد الإفاقة من السكر.

**Document 12** Al-Jaziri, *Al-Fiqh Ala Al-Mathahib Al-Arba'ah*, vol. 4, 34.
Guardianship

"The *balighah* whether a virgin, widow, or divorcée, is not compelled to obey anyone. Her marriage is not subject to a guardian's approval. She has the right to marry whomever she wishes on the condition of his suitability."

المصدر : كتاب الفقه على المذاهب الأربعة ج٤، ص٣٤.

أما البالغة سواء كانت بكراً أو ثيباً فلا جبر عليها لأحد ولا يتوقف نكـاحها على ولي بـل لها أن تزوج نفسها لمن تشاء بشرط أن يكون كفأ

**Document 13** Sabiq, *Fiqh As-Sunnah*, vol. 2, 87.
Guardianship

"A guardian's justice is not a requirement because corruption does not negate a marriage's suitability."

المصدر : كتاب فقه السنّة ج٢، ص٨٧.

ولا تُشْتَرَطُ العَدَالَةُ في الوليّ، إذِ الفِسْقُ لا يَسْلُبُ أَهْلِيَّةَ التَزويج

**Document 14** Al-Jaziri, *Al-Fiqh Ala Al-Mathahib Al-Arba'ah*, vol. 4, 27.
Guardianship

295

"They [most scholars] agreed marriage is valid even if done as a joke. Should a father say, 'I have married off my daughter to you,' and the man says, 'I accept,' while they laugh, the marriage goes ahead. It is like divorcing or freeing slaves, which go ahead even if done as a joke."

المصدر : كتاب الفقه على المذاهب الأربعة ج٤، ص٢٧. مستند رقم ١٤

(٢) اتفقوا على أن النكاح ينعقد ولو هزلاً ، فإذا قال شخص لآخر، زوجتك ابنتي فقال : قبلت ، وكانا يضحكان انعقد النكاح . كالطلاق والعتق فإنهما يقعان بالهزل .

## Document 15 Al-Jaziri, *Al-Fiqh Ala Al-Mathahib Al-Arba'ah*, vol. 4, 303. Different Schools of Thought

"A fundamental belief is that following a particular *mujtahid* [highest religious scholar] is not required. It is therefore allowed to follow any *mujtahid* of the Muslim nation in a ruling if it is confirmed to be his saying or thought."

المصدر : كتاب الفقه على المذاهب الأربعة ج٤، ص٣٠٣. مستند رقم ١٥

ومن القواعد الأصولية المقررة أن تقليد المجتهد ليس واجباً، فلا يجب الأخذ برأي مجتهد بعينه ، وحينئذ يجوز تقليد أي مجتهد من مجتهدي الأمة الإسلامية في قول ثبتت نسبته إليه ، ومتى ثبت أن ابن عباس قال ذلك فإنه يصح تقليده في هـذا الرأي كتقليد غيره من الأئمة المجتهدين

## Document 16 Ibn Qodamah, *Al-Moghni,* vol. 6, 644.
*Mut'ah* Marriage

"In *mut'ah* marriage, a man marries a woman for a period of time. If a man says: 'I have married my daughter off to you for a period of one month or one year or until the end of the season or the arrival of pilgrimage,' whether or not the time period is known, the marriage is invalid. Ahmad said, '*Mut'ah* marriage is forbidden.' Abu Bakr said, in another *hadith*, it is *makrooh* [not recommended], but not *haram* [forbidden] because Mansour [Ibn Hazim] asked Ahmad about it, and he said: 'Avoiding is more to my liking.'"

معنى نكاح المتعة أن يتزوج المرأة مدة مثل أن يقول زوجتك ابنتى شهر
أو سنة أو إلى انقضاء الموسم أو قدوم الحاج وشبهه سواء كانت المدة معلومة أو
مجهولة فهذا نكاح باطل نص عليه أحمد فقال : نكاح المتعة حرام ، وقال
أبو بكر فيها رواية أخرى أنها مكروهة غير حرام لأن ابن منصور سأل أحمد
عنها ؟ فقال : يجتنبها أحب إلي ، قال فظاهر هذا الكراهة دون التحريم ،

**Document 17** Ar-Rafi'i, *Islamuna fit Tawfeeq Bainas-Sunnah wash-Shi'ah*, 153.
*Mut'ah* Marriage

"Unbiased researchers who look closely at the *hadiths* of those who rule for and against allowing *mut'ah* must reach two conclusions. The first is the Shi'ah should not be slandered because they ruled to allow *mut'ah*. It is supported by evidence, especially after everyone agreed *mut'ah* was present at the time of the Prophet (pbuh) and after some of the grand Sunni scholars narrated that the *mut'ah* verse in the *Qur'an* was not *mansookh* [voided by a later verse]. Az-Zamakhshari mentioned in his *Qur'an* commentary *Al-Kashshaf*, narrated from Ibn Abbas, that the *mut'ah* verse is among the *muhkamat* [verses that may never be voided]. It is also untenable to say the verse **for the enjoyment you have had of them, give them their a'jer [dowry] as a duty, 4:24,** is canceled by a *hadith* because the *Qur'an* is *yeqeeni* [definite] and a *hadith* is *dhenni* [indefinite]. Moreover, those who say the *mut'ah* verse was canceled disagree on the source of this: Is it the *Qur'an* or the *Sunnah* or *Ijmaa'* [consensus among scholars]? And they disagree on the time when this claimed cancelation occurred: Was it during the battle of Awtas, Hunain, Khaiber, or Tabook, or the *Fateh Mecca* [conquest of Mecca], or the *Hujjat al-Wadaa'* [farewell pilgrimage], or any other definite time?"

ويخيَّـل إليَّ أن البـاحث المنصف اذا دقق فيـما رواه المجـوزون للمتعـة والمانعون لها لا بدَّ وان يخرج بنتيجتين اثنتين : **أولاهما** : أنه لا ينبغي - بحال - التشنيع على الشيعة الإماميـة بسبب قولهم بـزواج المتعة استنـاداً الى ما تقـدَّم من الأدلة التي استندوا اليهـا خصوصاً بعد ان اتفق الجميـع على ان « المتعـة كانت مـوجودة في زمن النبي « صلى الله عليه وآله وسلم » وبعد ان روى بعض كبـار علماء السنة ان آية المتعة الواردة في القرآن الكريم غير منسوخة كالزمخشري الذي ذكر في الكشاف نقلاً عن ابن عباس ان آيـة المتعة من المحكمـات . علاوة عـلى أنَّ القائلين بنسخ آية المتعة هذه لم يتفقوا على المصدر الذي صار به النسخ : أهو الكتاب او السنة او الاجـماع ؟ كما لم يتفقـوا على الـزمان الـذي صار فيـه النسخ ايضاً : أهو في غزوة « أوطاس » أو في غزوة « حنين » او في غزوة « خيبر » او في غزوة « تبوك » او في « فتح مكة » او في « حجة الوداع » او في اي وقت آخر على سبيل القطع وبإجماع القائلين بالنسخ . علماً بأنه لا يستساغ القول بأنَّ آية ﴿ فما استمتعتم به منهنَّ الخ . . . ﴾ . منسوخة بالحديث لأنَّ النص القرآني يقيني ونص الحديث ظني واليقين لا يزول بالشك .

## Document 18 *Sahih Muslim,* vol. 5, An-Nawawi's commentary, 179. *Mut'ah* Marriage

"Mohammed Ibn Abdullah Ibn Numayr Al-Hemdani said that Ubayy and Waki' and Ibn Bishr said that Ismael said that Qays said: 'I heard Abdullah saying: **'We were undertaking a conquest, alongside the Messenger of Allah (pbuh), with no women, so we said: 'May we masturbate?' He forbade us to do this, then gave us permission to marry a woman in exchange for a dress for a limited term;'** then Abdullah recited: **Believers, do not forbid the good things God has made lawful to you; (but) do not exceed the limits: God does not love those who exceed the limits. 5:87.**

"And 'Uthman Ibn Abi Shaybeh said that Jarir said that Ismael Ibn Abi Khalid told us the same thing using this narration chain, then he recited the verse without saying that Abdullah had recited it.

"And Abu Bakr Ibn Abi Shaybeh said that Waki' said that Ismael told us using the same narration chain and said: 'We, when young, said:

**'Oh, Messenger of Allah! May we not masturbate?'** but did not say 'during a conquest."

"And Mohammed Ibn Beshshar said that Mohammed Ibn Ja'far said that Ibn Shu'beh said that 'Amr Ibn Dinar said that he heard Al-Hasan Ibn Mohammed narrating that Jabir Ibn Abdullah and Salamah Ibn Al-Akwa' said: 'The representative of the Messenger of Allah (pbuh) came out to us and said: **'When the Messenger of Allah (pbuh) gave you permission to carry out testemti'oo [sexual enjoyment], he meant the mut'ah of women.'**

"Yezid, by which he meant Ibn Zuray', said that Rawh, by which he meant Ibn Al-Qasim, said that 'Amr Ibn Dinar narrated from Al-Hasan Ibn Mohammed from Salamah Ibn Al-Akwa' and Jabir Ibn Abdullah: **'The Messenger of Allah (pbuh) came to us and gave us permission for mut'ah.'** And Al-Hasan Al-Halawani said that Abdul Rezzaq said that Ibn Jurayj said that 'Ata said: 'Jabir Ibn Abdullah came for 'umrah and we came to him in his house; and the people asked him about things, then they mentioned mut'ah, so he said: **'Yes, we carried out istemta'na [sexual enjoyment] at the time of the Messenger of Allah (pbuh), Abu Bakr, and Omar.'**"

"Mohammed Ibn Rafi'i said that Abdul Rezzaq said that Ibn Jurayj said that Abu Zubair said: 'I heard Jabir Ibn Abdullah saying: **'We used to carry out nestemti' [sexual enjoyment] for a handful of dates or flour, at the time of the Messenger of Allah (pbuh).'**"

المصدر : صحيح مسلم بشرح النووي، ص١٧٩ ـ المجلد الخامس. **مستند رقم ١٨**

ماجاء في نكاح المتعة

حدثنا مُحَمَّدُ بنُ عَبْدِ اللهِ بنِ نُمَيْرٍ الهَمْدَانِيُّ حَدَّثَنَا أَبِي وَوَكِيعٌ وَابنُ بِشْرٍ عَنْ إِسْمَاعِيلَ

عَنْ قَيْسٍ قَالَ سَمِعْتُ عَبْدَ اللهِ يَقُولُ كُنَّا نَغْزُو مَعَ رَسُولِ اللهِ صَلَّى اللهُ عَلَيْهِ وَسَلَّمَ لَيْسَ لَنَا

نِسَاءٌ فَقُلْنَا أَلَا نَسْتَخْصِي فَنَهَانَا عَنْ ذَلِكَ ثُمَّ رَخَّصَ لَنَا أَنْ نَنْكِحَ المَرْأَةَ بِالثَّوْبِ إِلَى أَجَلٍ ثُمَّ

قَرَأَ عَبْدُ اللهِ يَا أَيُّهَا الَّذِينَ آمَنُوا لَا تُحَرِّمُوا طَيِّبَاتِ مَا أَحَلَّ اللهُ لَكُمْ وَلَا تَعْتَدُوا إِنَّ اللهَ لَا يُحِبُّ

المُعْتَدِينَ وحَدَّثَنَا عُثْمَانُ بْنُ أَبِي شَيْبَةَ حَدَّثَنَا جَرِيرٌ عَنْ إِسْمَاعِيلَ بْنِ أَبِي خَالِدٍ بِهَذَا الْإِسْنَادِ

مِثْلَهُ وَقَالَ ثُمَّ قَرَأَ عَلَيْنَا هَذِهِ الْآيَةَ وَلَمْ يَقُلْ قَرَأَ عَبْدُ اللهِ وحَدَّثَنَا أَبُو بَكْرِ بْنُ أَبِي شَيْبَةَ

حَدَّثَنَا وَكِيعٌ عَنْ إِسْمَاعِيلَ بِهَذَا الْإِسْنَادِ قَالَ كُنَّا وَنَحْنُ شَبَابٌ فَقُلْنَا يَا رَسُولَ اللهِ أَلَا نَسْتَخْصِي

وَلَمْ يَقُلْ نَغْزُو وحَدَّثَنَا مُحَمَّدُ بْنُ بَشَّارٍ حَدَّثَنَا مُحَمَّدُ بْنُ جَعْفَرٍ حَدَّثَنَا شُعْبَةُ عَنْ عَمْرِو

ابْنِ دِينَارٍ قَالَ سَمِعْتُ الْحَسَنَ بْنَ مُحَمَّدٍ يُحَدِّثُ عَنْ جَابِرِ بْنِ عَبْدِ اللهِ وَسَلَمَةَ بْنِ الْأَكْوَعِ

قَالَا خَرَجَ عَلَيْنَا مُنَادِي رَسُولِ اللهِ صَلَّى اللهُ عَلَيْهِ وَسَلَّمَ فَقَالَ إِنَّ رَسُولَ اللهِ صَلَّى اللهُ عَلَيْهِ

وَسَلَّمَ قَدْ أَذِنَ لَكُمْ أَنْ تَسْتَمْتِعُوا يَعْنِي مُتْعَةَ النِّسَاءِ وحَدَّثَنِي أُمَيَّةُ بْنُ بِسْطَامٍ الْعَيْشِيُّ حَدَّثَنَا

يَزِيدُ يَعْنِي ابْنَ زُرَيْعٍ حَدَّثَنَا رَوْحٌ يَعْنِي ابْنَ الْقَاسِمِ عَنْ عَمْرِو بْنِ دِينَارٍ عَنِ الْحَسَنِ بْنِ مُحَمَّدٍ

عَنْ سَلَمَةَ بْنِ الْأَكْوَعِ وَجَابِرِ بْنِ عَبْدِ اللهِ أَنَّ رَسُولَ اللهِ صَلَّى اللهُ عَلَيْهِ وَسَلَّمَ أَتَانَا فَأَذِنَ لَنَا

فِي الْمُتْعَةِ وحَدَّثَنِي الْحَسَنُ الْحُلْوَانِيُّ حَدَّثَنَا عَبْدُ الرَّزَّاقِ أَخْبَرَنَا ابْنُ جُرَيْجٍ قَالَ قَالَ عَطَاءٌ

قَدِمَ جَابِرُ بْنُ عَبْدِ اللهِ مُعْتَمِرًا فَجِئْنَاهُ فِي مَنْزِلِهِ فَسَأَلَهُ الْقَوْمُ عَنْ أَشْيَاءَ ثُمَّ ذَكَرُوا الْمُتْعَةَ فَقَالَ

نَعَمِ اسْتَمْتَعْنَا عَلَى عَهْدِ رَسُولِ اللهِ صَلَّى اللهُ عَلَيْهِ وَسَلَّمَ وَأَبِي بَكْرٍ وَعُمَرَ حَدَّثَنِي مُحَمَّدُ بْنُ

رَافِعٍ حَدَّثَنَا عَبْدُ الرَّزَّاقِ أَخْبَرَنَا ابْنُ جُرَيْجٍ أَخْبَرَنِي أَبُو الزُّبَيْرِ قَالَ سَمِعْتُ جَابِرَ بْنَ عَبْدِ اللهِ

يَقُولُ كُنَّا نَسْتَمْتِعُ بِالْقُبْضَةِ مِنَ التَّمْرِ وَالدَّقِيقِ الْأَيَّامَ عَلَى عَهْدِ رَسُولِ اللهِ صَلَّى اللهُ عَلَيْهِ وَسَلَّمَ

**Document 19** Shaltout, *Fatwat Jawaz Al-Ta'abod Be Math'hab Ash-Shi'ia Al-Imamia* [*Fatwa on Allowing Following of the Shi'ite Imamate School of Thought*]
Different Schools of Thought

Dar At-Taqreeb Bainal-Mathahib Al-Islamiah
Office of the Sheikh of Al-Azhar Mosque
In the name of Allah the Beneficent, the Merciful

The *fatwa* issued by his Eminence the Grand Scholar Sheikh Mahmoud Shaltout, the Sheikh of Al-Azhar Mosque, on allowing following of the Shi'ite Imamate school of thought:

His Eminence was asked, "Some people believe, for a Muslim's worship and transactions to be done correctly, he must follow one of the four known schools. Neither the Shi'ite Imamate nor the Shi'ite Zaidi's schools are among them. Does your eminence agree with this opinion and its absoluteness, and so prohibit following, for example, the Shi'ite Imamate Ithna'ashari school?"

His Eminence replied,

"(1) Islam does not require Muslims to follow a particular school, but we say: every Muslim has the right to follow at the beginning any school that has been narrated correctly and whose rulings are written in its books. Whoever follows a school has the right to change to another – any school – and there is no *haraj* [circumstance leading to extreme embarrassment or difficulty] on him in this.

"(2) The Ja'fari school known as the Shi'ite Imamate Ithna'ashari school is Islamically allowed to be followed like all the Sunni schools.

"Therefore, Muslims should know this, and get rid of loyalty without truth to certain schools. The religion of Allah and His *Shari'ah* do not follow a school nor are they the property of one school, as all are *mujtahideen meqbooloon* [highest religious scholars trying, to the best of their ability, to formulate rulings acceptable to Allah]. Those incapable of formulating rulings are allowed to follow schools and to act according to the schools' rulings in jurisprudence if the *'ibadat* [acts of worship] or *mu'amalat* [dealings with people] are not changed."

Your eminence the honorable scholar Mohammed Taqi Al-Qommi
General Secretary of Jama'at At-Taqreeb Bainal-Mathahib Al-Islamiah
Peace and mercy of Allah upon you.

It is my pleasure to send your Eminence a copy, signed by me, of the *fatwa* I have issued on allowing following the Shi'ite Imamate school. I ask you to kindly keep it in the archives of Dar At-Taqreeb Bainal-Mathahib Al-Islamiah, the establishment of which we both contributed to. May Allah guide us to succeed in achieving its message.

Peace and mercy of Allah upon you.
The Sheikh of Al-Azhar Mosque
Signature of Mahmoud Shaltout

The *fatwa* was photocopied on the 17th *Rabi' Al-Awwal* 1378 AH [1958 AD] in Cairo.

المصدر : الوحدة الإسلامية أو التقريب بين المذاهب السبعة، ص٢٢. مستند رقم ١٩

* * * * *

# Selective Bibliography

\* \* \* \* \*

Note: Authors are listed according to the English alphabetical order. Symbols that are not used in English do not affect the order in which the terms are listed.

Not all books printed in the Arabic countries contain standard publication information. The references cited here are as complete as possible.

## Books and Reports

Abdul Mohsin, Ali Abu Abdullah. *Ta'addod Al-Zawjat Bainal-'Ilm wal-Din* [*Polygamy Between Science and Religion*]. Beirut: Dar As-Safwa, 1997.

Al-'Amini, Ibrahim. *Nizam Al-Hayat Az-Zawjiyah* [*The System of Marriage*]. Beirut: Dar Al-Hadi, 1994.

Al-Bahrany, Yousif Ibn Ahmed. *Al-Hada'iq An-Nadirah* [*Fresh Gardens*], vol. 23. Beirut: Dar Al'Adwa', 1993.

Al-Bayhaqi, Ahmed Ibn Al-Hussein Ibn Ali. *As-Sunan Al-Kubra* [*Greatest Laws*], vol. 7. Hyderabad, India: Da'irat Al-Ma'aref Al-'Osmani mya, 1936.

Al-Bukhari, Mohammed Ibn Ismael. *Sahih Al-Bukhari* [*Al-Bukhari's Authentic Hadiths*]. Beirut: Dar-Ihya'a Al-Torath Al-Arabi (no year).

Al-Bukhari, Mohammed Ibn Ismael, Abul Hussein Muslim Ibn Al-Hajjaj Al-Nisapuri, Abu Abdullah Mohammed Ibn Yazid Ibn Maja al-Rab'i, and Abu Dawood. *Al-Mut'ah wa Mashroo'ietuha fil Islam* [*Mut'ah and Its Lawfulness in Islam*]. Beirut: Dar Az-Zahra', 1991.

Al-Dubai'i, Sheikh Ibrahim Ibn Mohammed. *Idah Hukmu Az-Zawaj Bi-niat Al-Talak* [*Clarifying the Order of Marriage with Hidden Intention to Divorce*]. (no city or publisher)1995.

Al-Hafani, Abdul Men'em. *Al-Mawsu'a An-Nafsiyah Al-Jinsiyah* [*Encyclopedia of Personality and Sex*]. Cairo: Madbouly Library, 1992.

Al-Jamili, Seyyid. *Al-Mashakeil Az-Zawjiyah Bainal-Tibb wal-Din* [*Marriage Issues Between Medical Treatment and Religion*]. Beirut: Dar Al-Hilal, 1994.

Al-Jaziri, Abdul Rahman. *Al-Fiqh Ala Al-Mathahib Al-Arba'ah* [*Jurisprudence in the Four Sects*], vol. 4. Beirut: Dar Al-Kutob Al-'Ilmiah (no year).

Al-Juwayr, Ibrahim Ibn Mubarak. *As-Shabab wa Kadayahu Al-Mu'asira* [*Youth and Their Contemporary Issues*]. Riyadh: Al-Baykan Library, 1994.

Al-Khouly, Sana'a. *Al-'Ailah wal-Hayat Al-'Ailah* [*The Family and Familial Life*]. Beirut: Dar Al-Nahda Al-Arabia, 1984.

Al-Kulainy, Abu Ja'far. *Al-Kafi* [*All-Encompassing*], vol. 5. Beirut: Dar At-Ta'aruf, 1995.

Al-Qabani. Sabri. *Hayatuna Al-Jinsiyyeh* [*Our Sexual Life*]. Beirut: Dar Al-'Ilm Lil Malayin, 1988.

Al-Qaradawi, Sheikh Yousif. *As-Sahwah Al-Islamiah Bainal-Ikhtilaf Al-Mashroo' wal-Tafarruq Al-Methmoo* [*The Islamic Awakening Between Good Differences of Opinion and Bad Divisiveness*]. Cairo: Dar As-Shuruk, 2001.

Al-Samarqandi Al-Hanafi, 'Alaa Eddine. *Tuhfatul Al-Fuqaha* [*Jewel of Fuqaha*], vol. 2. Cairo: Al-Matba'a Al-'Amiriya (no year).

Al-Shati, Adnan. *Az-Zawaj wal-'Ailah* [*Marriage and Family*]. Khaldiya: Kuwait University, 1997.

Al-Shawkani, Mohammed Ibn Ali Ibn Mohammed. *Naylul Awtar* [*Achieving Aims*], vol. 6. Beirut: Dar Al-Fikr, 1994.

Al-Tarmaneeni, Abdul Salam. *Kitab Az-Zawaj 'Indal Arab* [*The Arab Marriage Book*]. Kuwait: National Council of Culture, Arts, and Literature, August 1984.

Al-Thaqib, Fahad. *Al-Mar'aa wat-Talak fil Moujtam' Al-Kuwaiti* [*Women and Divorce in Kuwaiti Society: Psychological, Social, and Economic Dimensions*]. Khaldiya: Kuwait University, 1999.

Ar-Rafi'i, Sheikh Mustafa. *Islamuna fit Tawfeeq Bainas-Sunnah wa Ash-Shi'ah* [*Our Islam Reconciles Sunnah and Shi'ah*]. Beirut: Mu'assasat Al-'Alami, 1984.

Ar-Razi, Abu Abdullah Fakhr Eddine. *At-Tafsir Al-Kabir* [*The Great Explanation*]. Beirut: Dar Ihya'a Al-Torath Al-Arabi (no year).

At-Tusi, Abu Ja'far. *At-Tahthib* [*The Discipline*], vol. 7. Najaf, Iraq: Dar Al-Kutob Al-Islamiah, 1959.

As-Sa'adawi, Nawal. *Ar-Rajul wal-Jins* [*Man and Sex*]. Beirut: Arabic Institute for Studies and Publication, 1982.

Az-Zahabi, Mohammed Hussein. *Ash-Shari'ah Al-Islamiah* [*Islamic Laws*]. Cairo: Dar Al-Kutob Al-Hadithah, 1983.

Az-Zirkili, Khayr Eddine. *Al-Munjid fil A'lam* [*The Helpful Encyclopedia of Personalities*]. Beirut: Dar Al-'Ilm Lil Malayin, 1999.

Badran, Badran Abul 'Aynain. *Al-Mirath Al-Muqaren* [*Comparative Heritage*]. Cairo: Dar Al-Ma'aref, 1971.

Bahrul Uloom, Seyyid Izzuddin. *Az-Zawaj fil Qur'an was-Sunnah* [*Marriage in the Qur'an and Sunnah*], 3rd ed. Beirut: Dar Az-Zahra', 1974.

Beirut Shari'ah Office. *'Ahada 'Ashara 'Aman fil Khidma Al-Moujtama'* [*Eleven Years of Serving Society*]. Beirut: Beirut Shari'ah Office, 1996.

Fadlullah, Seyyid Mohammed Hussein. *Dunyal Mar'ah* [*The World of Women*]. Beirut: Dar Al-Malak, 1997.

---. *Kitab Al-Nikah* [*The Marriage Book*]. Beirut: Dar Al-Malak, 1996.

---. *Te'emmulat Islamiah Hawl Al-Mar'ah* [*Islamic Philosophy of the Woman*]. Beirut: Dar Al-Malak, 1997.

Fawzi, Ibrahim. *Ahkamul Usrah fil Jahiliah wal-Islam* [*Family Law Before and After Islam*]. Beirut: Dar Al-Kalima, 1983.

Hunaif, Abdul Wadood and Abdul Aziz Al-Ghamidi. *Al-'Unoosah* [*Spinsterhood*]. Mecca Al-Mukarramah: Dar 'Arraya, 1998.

Ibn Anas, Malik. *Al-Muatta'* [*The Foothold*]. Beirut: Dar Al-Gharb Al-Islami, 1984.

Ibn Baz. Sheikh Abdul Aziz. *Majmoo' Fatawa wa Maqalat Mutanawwi'ah* [*A Total of Various Rulings and Articles*], vol. 4. Mecca Al-Mukarramah: (no publisher or year.)

Ibn Hanbal, Ahmad. *Musnad* [*Predicate*]. Beirut: Dar Ihya'a Al-Torath Al-Arabi (no year).

305

Ibn Qodamah, Abu Mohammed Abdullah. *Al-Moghni* [*The Sufficient*], vol. 6. Beirut: Dar Ihya'a Al-Torath Al-Arabi, 1993.

Kamal, Abdullah. *'Adda'ara Al-Halal* [*Lawful Prostitution*]. Beirut: Cultural Library, 1997.

Kamal, Ali. *Al-Jins wan Nafs* [*Sex and Soul*]. Beirut: Arabic Institute for Studies and Publication, 1994.

Moghniyah, Sheikh Mohammed Jawad. *Al-Fusool Ash-Shari'ah* [*Sections of Law*], 3rd ed. Beirut: Dar Ath-Thaqafah, 1974.

Moir, Anne and David Jessel. *Brain Sex: the Real Difference between Men and Women* [*Jins Ad-Deemagh*]. Trans. Badr Al-Munayyis. New York: Carol Publishing, 1991.

Muslim Ibn Al-Hajjaj Al-Nisapuri, Abul Hussein, *Sahih Muslim* [*Muslim's Authentic Hadiths*], vol. 5. Beirut: Dar Ibn Hazim, 1995.

Ni'mah, Sheikh Abdullah. *Daleel Al-Qadaa' Al-Ja'fari* [*References for Shi'ah Judges*]. Beirut: Dar Al-Balagha, 1996.

*Qur'an* [*The Koran*].

Sabiq, Sheikh Seyyid. *Fiqh As-Sunnah* [*Doctrine of the Sunnis*], vol. 2. Beirut: Dar Al-Kitab Al-Arabi, 1971.

Shaltout, Mahmoud. *Fatwat Jawaz Al-Ta'abod Be Math'hab Ash-Shi'ia Al-Imamia* [*Fatwa on Allowing Following of the Shi'ite Imamate School*]. Cairo: Dar At-Taqreeb Bainal-Mathahib Al-Islamiah, Office of the Sheikh of Al-Azhar Mosque, 1958.

Tahiry, Habib. *Mashakeil Al-Ousra wa Turuk Halluha* [*Family Problems and Their Solutions*]. Beirut: Dar Al-Hadi, 1997.

*Wasa'il Ash-Shi'ah* [*The Ways of the Shi'ah*]. Beirut: Dar Ihya'a Al-Torath Al-Arabi, 1991.


**Periodicals**

*Al-Anba'a* [*The News*] [Kuwait]. 28 July 1999: (no page no.).

*Al-Majallah* [*The Magazine*] [London, U.K.]. 20 July 1996: 70.

*Al-Qabas* [*The Firebrand*] [Kuwait]. __ Sep. 2002 (no specific date): 20.

*Al-Qabas*. 9 Aug. 2003: 12.

*Al-Qabas*. 6 Dec. 2003: (no page no.).

*Al-Watan Al-Arabi* [*The Arab Country*] [Lebanon]. 8 May 1986: (no page no.).

*Al-Yawm* [*Today*] [Bahrain]. 9 July 1986: 14.

*As-Safir* [*The Ambassador*] [Lebanon]. 12 Feb. 1999: 7.

*As-Safir*. 17 June 1999: (no page no.).

*Khaleej [Gulf] Times Online* [U.A.E.]. 5 Sept. 2005: www.
   khaleejtimes.com.
*Kull Al-Ousra [All the Family]* [U.A.E.]. 4 Jan. 1995: 166.
*Kullun Naas [All the People]* [Egypt]. __ Jan. 1997 (no specific date): 27.
*Zahratul Khaleej [Flower of the Gulf]* [U.A.E.]. 18 Dec. 1993: 88.
*Zahratul Khaleej.* 22 July 2000: 65.
*Zahratul Khaleej.* 5 Aug. 2000: 23.

\* \* \* \* \*

# Index

* * * * *

Note: Terms are arranged according to the English alphabetical order. Symbols that are not used in English do not affect the order in which the terms are listed, with the exception of words beginning with the gutteral stop. These words are listed before the entries beginning with "a."

See the Glossary for the pronunciation and definition of the Arabic terms.

## B

bachelors 49, 50, 51
Badran, Badran Abul 'Aynain 206
Bahrain 26, 265
Bahrul Uloom, Izzuddin 57, 62, 63, 168
*baligh* 68, 69, 264
*balighah* 67, 68, 149, 264, 294, 295
Beirut 1, 19, 22, 26, 49
birth control 99, 152, 188, 273
black magic 31
boredom 31
breastfeeding 202, 203, 205, 221
brotherhood 39, 73, 148
*buloogh* 69, 71, 77, 78, 264
Burayd 69
business contracts 63, 64, 66, 67, 122, 132, 210, 276, 294

## C

calendar conversion 263
Caliph 73, 196, 264
call for Islam 51, 264
career 15, 29, 30, 106, 123, 167, 174, 175, 228, 260
caretaking 29
change after marriage 30
chaperon 38, 39
child's ancestry 43, 45, 63, 101, 102, 104, 203, 210, 220, 221, 265, 294
childbearing 99, 283
childbirth 29, 203, 207, 260
children 2, 5, 6, 7, 8, 12, 14, 16, 19, 24, 25, 26, 27, 29, 43, 44, 45, 46, 50, 63, 75, 78, 80, 83, 85, 95, 96, 99, 101, 102, 104, 106, 110, 115, 116, 120, 122, 123, 124, 125, 126, 129, 135, 136, 137, 141, 146, 149, 150, 151, 152, 153, 156, 157, 158, 162, 163, 165, 167, 170, 172, 174, 177, 179, 183, 184, 187, 188, 189, 190, 192, 193, 195, 202, 203, 205, 206, 210, 216, 220, 221, 223, 224, 225, 227, 228, 231, 232, 242, 245, 253, 254, 255, 256, 260, 265, 283
children, travel abroad of 123, 260
child marriage 78, 183
child support 12, 43, 125, 210, 260
Christianity 24, 238, 240
Christians 22, 37, 38, 40, 144, 237, 238
*coitus interruptus* 188, 264, 284
companionship 39, 40, 47, 116
comparison 66, 163, 229, 271
compatibility 3, 5, 36, 37, 41, 45, 73, 83, 97, 115, 125, 128, 142, 145, 155, 156, 160, 176, 177, 206, 216, 217, 219, 242
competence 56, 71, 73, 74, 75, 76, 80, 81, 105, 106, 107, 108, 109, 116, 132, 140, 150, 157, 162, 172, 173, 174, 177, 190, 192, 201, 223, 267, 271
conscience 45, 90, 96, 101, 131, 143, 144, 187
consummation of marriage 41, 66, 69, 120, 146, 164, 278, 292
corruption 51, 69, 74, 101, 106, 140, 166, 211, 282, 296
courts 24, 26, 27, 31, 32, 42, 43, 44, 45, 49, 53, 60, 80, 95, 108, 123, 124, 135, 148, 149, 224, 226, 245, 253, 274, 292
cousins 84, 159, 164
covenant 57, 245, 257, 277
crime 12, 24, 26, 30, 40, 83, 138, 174, 205, 260
custody 12, 123, 137, 157, 223,

260

customs and traditions  12, 14, 22, 27, 31, 38, 42, 60, 76, 77, 85, 86, 87, 88, 103, 107, 114, 122, 146, 185, 214, 222, 232, 234

# D

*da´wah*  51, 264

daughters  2, 6, 7, 8, 9, 11, 19, 20, 21, 37, 42, 60, 68, 73, 84, 106, 107, 110, 139, 140, 141, 149, 151, 152, 153, 157, 167, 168, 170, 171, 173, 195, 196, 215, 222, 225, 273, 278, 282, 283, 296, 297

decision-making  30, 78, 121, 151, 183, 259, 260, 264

defloration  141, 146

denial of marriage  43, 44, 61, 63, 101, 104, 110, 289

denial of paternity  43, 44, 101, 104, 110, 177

Dhahiri school  264, 289

*dhenni*  198, 264, 297

dinar  264

disabilities, physical  29

divorce, causes of  27, 28, 32, 33, 175

divorce, extra payment  19, 41

divorce, planning for  122, 123, 124, 223, 224, 226, 260

divorcées  19, 26, 42, 46, 49, 50, 70, 71, 80, 93, 94, 115, 144, 156, 164, 192, 204, 232, 249, 253, 255, 275, 282, 294, 295

divorce and children  24, 25, 85, 96, 122, 123, 124, 125, 158, 223, 224, 256

divorce and society  24, 80, 85

divorce and women's freedom  25

divorce procedure  32

divorce statistics  25, 26

divorce story  8, 19

DNA testing  102, 110, 136

*dofoof*  264, 289

dowry  19, 41, 44, 46, 56, 57, 58, 59, 60, 62, 76, 81, 93, 99, 100, 107, 109, 121, 123, 138, 145, 155, 156, 173, 177, 189, 196, 198, 201, 203, 204, 206, 215, 223, 224, 242, 243, 244, 249, 250, 259, 272, 276, 277, 291, 293, 297

dowry paid by woman  60

dowry repayment  19, 60, 87, 93, 204, 259, 268

dowry size  58, 59, 60, 109, 110, 123, 223, 252, 259, 281

drug use  30, 31

drums  105, 138

Dubai  50, 273

# E

education  19, 20, 21, 29, 30, 36, 43, 44, 74, 110, 115, 121, 123, 138, 152, 157, 164, 167, 175, 176, 177, 183, 185, 186, 191, 194, 195, 228, 260

Egypt  25, 43, 44, 46, 49, 60, 71, 78, 95, 263, 274, 291, 292, 302

emotion  141, 216

engagement  19, 38, 39, 40, 41, 42, 78, 80, 92, 93, 241, 249, 264, 269

# F

Fadlullah, Mohammed Hussein  59, 73

false information  29, 143, 208, 230, 259

family choosing spouse  4, 7, 37, 67, 68, 70, 84, 106, 107,

314

315

316

negativity 134, 139, 146, 162, 164, 212
neglect 29, 30, 44, 86
nestemti' 267, 270, 285, 299
new order 52
Ni'mah, Abdullah 56
nikah 120, 270
non-fixed features 109, 110, 111, 124, 154, 156, 181, 218, 237
non-Muslims 4, 74, 198, 205, 237, 240, 241, 243
non-virgins 41, 60, 69, 115, 144, 145, 156, 158, 161, 163, 164, 209, 272, 273
nostalgia 192

## O

Oman 265
Omar 197, 284, 285, 299
Omran bin Hussein 197, 284
oukeya 60, 270
overstepping boundaries 97, 127, 128, 129, 132, 136, 147, 153, 250

## P

Pakistan 60
parents 2, 3, 25, 27, 41, 43, 44, 50, 53, 72, 75, 80, 82, 84, 89, 92, 93, 95, 97, 102, 123, 124, 136, 140, 141, 145, 146, 147, 150, 151, 152, 153, 160, 174, 179, 180, 182, 183, 188, 189, 190, 191, 194, 195, 203, 221, 224, 236, 245, 265
passports 43, 123
past vs. present 32, 48, 102, 110, 121, 152, 171, 182, 183, 184, 257
paternity 92, 102, 110, 136, 146, 174, 186, 188, 189, 190
pause between contracts 133
pbuh 271

peace be upon him 271
permanent contracts 80, 93, 101, 121, 163, 177, 202, 203, 207, 211, 243
permanent marriage 47, 80, 92, 94, 96, 97, 98, 108, 115, 121, 125, 129, 132, 135, 136, 137, 140, 145, 147, 149, 155, 156, 157, 158, 160, 161, 164, 166, 173, 175, 176, 186, 187, 188, 189, 190, 191, 192, 193, 195, 196, 201, 202, 203, 204, 205, 206, 207, 208, 213, 214, 215, 216, 219, 220, 222, 231, 235, 244, 251, 252, 254, 266, 268, 269, 272
physical attraction 30, 39, 73, 74, 84, 92, 99, 141, 186, 217, 218, 219, 283
physical illness 9, 24, 31, 50, 51, 191, 205, 206, 260
pilgrimage 196, 197, 266, 297
pillars 56, 264
positives 13, 20, 35, 36, 162, 207, 212, 213, 219, 229, 234, 236
positivity 134, 162, 222
pregnancy 43, 80, 135, 136, 144, 157, 177, 210, 215, 241
Prince Salman Social Center 26
privacy 92, 114, 115, 148, 152, 159, 163, 259
privacy, lack of 39
Prophet's (pbuh) companions 52, 62, 65, 196, 232, 271, 290
Prophet's (pbuh) wives 62, 70, 165, 168, 233, 264, 265, 268, 272, 274, 282, 283, 290
Prophet Mohammed (pbuh) 52, 57, 58, 59, 62, 64, 65, 68, 70, 81, 88, 99, 107, 130, 131, 144, 147, 165, 168, 169, 170, 171, 172, 187, 196, 197, 198, 200, 231,

232, 233, 235, 268, 269,
273, 278, 281, 282, 283,
284, 285, 288, 289, 290,
297, 298, 299
prostitution 50, 65, 208, 209, 210,
211, 282
proxy 57, 100, 146, 249, 250, 267,
271
puberty 77, 105, 110, 148, 149,
195, 264

# Q

Qatar 26, 88, 89, 265
Qays 298
*qintar* 60, 271
*qismaw wa naseeb* 226, 227, 271
*qiyas* 66, 271
*qubool* 57, 100, 106, 244, 249,
250, 267, 271, 296
*Qur'an* 271
*Qur'anic* verses 13, 14, 41, 59, 62,
80, 263, 264, 267, 270, 273
*Qur'anic* verse quotation 47, 57,
58, 59, 60, 62, 63, 64, 65,
69, 71, 72, 81, 82, 86, 88,
89, 120, 138, 139, 157, 158,
163, 164, 168, 169, 174,
196, 198, 211, 227, 231,
235, 254, 256, 257, 275,
297, 298

# R

*rabbaiani* 174
*Rabi' Al-Awwal* 271, 302
*rafeeqah* 116, 271
*raj'ee* 271
*rashid* 68, 69, 149, 271
*rashidah* 67, 68, 69, 106, 141,
149, 151, 271
Ras Al-Khaimah 273
Rawh 284, 299
reconciliation 32, 120, 216, 270,
271
*reeba* 112, 271

rejection of Islam 104, 205
relationship counseling 4, 5, 23,
259
religious differences 28, 31, 33
religious obligations 32, 76
remarriage 71, 120, 140, 158,
192, 204, 220, 270, 275
renegotiation 260
reproduction 186, 188, 190
reputation 19, 42, 93, 94, 104,
160, 161, 164, 171, 185,
236, 242
rescue marriage 211
responsible character 78, 149,
271
Rezzaq, Abdul 285, 299
right to divorce 87, 123, 260, 267
Riyadh 26
romantic love 40, 73, 132, 175,
178, 217, 224, 230
*roshd* 78, 149, 150, 151, 195, 271

# S

Sa'd Ibn Muslim 69, 188
Sabiq, Seyyid 46, 51, 287, 294,
295
*sadaq* 58, 272
*sadaqah Shari'ah* 243, 272
*sadd bab ath-thara'ia'* 113
Safiah 62, 272, 290
*safih* 69, 272
*safihah* 67, 272
*sahih* 272
*Sahih Al-Bukhari* 197
*Sahih Muslim* 197, 284, 298
Salamah Ibn Al-Akwa' 197, 284,
299
Satan 13, 81, 281
satisfaction 14, 37, 50, 73, 74, 89,
100, 175, 176, 189, 195,
201, 256, 257, 282
satisfaction, lack of 31, 33
Saudi Arabia 26, 51, 52, 265, 287,
291

Printed in the United Kingdom
by Lightning Source UK Ltd.
109556UKS00002B/46-1008